JULIA LAWLESS

THE BOTANICAL HOME

YOUR COMPLETE GUIDE TO USING PLANTS TO SCENT, CLEANSE AND ENHANCE YOUR HOME

ROBERT HALE

Contents

Introduction

At Home with Nature

'Nature is not somewhere to visit, it is home.'

Gary Snyder, *Practice of the Wild*

Nature is an essential component in all our lives. It is the basis on which civilisation is founded, yet sometimes we can forget this essential connection. Recognising and honouring our interdependence with nature is key to re-establishing a meaningful relationship with ourselves and with our environment. Direct interaction with nature can also be a grounding force amid the ups and downs of our daily lives – it brings us down to earth and reminds us that we are a part of the natural world. The vibrant green scent of aromatic herbs; the brilliant radiance of a vase of fresh flowers; the grainy textural feel of wood; the enveloping warmth from the flickering flames of an open fire – all these sensory experiences raise simple but primeval emotional responses within us, which are comforting, nourishing and reassuring. By surrounding ourselves with elements from nature in our homes, we are simultaneously elevating our senses and soothing our souls at a primal level. Bringing plants and greenery indoors is one of the most effective ways to create a healing environment – a well-being sanctuary in which to regenerate and recharge from the overload of our modern lives.

Scientific studies are increasingly demonstrating that contact with nature is inherently therapeutic, whether this is by walking in a forest or park, or simply by seeing a garden or some greenery through a window. If we live in an urban environment this is not always so apparent, but even the most basic relationship with the natural world, such as caring for a house plant, can have a profound impact on our sense of well-being and help lift our spirits. Plants play an indispensable role in our lives because without them we would not even have oxygen to breathe. In fact, plants and humans live in a natural synergy – we breathe in oxygen and breathe out carbon dioxide while plants breathe in carbon dioxide and breathe out oxygen. Some house plants can even help to purify the air within our homes, reduce toxins, remove airborne mould or damp and improve sleep quality.

Throughout these pages, we will explore lots of ways through which we can create a healing sanctuary by inviting nature into our homes. This means incorporating design features that blur the division between the inside and outside, so we enjoy living in a green haven – a place in which to retreat from the world, providing refuge and protection. By embracing nature in all its aspects, our home can become a source of well-being where we feel nourished and uplifted, a sacred space that nurtures our entire being. In symbolic language, our home represents our inner psyche, so it is important that we feel comfortable and at ease within our dwelling and that we take care of it.

When we combine the benefits of natural

aromatics with the power of ritual, we can effectively purify and sanctify a space, on both an outer and an inner level. Fragrant plants and incense have been used for thousands of years to elevate our consciousness and make a direct connection with the divine. Recipes created in a modern stillroom provide multiple natural ways to cleanse, enhance and look after our homes using pure botanical ingredients that are biodegradable and non-toxic. Many essential oils, for example, can multitask as purifying air fresheners, eco-friendly disinfectants, household hygiene products and natural insect repellents, as well as being therapeutically invaluable for combatting airborne infections and a wide range of stress-related conditions when used in room vaporisers.

The creation of a healing and sustainable home is also about being aware of the challenges facing our society today. Confronted by such enormous ecological issues as global warming and the destruction of natural habitats, we urgently need to return to a more environmentally conscious way of living, to renew our connection with nature and to utilise the limitless healing potential of botanicals as an everyday practice. By incorporating the lifestyle suggestions presented in this book, we can begin to move away from the habits that further destroy our ecosystems and instead make an individual step towards addressing some of these important environmental issues. In her book, *60 Days to a Greener Life*, Heather White reminds us that it took one generation to change the lives of women forever by petitioning for the vote and that a collective effort today can bring about a widespread change of attitude towards our environment:

> *'Individual action drives culture change, and without culture change, global policies and market solutions will not work.'*

I would like to invite you to take a walk through history, with herbs and aromatic plants as your companions, since botanicals have always played a central role in our evolution. The story begins with humans perceiving themselves as inseparable from nature and therefore treating it with reverence and respect. Then gradually human nature and the natural environment became divorced from each other, due to the prevailing religious, philosophical or scientific beliefs of the time. Today, as a result, and with the natural world in crisis, there is the need to reconnect to our past, not in the sense of trying to resurrect primitive patterns of thought, but by reimagining our role as an intrinsic part of nature and by taking care of the natural environment in all its aspects. Developing a daily practice of sustainability can help mould the future through changing our perception of what it means to live ethically and by prioritising environmental stewardship for future generations.

I have always considered myself a nature devotee and continue to find the richness of the plant kingdom a never-ending source of beauty, wonder and wisdom. Whether I am in the city or the countryside, I like to have a display of seasonal flowers on my kitchen table, in pots or in vases, so I can trace the changing botanical moods of the year. Just seeing the frothy whiteness of a jug full of freshly picked cow parsley in early summer, or waking up to a miniature posy of wildflowers on my bedside table early in the morning, reminds me to appreciate the little things in life. In addition, spending time alone in nature and being in touch with the elements has always provided solace and healing for me during difficult times.

I'm aware that my Finnish heritage and background have also played a vital role in creating my deep connection and reverence for nature, as has my work with botanical products in our family business, 'Aqua Oleum', for over forty years. Over this period, I have written many books that detail the therapeutic uses of herbs and aromatic oils, mainly as skincare, medicinal or cosmetic agents – while in this book, I set out to explore the value of botanicals in the context of the environment by focusing on their benefit within our homes, rather than on our bodies.

I have also been fortunate to design several gardens, each with a different character, over the past three decades. Perhaps the most ambitious of these projects was taking on a property with an overgrown three-acre plot at the foot of the Epynt mountains in Wales. The traditional longhouse and adjoining barn had once been the principal farm for the local area and occupied an ideal, south-facing position overlooking a river valley. As a keen gardener, I enthusiastically set about landscaping the surrounding land, including creating an extensive vegetable plot. However, I did not factor in the turbulent mountainous weather with frequent heavy rainfall, sudden high winds and temperatures that would sometimes plunge to −15°C! I therefore made plenty of mistakes, such as trying to keep an olive tree alive on the southern terrace of the farmhouse by wrapping it in fleece over winter, only for it to eventually die due to the ongoing cold and damp. Nevertheless, I was able to gain a great deal of experience in cultivating and growing a wide range of plants organically, especially those herbs and aromatics as detailed in Part 2 of this book. My enduring lesson from these experiences has been to develop a more naturalistic style of gardening, by choosing plants that are automatically suited to the specific climate and habitat of a given environment by nature.

How to Use This Book

Part 1 of this book covers how to grow herbs and flowers at home, as outlined in Chapter 1, which provides a good basis for connecting with nature. Nurturing seeds and creating a garden embodies a form of environmental stewardship on a personal level. Learning how to prepare plants in many ways, to enhance our homes in a modern stillroom, develops this theme as part of an age-old tradition. Using botanicals as home-hygiene agents and purifying and cleaning internal spaces provides another vital step in caring for the environment by reducing the need for chemical products. Chapter 4 deals with the power of perfume and incense as a central focus of early civilisations, including the psychology of scent and the value of aromatics as mood adaptogens. Recognising the healing potential of nature and introducing botanically based rituals back into our lives is also a traditional way of paying respect to nature. Finally, Chapter 6 explores how to merge the inner and outer spaces of our homes and introduces ways to bring nature indoors directly. Specific rituals and recipes accompany each chapter that suggest practical ways to utilise the healing power of plants and the well-being benefits of living close to nature.

Part 2 of this book provides an in-depth guide to growing and preparing a wide range of specific plants and how to use them within the home. The magic and folklore of individual herbs and aromatics is also touched upon in this section as it is a fascinating area of study. This book can therefore be read as an overview of our relationship with botanicals from the earliest civilisations right up to the present day, including their history, folklore and magic. It also provides a step-by-step guide on how to create your personal well-being sanctuary as a refuge from the stresses of everyday life. In addition, it can be used as a practical textbook on how to grow, prepare and use a wide range of plants in the home, together with a detailed and clear presentation of over forty individual species in an A–Z format. It is my hope that you will find these pages, along with the beautiful images, both informative and inspiring.

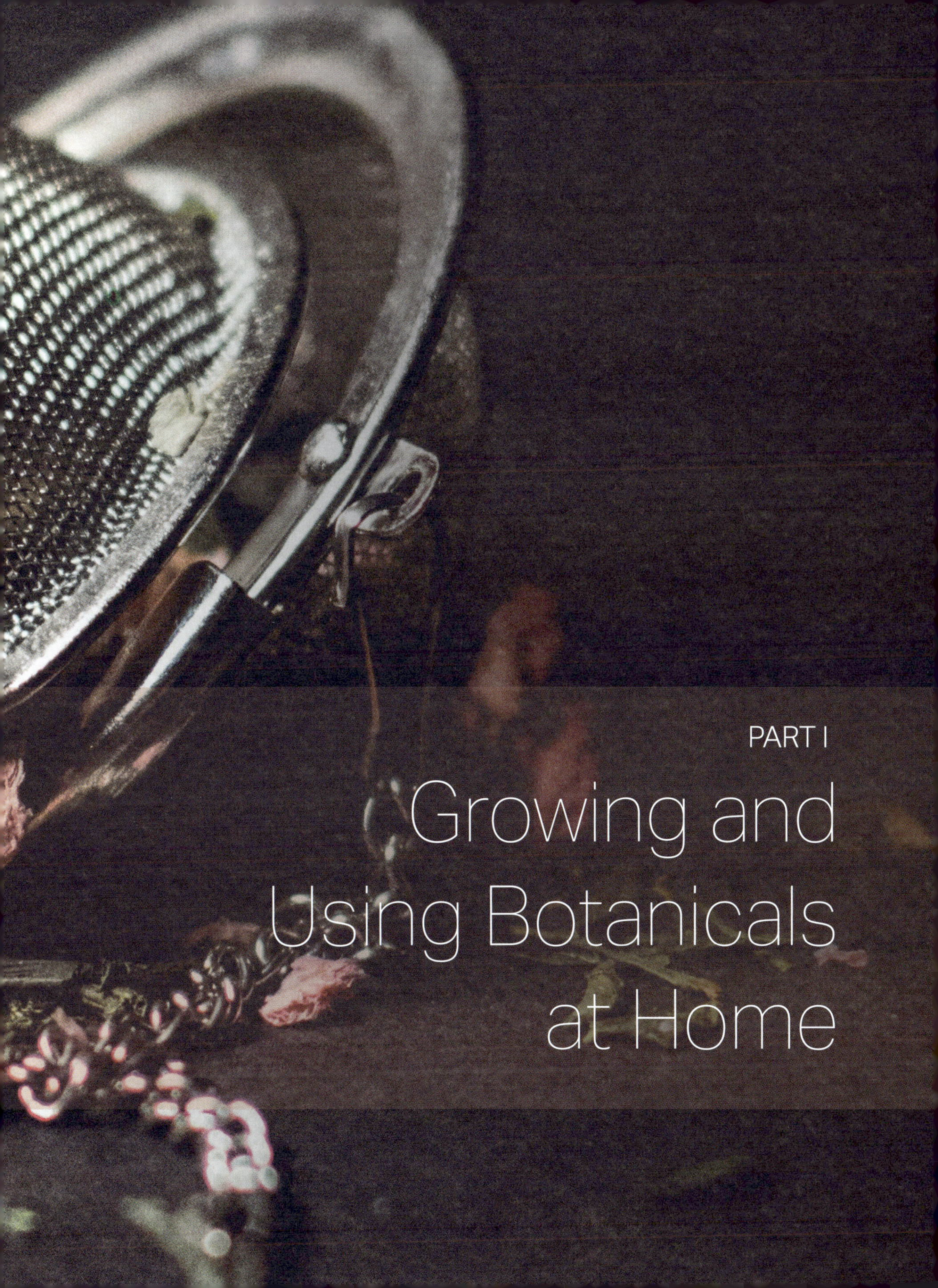

PART I

Growing and Using Botanicals at Home

Chapter 1

Growing, Gathering and Drying Plants

'Herbs are the bridge between nature and healing.'

Rosalee de la Forêt, ***Alchemy of Herbs***

Herbs have been used for thousands of years by all cultures alike and were the first botanical species to have been cultivated by humankind. Herbal treatment is the earliest form of medicine, and consequently, the main reason for growing plants was originally for their therapeutic benefits. Before the advent of modern drugs, plant medicine was the principal way of combatting all kinds of illness, including contagious diseases, infection and injury.

In Western civilisation, ancient herbals date back to *De Materia Medica,* written in the first century CE by the Greek physician Dioscorides. In this great work, he describes the medicinal use for over 500 'flowers and sweet-scented things' and how to grow, gather and store them, detailing plants that mainly came from the Mediterranean region. Over the next 1,500 years, herbals expanded their repertoire to include plants with culinary and household uses too, often mixed in with an archaic blend of myth and magic.

The range of plants that we call herbs has continued to change over the centuries in Europe. At one time, many familiar flowers, such as pinks, peonies, roses and irises, were termed 'herbs', as were most of our common vegetables. Some wild species, such as sweet woodruff and meadowsweet were also called herbs, since they were commonly grown for household hygiene purposes. It was only later, as the study of plants became more specialised, that they were classified into distinct species, as showcased in botanical gardens around the world. According to the contemporary *Oxford English Dictionary,* herbs are 'plants of which the leaves, stems or flowers are used for food or medicine, or in some way for their scent or flavour'. Although many of the plants we now call herbs are fragrant, however, this is not true of all of them: for example, the common plantain *(Plantago major)*, celebrated by the Anglo Saxons as the 'mother of all herbs', is not aromatic and contains no essential oils.

The Herb Garden

With the conquest of Britain, horticultural knowledge that had spread throughout the Roman Empire was initially preserved in the monasteries. The Romans also brought with them many familiar herbs from the Mediterranean, such as chives, parsley, onions, fennel, rosemary and thyme. These plants adapted well to more temperate climes and form the basis for the herb gardens that are a familiar sight in the UK today. This herbal legacy bequeathed by the Romans also proved invaluable for the development of herbal medicine in Britain. It was only later in Europe, starting with the medieval physic garden, that outdoor spaces also became places for recreation and enjoyment. As the cultivation of plants purely for pleasure and for appreciation of their aesthetic beauty developed, the nature of gardens also changed to accommodate these changes. The secular pleasure gardens of the Middle Ages were the domain of the nobility and the wealthy, known as 'Gardens of Delight', and featured an array of scented plants, such as roses and honeysuckle. Then with the Renaissance influence, the features of the medieval herb gardens became grander and more classical in structure, with formal walkways and box hedging to contain the aromatic planting.

As the passion for creating gardens spread, it reached new heights in the period of the great plant hunters during the eighteenth and nineteenth centuries. Many of the exotic plants found in European and American gardens today come from as far afield as Burma, Tibet, China, Japan and the West Indies. Perhaps the best known of these explorers was Joseph Banks who brought back specimens of around 1,300 new plant species. However, alongside the historical development of the garden, there has always existed the more common usage of herbal folk remedies known as 'simples'. These were indigenous plants used by local people as remedies for common ailments and for household purposes, where the knowledge of how to use them was often handed down by word of mouth. For example, growing up in the countryside, I was taught early on how to rub a crushed dock leaf or some lemon balm onto a nettle sting to soothe the pain. It was also common practice in my family to put a few lavender sprigs under the pillow or in bath water to aid restful sleep before retiring. These are the same botanicals that form the basis for preparation in the stillroom:

> *'When we align ourselves with the wisdom of herbs, we tap into the ancient knowledge that has been passed down through generations.'*
>
> **Rosalee de la Forêt, *Alchemy of Herbs***

Growing herbs and flowers at home for their culinary and household usage, as well as for their inherent healing properties, is therefore part of an age-old tradition that is both practical and enjoyable. My Finnish grandmother and my mother always had extensive herb gardens. I too have always focused on cultivating a wide range of aromatic plants, especially herbs and those species used to produce essential oils. Being surrounded by a range of fresh botanical plants is not only a natural way to look after our health but also an ecologically aware manner to care for our home, our families and the environment.

We do not need a large space to enjoy the numerous benefits that herbs and aromatics can bring to our everyday life. A personalised garden can range from a window box or a small yard with pots, right up to a large outdoor plot. Since most herbs and aromatic plants are tolerant of poor soil conditions or being grown in containers, it is possible to create a botanical sanctuary wherever we live. Most herbs also mature quickly, ensuring we will always have a crop that is available to use either fresh or dried for inclusion in our aromatic recipes.

Most herbs are easy to grow from seed, such as dill, coriander, fennel and parsley, as well as many other valuable household plants, including marigold, borage and lemon balm. Lots of these plants will also self-seed readily all around the garden once established. Allowing plants to self-seed is a natural step towards rewilding parts of a garden and a way of encouraging animals, birds and pollinating insects to find their homes there. Apart from the fact that I find it satisfying to nurture plants from seed to maturity, it is also by far the most economical way to establish a garden, whether this is in a window box, in pots or by establishing plants directly in the soil. Alternatively, seeds for most common herbs and flowers are available from shops. Many species can also be bought as small plants from garden centres or grown from cuttings. More tender plants, such as lemon verbena or gardenia, need the protection

of a greenhouse or a warm windowsill, or at least a sheltered position in the garden to thrive.

Growing Plants from Seed

Cultivating plants from seeds you have gathered yourself is one of the greatest pleasures of gardening. Firstly, it is important to collect the seeds of each plant at the perfect stage of ripeness, usually from September onwards, although this can vary according to each species and the prevailing weather conditions. Prolonged periods of hot, dry weather will often cause flowering plants to bolt so they may produce seeds earlier in the season than normal. This means it is good to keep an eye on each species and, once the plant has flowered, watch for the seed heads to turn from green to brown or black, indicating they are ripe and ready to harvest. Seed is generally set about two months after flowering and the seed heads can ripen quickly so it is important to catch them just before they open their pods and shed the seeds themselves!

It is vital to collect the seeds on a dry, sunny day, because if they retain any residual moisture from rain or dew, then it is easy for them to spoil and develop mould. It is also best to cut the whole stem off with the seed heads attached and place them in a paper bag immediately. This helps to keep any small seeds from escaping – if you write the name of the plant on each paper bag beforehand, it also ensures that you know which seeds belong to which plant. Then once you have gathered all the seeds you need from a particular species, carefully lay them out on some white paper on a kitchen table, in a shed or greenhouse so you can easily extract and sort the seeds. If some pods don't open readily when they are dry, gently crush the capsules to release their seed then clean off any surrounding material attached to them, as this could rot and lead to the seed becoming damp or diseased. Some seeds, such as coriander, are tiny, so it may take some patience to extract and separate them all out.

Once the seeds are all sorted by species, lay them out to dry on some greaseproof or waxed paper on a greenhouse bench, warm windowsill or in an airing cupboard for about one week. However, too much heat can be detrimental to the drying process and prevent the seeds from germinating. The main thing is to ensure that all the seeds are spread out in a single layer so the air can get to each one and to let them dry naturally. Paper towels placed on a serving tray can also provide a good method, so long as the seeds are spread thinly so they dry quickly, but in this case, you need to be careful the seeds don't stick to the paper towel.

An even better way to get maximum air contact is to dry the seeds on a type of fine mesh or screen as this way they dry from the bottom as well as the top. It is also good to gently stir the seeds around quite frequently, as this encourages more air contact, evens out the drying process and helps to break up clumps of seeds that stick together and prevent rot from developing. After about a week or so, once you are satisfied that the seeds are thoroughly dry, place them in a small envelope or glass jar and label each species carefully. A silica sachet can be added when you seal each container to help eliminate any moisture. Finally, you need to store your seeds in a cool, dry place, for example in a dark cupboard or in a fridge until required, since most seeds will remain viable in this way for many years.

Once you have your store of gathered seeds, you will need to decide where to grow your herbs and aromatic plants. In nature, the seeds simply lie on the ground from the moment they are released to wait for germination in the spring – or once the conditions are right – then emerge as self-seeded specimens. You can use the principle of lunar-phase gardening to discern the right time for the sowing of seeds. The principle is quite simple: when the moon is waxing, this is a good time for planting seeds that yield fruit above ground; when the moon is waning, the time is right to plant root crops with edible parts below the soil. The growth of crops is influenced by the moon phases because, just like the tides of the ocean, the moisture levels in the soil rise and fall with these cycles. At both the new-moon and full-moon high tide, there is more water being pulled to the surface of the soil, so the seeds and plants are better able to soak it up, which benefits both germination and growth.

When early spring arrives and it begins to get warm, having taken note of the moon phase, your seeds can be sown into pots or trays in a greenhouse or on a windowsill to germinate. If the seeds are tiny, sprinkling them into trays is the most effective method. Most herbs and aromatics, especially those from the Mediterranean, require well-drained soil and, in most cases, gravel or vermiculite can be added to the seed compost. It is best to always use low-nutrient soil in the beginning and move progressively up into higher nutrients as the plants mature, according to their individual needs. To keep the soil moist, a polythene bag can be placed over the pot or tray to stop the emerging seedlings from drying out. Some seeds that are tough benefit from being soaked beforehand in warm water. I like to sow tiny parsley seeds (which do not like to be transplanted), into shallow rows of fine soil outdoors into which I have previously poured a jug of boiling water, to help them germinate quickly.

Then at a certain point, you will need to thin the seedlings out to allow the remaining plants to grow robust and healthy. Once the plants can be handled individually, it is time to gently transfer them into small pots. Later still, they can be transplanted into larger containers or out into the ground. Some small herbs, such as coriander, can simply be left to grow in their pots and more seeds can be re-sown at intervals to ensure a continuation of the crop. There is also an advantage to keeping certain herbs in pots in the kitchen, such as basil, as they not only look and smell lovely but also help to keep flies away. Certain areas of the garden can also be dedicated to rewilding, for example by sowing wildflower seeds in place of a lawn, to encourage biodiversity.

Foraging in the Wild

If you don't have a garden, yard or window box to grow your herbs and flowers, then foraging for wild plants can be enriching. This is a great way to get to know the botanical treasures on your doorstep, especially if you live in the countryside. Otherwise taking regular day trips to local nature spots, notebook in hand, can make a welcome change to life in a city, while at the same time expanding your knowledge of the region. Wherever you live and in whatever country, it is always possible to become more familiar with the natural world around you. When out foraging, remember to take a basket or a suitable container with you, a pair of thornproof gloves and a sharp, folding knife or some secateurs.

I spent every long summer in Finland until late into my teens, so during this period I developed a strong affinity with the Finnish landscape. Finland is a beautiful place to spend time outdoors in the summertime and become one with nature. The whole country has a small population – around the same number as Bristol – yet it covers a vast area made up of forests, lakes and islands, where much of the land has remained unchanged and untouched since the last ice age. When the glaciers gradually receded northward, they left behind a trail of enormous granite boulders and sudden outcrops of rock scattered unexpectedly across the landscape. To walk through the forests or along the rocky shorelines inevitably evokes a sense of being somewhere remote and primeval. I also naturally adopted many of the Finns' national customs, including foraging for wild plants and mushrooms.

The Finns are famous for their botanical knowledge, so foraging has always been an important aspect of the Nordic lifestyle that has endured for centuries. A Finnish study by The Natural Resources Institute indicated that 66 per cent of Finns go foraging at least once a year, whether they live in the town or countryside. In Finland, the so-called 'everyman's right' or 'the right to roam' law means that people are permitted to camp, swim, fish and forage virtually anywhere in the land – thus everyone is permitted to go foraging freely, apart from in private gardens or on protected nature reserves.

The benign and temperate weather of the British Isles also ensures that there are plenty of plants available to gather on foraging expeditions; you just need to learn to identify them well. Today, foraging is now enjoying a surge of popularity internationally as an enjoyable outdoor pastime and a way to get closer to nature – even many restaurants now use wild herbs in their dishes – quite apart from the economic benefits of gathering your own botanical goodies. Many useful plants, such as St John's Wort, wild garlic, nettles, sweet woodruff, dandelion, yarrow and comfrey, grow wild and plentifully in the UK and can be gathered as part of a foraging expedition. In addition, many of these species can be used to produce stillroom recipes at home.

All sorts of mushrooms and berries can also be found growing wild in parts of the British Isles. Of course, the favourite berry that is commonly gathered in the autumn across the UK is the blackberry (*Rubus fruticosus*), which is delicious made into jams and crumbles; however, the berries and leaves can also be used to make an excellent cloth dye. I have also gathered sloe berries (*Prunus spinosa*) on many occasions, which can be used to flavour gin, which turns a delicious bluish-purple colour, while the juice of the fruit can be used to dye linen a reddish colour that washes out to a lovely pale hue. Rosehips from the wild rose (*Rosa canina*) are also plentiful later in the year and are high in vitamin C. They can be used to make a delicious jelly or can also be used to prepare rosehip seed oil. Elderberry (*Sambucus nigra*) is a common shrub in Britain that grows in hedgerows and woodlands, having sweet-scented, creamy-white flowers that are ideal for infusing into cordials or for making sparkling wine.

Wildflowers were traditionally foraged at midsummer in Britain to make garlands and to decorate the home, often in association with their symbolic significance. For example, oxeye daisies are prolific in summertime, growing along roadsides, and make lovely wildflower arrangements. According to folklore, these are known as 'moon daisies' because of the way their translucent petals glow at dusk. It is also customary to gather evergreens during the colder months, especially at Christmas, and to celebrate the winter solstice by bringing greenery indoors.

There are, however, a few basic guidelines to keep in mind when collecting plants from the wild, whatever the location or country, so always take the following precautions into account:

- Always carry a precise botanical field identification guide with you.
- Never pick any species that you cannot 100 per cent identify.
- Only pick a small proportion of each plant and never strip an area of a specific species.
- Don't use plants growing near polluted roadsides or fields sprayed with pesticides.
- Never dig a plant up from the roots or pick a rare species.
- Ensure you don't trespass on private land.

I also like to always remember the Finnish Sámi's inherent respect for nature before harvesting any plant from the wild. For the Sámi people, like the Native Americans, all plants are animate, as are the rocks, mountains, springs and streams – all are imbued with their own spirit. Concepts of an external environment are alien to the Sámi, as traditionally they see themselves as a part of nature, not outside of it. It is therefore natural for indigenous cultures such as these to treat each plant and the whole of the natural world with respect as well as with an attitude of gratitude for what is given. This is known as an 'honourable harvest' since it also ensures sustainability of each species for future generations, as Robin Wall Kimmerer recounts in her classic book on Native American wisdom, *Braiding Sweetgrass*:

> *'When I ask my elders about the ways our people lived in order to keep the world whole and healthy, I hear the mandate – to take only what you need.'*

Foraged Plants for Making Wreaths and Garlands

A traditional way of using plants gathered in the wild is to make them into wreaths or garlands. Traditionally, wreath-making has a strong association with festivals, seasonal rites or celebrations where the plants used carry strong cultural associations. For example, pine, bay, holly, ivy and mistletoe are the traditional plants to use for wreath-making at the winter solstice to hang on the front door, where each of these evergreens have a symbolic meaning. For example, mistletoe is a plant sacred to the Druids and is now used to kiss beneath. A wreath or sprigs of greenery also make lovely displays placed on the dining table at Christmas. Arranging candles or night lights in the centre of the wreath so their lights illuminate the greenery makes for a beautiful centrepiece. However, be careful that the plant material is kept well away from any candles or naked flames.

Wildflowers are gathered at May Day and at midsummer to make garlands as part of the age-old custom in honour of the Goddess Flora. However, there does not need to be a special occasion to be creative with nature. I once made a wreath purely of woven clematis creepers that looked so attractive as it dried naturally that I simply hung it against a white wall in the hallway to display the intricacy of its structure. Whatever the time of year and wherever you go foraging, remember to take a basket or a large bag with you to gather plant materials so they don't become crushed.

The equipment you will need includes a bag or basket for collecting botanical materials, sharp scissors or secateurs, twine or florist wire, colourful ribbons (optional).

Method

1. First, collect twining or pliable plant material, such as willow wands, dogwood shoots, hazel tips, hops, old man's beard or clematis, as this will form the base for your wreath.
2. Then gather foliage, flowers and other decorative materials of your choice. It is best to collect all your materials on dry days – it is important that they are not damp when you start working with them or they may start to rot.
3. Begin by winding and threading your base materials, which are pliable, together to form a circular frame and then tie them in place using twine or florist wire.
4. Continue to thread more stems together until you have made a complete ring or circle three strands thick and no more than 30cm (12in) in diameter.
5. Add more twigs starting at different points, weaving in and out of the ring to strengthen it until it easily holds its shape.
6. An easy alternative is to use a ready-made wire structure or frame which can be bought from florist shops as a base. However, I prefer to make my own naturally foraged base.

7. Fix the materials or small bunches one at a time to the wreath base using wire or strong thread, laying each new bunch so it overlaps the former and conceals the wiring.
8. Gradually work your way all around the wreath, always laying the bundles in the same direction until the circle is completed and full.
9. Choose the foliage that is suited to the season and occasion, such as pine, cypress, juniper, holly and sprigs of mistletoe in the winter months. Some plants such as bay and rosemary are available at any time of year since they are both evergreen – these have been used for making protective wreaths especially.
10. Decorate this with holly berries, rosehips or any other small items that you find, which can be fixed to the wreath using florist wire. Alternatively, in summer, you can bind together small bunches of fresh plants that dry well, such as wild yarrow, love-in-the mist and lavender, then attach them using florist wire.
11. Additionally, you can embellish the wreath with anything else you wish, such as colourful ribbons or other items found outdoors, such as fir cones or small seed heads.
12. Finally, attach a looped wire or ribbon to hang it on your front door, or if you wish, in a suitable place indoors.

Cutting and Harvesting

Plants to be harvested for use in floral arrangements, stillroom recipes or for drying should always be picked with a good length of stem, just before they come into full bloom on a warm day. The best time of day for picking herbs and flowers is in the early morning after any dew has vanished, as it is essential that all plants are completely free of damp before they are harvested, otherwise they may start to turn mouldy. Check that all parts of the plant are healthy and remove any rotten or discoloured bits, which can be composted or returned to nature. Leaves especially should be harvested when they are young as this is when they are at their most vibrant. Seeds however should be left to sun-ripen for as long as possible on the plant before they are gathered, and berries collected only once they are completely ripe.

When it comes to harvesting herbs, most annuals can be harvested at least twice in a single season – the first time it is important not to trim them too much or they will not be able to recover in time for harvesting later in the season. Most herbs can also be harvested early on in their growing season, and it may even be possible to harvest perennials up to three times in a single season – but be careful not to cut into any woody growth, especially later in the year. In some instances, it is true to say that the more you pick the more a plant will grow – for example, chives will recover quickly and produce new growth soon after they have been trimmed. There is an old country tradition that says it is preferable for culinary herbs to be picked by hand rather than cut using a metal tool, and some East Asian cooks still maintain that plants retain their flavour better when harvested in this way.

Roots should be dug up in the autumn when they have completed their growing season and are at their peak. Lift them from the soil with a fork or trowel, taking care not to damage the outer skin. Wash them free of soil and remove any remains of their top growth. For drying larger roots, it is best to slice them into smaller sections for handling with ease as they generally take longer to dry than leaves or flowers and may also require a higher temperature to fully eliminate any moisture.

Flowers for floral arranging are best cut when they are in bud, but not fully open, and it is also best to trim off the lower leaves and any unwanted branches at the same time as picking. As soon as the flowers are cut, they should be plunged into water as soon as possible after picking to ensure they have a long life. If you are picking flowers from your garden, it is good to have an appropriate container nearby or ideally to take a bucket of water around the garden with you. During the day, particularly in the summer months with the increased heat, most plants will transpire more and so will become moisture-deficient quite quickly. This means they are more likely to droop as soon as they have been cut in hot weather so try to pick them in the cool of the morning. Plants that have had the opportunity to restore their moisture balance overnight will be more able to withstand the trauma of being cut – even when gathering plants from your garden, it is good to always remember the wisdom of making an 'honourable harvest'.

When harvesting botanicals from the garden generally, always try to use a pair of good-quality secateurs or scissors when you cut any plants – and they must be super sharp. If they are blunt, there is the danger you will crush the stem and this could damage the parent plant, whether you are foraging in the wild or picking plants from your garden. Be aware of the overall picture when you are harvesting any species and just take one or two stems from each plant rather than all the flowers from one specimen, much as you would if you were gathering from the wild. As you become more experienced with the process of harvesting, you will discover that some plants naturally respond well to being picked, whereas others tend to droop directly. If this is the case, try searing their stems a little, for example by placing them in a jug of boiled water. In all cases, it is important to

always slice off a small portion from the bottom of the stem so that the plant can take in water more easily.

In the garden, many plants benefit from being trimmed back as a matter of course after flowering and before autumn, since clipping off all the old flowering stems encourages new healthy growth. I always like to see what can be used for floral displays from these offcuts rather than discarding them outright. In the case of tender plants, however, major pruning should be left until spring to prevent any exposed stems from frost damage or the chilling effects of cold weather.

Drying Plant Materials

Plant material for drying should be hung in small, loose bunches with natural string or twine in a dark, well-ventilated place such as a darkened room, an old cupboard or a dry shed. Alternatively, the botanical items can be laid out on newspaper-lined trays or on a raised mesh and slid under the bed or a chest of drawers. In this case, the plant material may need to be turned over by hand several times during the first few days if they are on sheets of newspaper. Another drying method is to make loose bundles of three or four cut stems that can be placed in brown paper bags, with the neck left open and pegged to a rope, then hung between hooks in a room.

A gentle heat from an Aga, open fire or airing cupboard can help speed up the drying process, but intense heat is destructive to the plants' properties. My Finnish grandmother dried herbs in her kitchen in this way above her stove, before storing them away carefully in a cool, dry attic space. When drying fragrant herbs, it is always best to keep them separate from each other, so the stronger scented ones do not overpower the more delicate species. Seeds should be dried without any artificial heat, however.

The main object of drying herbs is to eliminate the water while retaining the essential oils and those parts of the plant that offer nutrients and

Instructions for Making a Traditional 'Sweet Jar'

A 'sweet jar' is an old-fashioned method for purifying and scenting a room using a range of botanicals. The recipe is intended as an aromatic inspiration rather than a step-by-step guide.

Ingredients

24 sweet bay leaves, torn into strips, 1 handful (each) of myrtle leaves, the red part of clove carnations, syringa or orange blossom separated from the green calyx, and violet flowers picked from their stalks, 6 handfuls of lavender blossoms, 1 handful (each) of sweet verbena leaves, thyme, balm, sweet marjoram and rosemary, 6lb (2.7kg) of bay salt (coarse sea salt) beaten fine, 4oz (110g) of orris root sliced, 2oz (55g) of beaten cloves, rinds of three Seville oranges and three lemons finely pared

Method

1. Dry bay leaves, myrtle leaves, clove carnations, syringa or orange blossom, violets and herbs (verbena, thyme, balm, sweet marjoram and rosemary) on a sheet spread in a sunny room.
2. Put them all into a large china jar, sprinkle with the pounded bay salt, and mix thoroughly.
3. In a short time, the flowers and leaves will become moist.
4. Stir the contents of the jar well every day for a month, adding a little bay salt occasionally. Keep the jar in the sun, closely covered with a china lid.
5. When the materials have been in the jar for a day or two, add the orris root sliced, beaten cloves and the rinds of Seville oranges and lemons finely pared, cut into strips and well beaten.
6. Cover the jar as before. Remove the lid to release the scent as required.
7. Jessamine (jasmine) flowers, myrtle or syringa, or orange flowers, well dried in the sun, can be added at any time to this mixture.
8. Never adulterate with synthetic scents bought at a shop!

therapeutic value. One of the main ways of ensuring this is to make sure the plants always have good airflow around them, since this process speeds up the drying time and so their aromatic qualities are preserved. After a few days have passed, check that your flowers and herbs are completely dry and brittle to the touch. If the plant material retains any moisture, then it will most likely rot or go mouldy. Don't throw away the woody stems of aromatic plants as you can use them as incense or as burning perfumes – *see* Chapter 4. Any single decorative dried flowers should also be retained to make beautiful, long-lasting recipes, such as adding to potpourri, once they have been properly dried.

Another quick method for drying plant material is to use a microwave oven. However, it is easy to 'overcook' herbs in this way as most soft-leaved botanicals only require about a minute. Freezing herbs is another way of preserving the nutritional and medicinal value of herbs and is becoming an increasingly popular method to prepare and store botanicals, being quick and easy. Freezing freshly harvested herbs such as parsley or chives, rather than drying them, is perhaps the most effective modern method of ensuring that all their essential oils and other therapeutic constituents remain intact, especially when they are to be used for culinary or medicinal purposes. In this case, it is enough to just wash the plant with water then shake them dry before putting them into individual sealed and labelled bags for freezing.

Whichever method you use, it is important to check the plant material is thoroughly dry before it is stored in an airtight container away from direct sunlight. A dark-tinted glass jar is ideal because if material is exposed to sunlight or too much heat, it will lose most of its aromatic potency, especially for therapeutic use or if it is to be used in cooking. It is important to store any seeds, leaves and flowers in airtight jars or containers, or in paper bags secured at the top, and remember to label them clearly. It is easy to forget which seed or herb is which, especially when they are dried, so have a pen and some blank labels ready to name them immediately and add the date they were prepared.

Most dried herbs can be stored for a year in this way, although some aromatics will last even longer without deteriorating. Freezing herbs, such as dill, fennel, parsley, tarragon and chives, ensures they have the longest shelf life and there is also no need to thaw them first if they are to be used for cooking. Many flower materials, such as lavender bundles, can look decorative hung upside down to dry without further preparation, but other materials are best enjoyed in the form of stillroom recipes.

Note: When making up recipes for culinary or therapeutic use, the dried herb is around three to four times as powerful as the fresh form, so this always needs to be considered when following instructions.

Recipes & Crafts

Dried Flower Arrangements

This is a lovely way to enjoy flowers at any time of year and an art form that has seen a resurgence in popularity in recent years. Dried arrangements offer a sustainable option for eco-friendly flower arranging and bridge the seasonal gap when there is little fresh in the garden. Roses, delphiniums, hydrangea, globe amaranth, celosia, pansies, lavender, eryngium, chrysanthemums, gypsophila, globe thistle, scabious, cornflowers, astrantia, peony, crocosmia, strawflowers, love-in-the mist, yarrow and statice all retain their colour well upon drying. Flowers need to be picked just before or as they open before any ageing occurs. Different types of tall grasses and large seed heads also make a stunning statement placed in large jars or vases. It is hard to beat the raw beauty of botanical materials when displayed in a naturalist manner. If well cared for, dried flower arrangements can last on average between three to four years.

Ingredients

Dried flowers, seed heads, greenery, grasses

Equipment

Secateurs, suitable containers for display, for example, pots, baskets or vases

Method

1. Ensure all the botanical materials are completely dry – they should be brittle to the touch (see instructions for drying earlier in this chapter).
2. Select specimens or flowers that work well together in form and colour.
3. Trim the stems and split them into small bunches of three or more stems.
4. Arrange the items according to the size of the container, for example, a low basket may require lots of small flower heads whereas a large jar may simply require a single or a few stand-out specimens.

5. Avoid placing the arrangement in direct sunlight to preserve the colour of the flower heads.

Making Dried Posies

I like to gather wild material from hedgerows or small items from the garden that dry readily, then bind them into loose hand-tied bundles or posies to display creatively. You can then simply hang them on the wall using raffia or offer them as a gift. You may wish to choose a single species according to 'The Language of Flowers' in Chapter 5, make a more naturalist mix of various botanicals, or simply use grasses or seed heads.

Ingredients

Dried flowers, seed heads, grasses, and so on

Equipment

Scissors, raffia for binding, ribbon, gift tag (optional)

Method

1. Ensure all the materials are completely dry before you begin to create the posy (*see* instructions for drying earlier in this chapter).
2. Trim the stems and make them into small bunches using multiple stems.
3. Secure with natural raffia, with a loop for hanging if required.
4. Add a ribbon for decorative effect and a gift tag if giving as a present.

Modern Potpourri Method

There are numerous traditional potpourri recipes available, for example, the moist 'Sweet Jar' blend shown earlier in this chapter. However, experimenting with new home-grown combinations can be exciting and can turn this classic craft into a modern art form. Incorporating more unusual items into the mix, such as large fir cones, dried citrus peel and over-sized seed heads, along with the more traditional dried petals from a wide range of flowers,

including roses, marigolds, lavender and lemon verbena, makes for a more unique display. The choice of an innovative container can also add a contemporary twist to this custom. This is also a creative way of using botanical materials that can be adapted to the changing seasons – *see* the summer and winter potpourri recipes later in this section.

Making potpourri is also a great way of 'recycling' cut flower arrangements, such as bunches of roses, tulips or delphiniums, as well as greenery such as sprigs of eucalyptus. Most modern recipes tend to omit the use of orris root powder, which was often added as a fixative in traditional blends. However, orris tends to leave a powdery residue so I prefer to use long-lasting natural aromatics as fixatives instead, such as vetiver, benzoin or frankincense oils. Another alternative to orris root powder is to use lavender blossom powder instead. The addition of raw spices, such as cinnamon sticks, cardamon pods or grated nutmeg, will also help to preserve the scent of a blend.

Ingredients

Essential oil, selected dried petals, buds and leaves, dried citrus peel or other items

Equipment

Glass bottle; mixing bowl, 1 litre (1.7 pint) glass preserving jar with a screw top, decorative bowl, jar or container

Method

1. Measure out and blend all the essential oils into a small glass bottle: the ratio to use is 50 drops of essential oil to every 500g (17.6oz) or 4–5 handfuls of dried plant materials you will be using.
2. Mix all the dry material, such as petals and seed heads, together gently.
3. Add half the total quantity of essential oils to this mixture.
4. Mix thoroughly then gently blend in the rest of the dried materials and the remaining essential oils.
5. Before putting the blended mix into the container, keep aside a few decorative ingredients, such as large seed heads or bark.
6. Put the blended mix into the glass preserving jar and seal the container.
7. Leave to mature in a dark place for five to six weeks, until mature.
8. Display in a wide ceramic bowl, glass dish or pot, arranging the reserved decorative ingredients artistically on top.
9. Your essential oils blend can be used to 'top up' the potpourri fragrance after a few weeks if required.

Summer Potpourri Recipe

Summer is when buds and flowers are at their most plentiful. All the classic scented potpourri ingredients are available at this time of year, such as roses, lavender, hydrangea, chamomile, chrysanthemums, calendula, lemon balm and peppermint, as well as many of those flowers that dry well, such as love-in-the mist, yarrow and statice. Harvest and dry the flowers as directed earlier in this chapter to ensure they retain no moisture before you begin, and use the same method as described for the 'Modern Potpourri Recipe'.

Ingredients

20 drops of lavender essential oil, 15 drops of geranium essential oil, 5 drops each of rose, bergamot and benzoin oils, 85g (3oz) or 1 handful each of mixed dried flower petals, lavender flowers, dried verbena leaves, dried hydrangea flowers, 42g (1.5oz) of rose buds (or petals)

Winter Potpourri Recipe

Autumn and winter are the perfect time for collecting dried seed pods, such as poppy seed heads or pinecones, while out walking or from the garden. Flower petals and other aromatic items,

such as orange or tangerine peel, can also be dried easily by laying them out on a sheet of newspaper and sliding them under a chest away from the light for up to ten days; you can then add these to your blend. Use the same method as described for the 'Modern Potpourri Recipe'.

Ingredients

20 drops of frankincense essential oil, 15 drops of juniper berry essential oil, 5 drops each of orange, clove and cardamom essential oils, 85g (3oz) or approximately 1 handful each of dried marigold petals, bay leaves, verbena leaves, dry orange peel, a selection of decorative seed pods, dried bark, pinecones (whatever is available), ¼ grated nutmeg; a few cardamom pods, juniper berries and cloves buds (as fixatives)

Herbal Sleep Sachets

Dried flower sachets have traditionally been used to promote sleep and soothe a restless mind. This practice derives from the habit of stuffing mattresses with scented plants. The Roman Emperor Nero reputedly slept on a mattress filled with fragrant grasses and dried rose petals; Edward III favoured chamomile, while Charles VI of France preferred lavender for scenting his bed and pillows. This recipe uses hops, lavender and chamomile but other suitable herbs include lemon balm and woodruff. If making larger pillows, you can use more dried hops to add bulk. Then simply place this herbal sleep sachet under your pillow or in the linen cupboard or drawer to promote a restful night. A sleep bag also makes a lovely gift. This recipe makes approximately four sleep bags.

Ingredients

170g (6oz) or approximately 2 handfuls each of dried hops, lavender and chamomile flowers mixed

3 drops each of rose geranium, chamomile, clary sage and lavender essential oils

Equipment

Paper to make a template, ruler, pen, scissors, fabric offcuts in linen, cotton or muslin (lining wadding if required), glass or ceramic mixing bowl, ribbon

Method

1. To make the sachets or bundles, make a square paper template, approximately 15cm × 15cm (6in × 6in) in width.
2. Using the template, cut your chosen fabric into four squares (plus wadding if required).
3. Carefully mix the dried flowers with the essential oils in a glass or ceramic bowl.
4. Lay a portion of the botanical blend into the centre of each of your fabric squares.
5. Close and seal each of the pouches with ribbon.
6. Place under the pillow or between sheets or linen.

Scented Spice Bags

Small bags of powdered aromatics have been used for centuries to perfume gloves, scarves, handkerchiefs and underwear. This recipe is for a unisex scented bag and has a slightly spicy bouquet. Patchouli oil is the classic fragrance used in India for scenting clothing and scarves with a long-lasting aroma, but not everyone is a fan of the aroma! This recipe is enough for one bag.

Ingredients

42g (1.5oz) or approximately half a handful each of dried lavender, dried lemon verbena, dried hops, 1 lightly crushed cinnamon stick, 1 tsp dried cloves, 5–10 drops of lavender essential oil, 5–10 drops of patchouli (or bergamot) essential oil

Equipment

Pestle and mortar, glass preserving jar with screw top, 2 pieces of quilted wadding about 15cm (6in) square, 2 pieces of plain cotton about 15cm (6in)

1. Mix and crush together the dried herbs, cinnamon, cloves and essential oils using a pestle and mortar.
2. Put in a glass jar, seal the top and leave for one to two weeks in a dark place.
3. Place a piece of wadding on each piece of a plain fabric square and sew around all the sides. With the fabric and wadding joined together, sew around three sides of the square.
4. Turn the right way around and stuff the aromatic herbal powder into the bag through the remaining open side. Stitch up the fourth side carefully.
5. Now make the outer casing of the bag in the same way as in step 3. Place the powder bag within the casing and use ribbons as ties or poppers to secure it.
6. Slip the bag inside clothing drawers, on shelving between linens or use to scent underwear or other items.

Moth- and Insect-Repellent Sacs

Traditionally, Indian shawls and cloth were scented with patchouli oil, not only for its exotic fragrance but also for the practical reason that it protected the cloth against moths. This can be an effective wardrobe deterrent if you like the smell of patchouli. Cedarwood is an effective essential oil to use for this purpose too. However, all kinds of powdered herbs, petals or spices can be used in making scented insect-repellent sacs, such as lavender, mugwort, rosemary, bay, peppermint and lemon balm. These aromatics, together with orris made from powdered iris root, are amongst the most traditional plants or oils used to keep clothes and linen free of moths and insects. Ants and spiders dislike the smell of peppermint oil if it is put in their path, while citronella oil helps deter mosquitoes and other insects.

An ancient recipe for protecting against moths combines cinnamon, cloves, caraway seed, nutmeg, camphor and orris root. The recipe below is a contemporary version, to leave clothes and woollens scented with a fresh aroma and is enough to make five bags.

Ingredients

85g (3oz) or approximately 1 handful each of dried lavender, lemon balm and peppermint, 3 bay leaves, 500g (17.6oz) orris root powder, 10 drops each of cloves, cedarwood and lavender essential oils

Equipment

Pestle and mortar, 5 facial cotton pads, jar or tin that can be sealed, 5 circular pieces of linen cloth 20cm (8in) in diameter, 5 lengths of ribbon

Method

1. Using a pestle and mortar, crush the dried herbs and leaves to a rough-textured powder. Add the orris root powder.
2. On each cotton pad, put two drops of each of the essential oils.
3. Put these, together with the crushed herbs and orris root mixture, into a sealed jar or tin for one week to infuse.
4. Divide the herb mixture into five portions, including a cotton pad with each.
5. Put one pad and one portion of the herb mixture onto one of the pieces of linen cloth, then draw together the cloth to form a gathered pouch.
6. Do the same for the remaining portions of herb mixture and pieces of fabric.
7. Use ribbon to secure the necks, leaving a loop to hang in your wardrobe or in your drawers.

Chapter 2

The Modern Stillroom

'There is no occupation that comes nearer to the work of gods than the occupation of distilling.'

J. Roundell and H. Roberts, *The Still-Room*

The term 'stillroom' dates back to medieval times in Europe, as it was an integral part of all great households. Part alchemical laboratory and part botanical kitchen, it was the place where plants were prepared to create all kinds of homemade condiments, such as flavoured oils, vinegars, jams and preserves, as well as delicious beverages, including beer and wine. It was also the room where herbs and flowers were dried and processed to make essential oils and floral waters to produce natural cosmetics, perfumes and medicines, plus a whole range of household items, using basic methods of blending, infusing and distillation; thus the term 'distillery' or 'still' room developed.

Yet this same ancient tradition can be traced back many thousands of years to East Asia. Perfectly preserved distillation apparatus made from terracotta and used to make primitive essential oils and perfumes have been discovered in the ancient Indus Valley civilisation at the foot of the Himalayas, dating to around 3000 BCE. Then in the Middle East, a more sophisticated distillation technique was discovered by the Arabic scholar and alchemist Avicenna during the tenth century CE, when it became possible to produce even purer essential oils and floral waters. The Arabs have always been renowned for their love of rosewater, which is still used extensively in their skincare formulations today as well as being an integral part of their everyday healing practices and culinary heritage. The practices of the stillroom are therefore not simply part of a medieval European tradition, but an ancient alchemical craft inspired by nature, whose lineage can be found within diverse cultures across the world.

The Origins of the Stillroom

Originally, the stillroom was used primarily for preparing aromatic substances of hygienic and medicinal value, alongside making flavoured vinegars and oils, botanical wines and cordials, as well as for drying culinary herbs. In larger houses, there was often another room used solely for the drying of plants, but in smaller households, both activities took place in the same place. The task of making these household items was largely carried out by the women of the household and often required a certain skill. The list of items that were once prepared in the stillroom is quite extensive, and includes:

- toiletries and cosmetics, such as essential oils, flower waters, eau de colognes, smelling salts, soaps, perfumes and pomanders
- medicines such as salves, tinctures, lozenges and poultices

- culinary delicacies like sweetmeats, candied flowers, pickled vegetables, jams, jellies, syrups, flavoured vinegars and oils
- fermented drinks such as beer, wine, liqueurs, cordials, herbal-infused drinks and tisanes
- household aids and cleaning agents such as furniture polishes, vegetable dyes, candles, insect and pest repellents
- dried scented items, such as herbs and spices, flowers and roots, potpourri, sweet jars, herbal sachets and strewing herbs
- other useful talismans, such as good luck charms and love potions.

Most of the recipes for stillroom preparations were passed on orally but some 'receipts' were preserved by families recording their medical, household and perfumery knowledge over generations in special handwritten books. Mary Doggett in 1682, for example, noted down one of the finest recipes for a 'sweet bagg' using a mixture of orris, rosewood, coriander seeds, oranges, cloves, lemon peel, damask leaves, marjoram, juniper, sweet flag and cypress roots.

In 1617, William Lawson wrote *The Countrie Housewife's Garden*, in which he not only described medicinal and culinary herbs but also those that are especially valuable for the stillroom in the preparation of home remedies, perfumes, soaps, potpourri, wines and vinegars. He recommended women have both a flower garden and a kitchen garden and advised mixing lavender and roses with growing vegetables and herbs. Lawson's potager-style arrangement, where vegetables, herbs and stillroom plants together with flowers for cutting are combined in an overall scheme, would make a good design for a modern aromatic garden since this kind of mixed planting has become increasingly popular in recent years.

Roses were grown extensively and used for making flower waters, while linens, writing paper and clothes were scented with aromatic herbs such as lavender as well as spices. A fragrant cosmetic water made from lily-of-the-valley, known as 'Aqua Aurea', was used as a beauty aid, while myrtle flowers were used to make a popular skin tonic called 'Angel Flower Water'. Scented water was also frequently sprinkled on the floors of Elizabethan rooms, which were commonly strewn with scented rushes or bay. The lemon-scented juice from the leaves and stem of lemon balm or the seeds of sweet cicely were used to polish heavy oak furniture and flooring, imparting their sweet perfume to the wood.

In a historical context, the stillroom contained a great deal of equipment and tools that were required in these traditional settings, for example: distillation apparatus used for extracting essential oils and floral waters from botanical materials; an alembic, used specifically for distilling alcoholic spirits or perfumes; a mortar and pestle; pots and glass containers for infusing plants in liquid, such as oil, vinegar or alcohol; scales to measure precise quantities of herbs, spices or other ingredients; funnels, stirring rods or spoons, sieves and strainers; plus a wide range of tinted glass containers, such as jars and bottles of various sizes and shapes, for storing and preserving remedies, aromatic oils and other preparations, along with tightly fitting seals or lids. In a modern setting, many of these traditional tools can be replaced by more advanced equipment, while the process of drying herbs or preserving foods using salt, for example, has been replaced by the method of freezing. Some techniques have also been outdated but many of the items, such as tinted jars, scales and a range of storage containers, remain invaluable for the modern stillroom even today.

The idea of the modern stillroom is essentially a room or an area where plant materials can be prepared to create a multitude of nature-inspired, handmade items to enhance our homes and sense of well-being. Today, it could be our kitchen, utility room, studio or garden shed – any space that can

be utilised for the art of working with natural materials to create health-giving products that enrich our everyday lives and our environment. The modern stillroom is also a place in which we can rediscover a sense of stillness within – a space in which we can touch a natural quiet and re-centre ourselves by practising age-old crafts and revisiting a time when life was not consumed at such a fast pace. Today, it is becoming clear, given the dis-stress levels of our society at large, that the benefits of modern technology and social media need to be balanced against our inherent inner need for simplicity, stillness and silence.

The Finnish Tradition

Over time, each culture interpreted the role of the stillroom in different ways, depending on their climate, environment and the botanical plants at their disposal. Whether in Finland, Norway, Britain, Japan, the Middle East or America – each nation developed its own botanical pharmacopoeia, systems of healing and well-being rituals – although many of these indigenous wisdom traditions have become buried or overlaid by time. When I spoke to a Japanese friend, where I extolled the beauty inherent in the ancient Zen traditions, such as ikebana, the art of Japanese flower arranging, I was reminded by her that many aspects of early Japanese culture have largely been overshadowed by commercial interests in recent years. Nevertheless, now there is a growing interest and enthusiasm to revive the integrity of these valuable cultural traditions and markers of national identity, and to recover the knowledge embedded in each heritage.

My botanical heritage is tied to the Finnish tradition due to my Scandinavian roots. I used to love exploring my grandmother's house in Rauma on the west coast of Finland when I was a child. This was a beautiful wooden L-shaped building that was set around a central, cobbled courtyard, like so many of the other old wooden houses

Preparing Aromatic Waters
– A Traditional Practice

The generality of plants will give their maximum amount of essence when they are dealt with in their fresh condition. A few, however, produce more when they are dry. The produce of the same kind may vary for diverse reasons: the moment of its harvest and the atmospheric conditions under which it is affected, the nature of the soil and the quality of the plants.

The proportion of water used is mostly three to four times the weight of the substance. The length of time for soaking varies from twelve to forty-eight hours according to the dryness and the divided state of the substance. Some light essences extracted from fresh flowers (from roses, for example) are obtained without previous maceration. The matter is placed in the still with the water into which it has been macerated. Sea salt is sometimes added for the purpose of retarding the point of boiling point.

Note: The directions described here are intended as inspiration rather than as a practical step-by-step guide.

Aromatic Waters

For the distilling of simple aromatic waters, about 4 litres (1 gallon) of water should be allowed to 1.8kg (4lb) of the fresh herb or 450g (1lb) of the dry herb, and about 2 litres (½ gallon) should be distilled over. Peppermint water, damask-rose water, orange-flower water, spearmint water and elder-flower water are prepared in this way. For dill water, caraway water, fennel water and cinnamon water, 450g (1lb) of the bruised fruit is mixed with 8 litres (2 gallons) of water, and 4 litres (1 gallon) is distilled.

Rosemary Water

This is made by mixing 4 litres (1 gallon) of water, 44 litres (11½ gallons) of rectified spirit, and 6.4kg (14lb) of rosemary flowers and leaves, and slowly distilling off 10 gallons over the water bath.

Simple Lavender Water

This is made in the same way, substituting lavender flowers for rosemary flowers and leaves.

Beauty Water

This is made by mixing 2 litres (½ gallon) of rectified spirits, 4 litres (1 gallon) of water, 450g (1lb) of the flowering tops of thyme and 1lb of marjoram, and distilling off 4 litres (1 gallon).

in Rauma. I was named Julia after my maternal grandmother, a remarkably capable and practical woman who was well versed in herbal lore, whom I simply called 'Mama'.

On the top floor of her home was a long passageway that ran the whole length of the property beneath the eaves. I can still vividly remember its unique aroma – a familiar sharp-green fragrance of herbs blended with the faint, soft-warm odour of ski wax, mixed with the musty smell of leather and an underlying faint tang of turpentine. This was Mama's winter larder, as it was here that she used to store a whole variety of household items over the long, cold months of the year. Flat, round rye breads were threaded on wooden poles along the rafters; labelled jars of dried aromatic dill, marjoram and parsley were kept tightly sealed alongside glass pots of pickled cucumber and cabbage on shelves along one wall; and at the far end, skis, skates and sledges were propped up alongside piles of reindeer skins. The room was also used to store some of Mama's kitchen basics, such as strings of garlic and onions dangling high up on hooks at the near end since these items were best overwintered in a cool, dark place.

The large kitchen overlooking the courtyard, however, was the place where Mama's herbs and other plants were generally prepared for use as home remedies, cooking and household items. This was her stillroom – the area used for preparing herbs and other botanicals. In the centre of the room was a long wooden table near to the window, while nearby, in the corner, was her favourite rocking chair. My mother, Kerttu, remembers the scene vividly from when she was growing up:

> *Mama's most important herb was parsley, which along with dill, marjoram, hops, and others were dried in bunches in the autumn, dangling at the ends of the short lengths of cotton, all strung on a long length of thin rope, stretching right across the kitchen stove. As scents are evocative for remembering old things, I remember it so well – the strong and heady smell emanating from these herbs, when they were hung up, and the stove was warm.*

Later, as a biochemist, my mother became involved with the research of essential oils and aromatic plants and helped encourage my fascination for herbs and the use of natural remedies. My mother would frequently use the kitchen table at home for her botanical experiments, both in making folk simples, such as handmade herbal blends and cosmetic preparations. Luckily, I still have many of my mother's recipes for creating therapeutic and toiletry products at home. Her notebooks include how to make creams and balms, as well as many other innovative aromatic products, such as blended flower waters and lotions. As a research chemist, she was familiar with using hands-on techniques, which included producing essential oils using a simple distillation method; I can still remember her experimenting with all sorts of potions on our kitchen table when I was a child.

Today, few of us have the luxury of having a room that we can put aside and use as a special stillroom. Instead, the kitchen table can be used for preparing most household items – much like my Finnish grandmother and mother – along with using a separate place for storing jars and drying herbs, such as a garden shed, garage or utility room. The fact that we can now readily freeze fresh produce for later use has made a massive difference to the way many plants and foodstuffs can be stored, especially over winter, compared to the more traditional methods.

Ingredients of Botanical Alchemy

The ingredients used in the stillroom include many common household items, such as bicarbonate of soda, glycerine, honey and sea salt as well as a whole range of vegetable oils, essential oils and various botanical extracts. Essential oils, which play a central role in many traditional recipes, occur naturally in a wide variety of different species and can be found in different parts of the plant: leaves (rosemary), bark (cinnamon), blossoms (neroli), fruit (orange), wood (cedar), resin (pine), gum (myrrh), roots (vetivert) or buds (clove). These aromatic oils can be separated from the raw plant material in several ways: some are produced by simply pressing the fresh peel of the fruit, as in the case with bitter orange, bergamot, lime and lemon, while the more delicate flower essences require a more complicated technique and comprise another category of aromatic substances called absolutes.

These compounds are produced nowadays by a complex process of solvent extraction, but originally all absolutes were made using the traditional 'enfleurage' method. This was a technique where delicately scented flowers, such as orange blossom or rose petals, were steeped in a fat or oil-based solvent over some time, until the base material became charged with scent. The resulting scented 'unguent' could then be separated further to isolate the perfume from the oily base. Although today the blossoms of flowers such as jasmine, frangipani and rose are used to produce absolutes on a commercial scale, at one time they were all extracted using this age-old method. A simple 'enfleurage' process for making exquisite natural perfumes using delicate flower petals is possible to carry out at home – *see* the 'Recipes & Crafts' section later in this chapter.

However, the main method of extraction for essential oils is by water or steam distillation. This applies to the majority of herbal oils including lavender, thyme, rosemary and sweet marjoram. In this case, the aromatic oil is extracted by passing steam through the fresh or dried herb. Traditionally in the stillroom, this was performed using special glass distillation apparatus, using a still or an alembic. For commercial, larger-scale production, this is often done at the site of the crop to be produced using mobile equipment.

However, a great deal of plant material is necessary to extract even a small amount of the pure essence, so producing one's own essential oils at home is largely impractical today, given the range of essential oils on offer.

Whereas essential oils are the aromatic components of fragrant plants, which are extracted mainly through steam distillation, flower waters or hydrosols are the natural by-product of this distillation process. These fragrant floral waters, such as rosewater, can be used as skincare agents, in toiletries and for culinary purposes. They also feature in many traditional stillroom recipes alongside essential oils and vegetable oils. Flower waters can be made at home using a variety of techniques – *see* the 'Recipes & Crafts' section later in this chapter.

Botanical or vegetable oils are generally produced by compression, from the seeds, nuts, fruit or kernels of a plant, such as sweet almond oil (kernel), grape seed oil (seed), coconut oil (nut) or olive oil (fruit). In the case of avocado, this thick, viscous oil is made from the actual pulp of the fruit, which is full of natural, healthy non-saturated fats. Cold-pressed oils are of the highest quality, as opposed to those that are subjected to heat during their extraction, since the former retain all their nutritional value.

Botanical or vegetable oils are also often called 'fixed' oils, being made up of dense liquid lipids or fats. Whereas essential oils are volatile in nature, all botanical or vegetable oils are stable – this means that if you spill a little vegetable oil on your sleeve it will stain your garment, whereas an essential oil, which is naturally volatile, will gradually evaporate, leaving no mark. Both essential oils and vegetable oils repel water, being hydrophobic, which makes them compatible with each other. That is why vegetable oils are commonly used as carriers for essential oils and are used in products like body oils. Botanical oils together with infused oils are therefore often called 'carrier' or 'base' oils in the context of aromatherapy, simply because they are used as the ideal medium for the application of essential oils to the skin. Notably, neither vegetable oils nor essential oils mix with water, which is why it is necessary to use equipment such as a bain-marie (double boiler) with heat to create a blended cream.

Unsaturated oils tend to be liquid at room temperature and are well known for their nutrition-rich, health-giving properties. The highest-quality unsaturated vegetable oils are cold-pressed from the fatty fruits and seeds whose names they bear. Oils such as olive, apricot kernel, grapeseed, sunflower seed and sesame are not only commonly used for their culinary benefits but are also frequently used in herbal preparations and natural toiletries due to their healing qualities. Saturated oils, sometimes called vegetable fats, tend to be solid at room temperature, such as coconut oil.

In the context of herbal medicine, infused oils are another important form of herbal preparation. In this process, the herb is steeped in a vegetable oil base such as olive oil or sunflower oil for a period of time. Gradually, the active therapeutic compounds of the herb dissolve into the base oil, so the resulting infused oil represents a whole herb extract of the plant, where the individual herbs impart their healing properties to the resulting infused oil.

It is easy to make your own infused herbal oils at home and the results can be spectacular! I regularly make my own infused oil using the freshly gathered yellow flowers of St John's Wort, which produces a wonderfully ruby-red oil once it has matured. In this case, the flowers are used fresh, since this ensures the main active ingredient, hypericin, is activated, thus imparting the dramatic red pigment characteristic of this powerful, healing oil. Many of the most useful plants for making infused oils can be grown at home, while others can be gathered wild. More exotic aromatic species, such as spices, may need to be bought as raw materials.

Making herbal teas is a similar process to making oil infusions, except that a tea or tisane is a water-based infusion of a herb or flower rather than an oil-based infusion. Herbal teas are also quite similar to flower waters since some modern methods for preparing flower waters mimic making a flower-based tisane.

The Kitchen Witch

Apart from the practice of drying, distilling and preparing botanical plants for use in toiletries and household items, the making of herbal oils, vinegars, tisanes and infusions as everyday home remedies and for their culinary benefits played a central role in the traditional stillroom. Aromatic culinary herbs have always been grown for their ability to flavour and enhance the preparation of food and drink. The preservative properties of plants were also considered to be invaluable before the advent of modern storage techniques, such as refrigeration, as were their aperitif and digestive properties. Many of the Mediterranean herbs such as bay, marjoram, rosemary and thyme, which all contain large proportions of bactericidal essential oils, were especially highly regarded in this respect, as were spices such as cloves, cardamom, cinnamon and ginger. A further advantage of most culinary herbs is that they can be grown in pots, tubs or window boxes that can be placed within easy reach of the kitchen door.

Herbal teas or tisanes have enjoyed a revival of interest in the last few decades as the numerous benefits of herbs in promoting well-being have become more appreciated. Today, the main plants to include in a medicinal herb garden are those that can be used to make refreshing and digestive tisanes or herbal teas for their health benefits. These can be made at home from a wide range of plants, including lime flowers, chamomile, mint, sage, lemon balm, verbena and fennel, and are one of the easiest ways of preparing home-grown

herbs for promoting good health and longevity.

Health-giving herbal teas can generally be made using either fresh or dried plant material. Dried plant materials are more concentrated – one teaspoon of dried material equals about three to four teaspoons of fresh material. Fresh herbs are often more potent and are likely to have a higher medicinal value, but dried plants are more readily available all year round. Whenever possible, infusions should be made using fresh herbs or flowers as soon as they have been picked.

Infused herbal oils have a multitude of everyday uses and are one of the most traditional ways of preparing plants, common to all cultures alike. These can be employed therapeutically, or to enhance the flavour of food by making herbal oils and delicious vinegars. These can then be added to salad dressings and numerous culinary recipes, to enhance the taste of vegetables and other foods, such as meat and fish dishes, as well as to aid digestion and as a preventative against bacterial infection.

Adding aromatic plant materials to oil or vinegar is simply one of the best ways of capturing the unique flavour of different herbs, such as basil, rosemary and garlic, as well as numerous spices, such as coriander, dill or fennel seeds. These are easy to make and simple to use in the kitchen, as well as being naturally therapeutic in their action. Making herbal tinctures, syrups, jams, cordials, wines and a whole range of other culinary delights are also traditional ways of preserving and enjoying botanical raw materials for inclusion in recipes. Making medicinal or culinary preparations from herbs and aromatics, however, is beyond the scope of this book because these are both vast subjects in themselves.

In the following section, I have included some suggestions for making essential oils, flower waters, botanical perfumes, flavoured oils and vinegars and a range of blended teas in some simple ways at home.

Some Traditional Stillroom Recipes

The recipes here are intended as aromatic inspiration rather than as a practical step-by-step guide.

Aromatic Vinegar for Smelling Salts

Digest in a bottle for four days, with frequent shaking, a mixture of 473ml (1 pint) of acetic acid (90 per cent), 1oz each of dried lavender flowers, thyme, and rosemary, and twenty grains each of powdered cloves and cinnamon. Strain, filter through blotting paper and bottle.

Toilet Vinegar

Mix 1oz of pure acetic acid with 473ml (1 pint) of water and digest therein, for two or three weeks, 125g (4oz) of fresh, or 2oz of dried, fragrant flowers or leaves. Among the best for the purpose are rose petals, lavender, elder blossom, rosemary and thyme.

Eau de Cologne

Mix 1 pint of rectified spirits (ethyl alcohol), 1oz of orange-flower water, 2 drams* of oil of bergamot, 2 drams of oil of lemon, 20 minims* of oil of rosemary, and 20 minims of oil of neroli. Allow the mixture to stand for a couple of months, thoroughly shaking at intervals. Filter, if necessary.

Lavender Water without Distillation

Mix a pint of rectified spirits (ethyl alcohol), 4oz of distilled water, three drams of oil of lavender, three drams of orange-flower water, five minims each of oil of cloves and oil of cinnamon, and four minims of otto of roses. Allow this mixture to stand for a fortnight, then filter through the carbonate of magnesia and bottle. Keep for three months before using.

Note: One dram is ⅛fl oz while a minim is roughly equivalent to one drop.

Recipes & Crafts

Preparing Flower Waters – Rosewater

Flower waters, such as rosewater, can either be made using fresh materials gathered from the garden or dried petals. This recipe uses fresh rose petals – just make sure they are a scented variety. Rosewater is used extensively in skincare and has always been a mainstay of perfumery work – there is an old saying, 'no perfume without rose'. Rosa centifolia is renowned as an aphrodisiac and a pronounced euphoric and soothing effect on the heart, so is good for grief and depression. Rosewater also makes a perfect and classic toner for all skin types and is lovely spritzed onto the skin as a light perfume. You can also use this method to make other scented waters such as lavender, rosemary or lemon balm (melissa) water.

Ingredients

5 large handfuls of fresh rose petals or other botanicals (if using dried petals, use less than half the quantity), spring water

Equipment

Heavy-bottomed saucepan, sieve, muslin, measuring jug or bowl, airtight tinted glass bottle with lid

Method

1. Rinse fresh rose petals under cold, running water to remove any dirt – skip this step if using dried rose petals.
2. Add the petals to a heavy-bottomed saucepan and pour in enough spring water to cover them.
3. Bring the water to a mild simmer, then turn off the heat and let the petals steep for about 10–15 minutes. They will release their colour into the water and then turn pale – the rose-tinted effect is stronger when using dried petals.
4. Line a fine-mesh sieve with a piece of muslin, then put the sieve over a large measuring jug or bowl to catch the liquid.
5. Pour the rose petal mixture into the sieve, then let the liquid cool.
6. Decant the rosewater into an airtight glass bottle. Tinted glass bottles are best, but a clear glass bottle will work if it is kept out of direct sunlight.
7. Don't forget to apply a label with the date.
8. The flower water is best used within two weeks.

A Modern Method for Making Hydrosols

Flower waters are light, aromatic, aqua-based fragrances that have been used since antiquity and are now enjoying a massive contemporary revival. Their sheer versatility makes them ideally suited to our modern life, where each flower water has a wide range of specific properties and benefits, for example as a light perfume, pillow spray or simply as a refreshingly cooling air freshener. Hydrosols are the natural by-product of essential oil distillation. Flower waters can also be produced by saturating pure essential oils in water for a set time (which varies according to each oil) to make sure the base has matured sufficiently to have become infused with a high level of aromatic constituents, then filtering. This means the resulting scent is true to that of the essential oil, lasts a long time and will also maintain its characteristic 'true-to-nature' fragrance. I have been involved in the production of a wide range of unique, handmade floral waters in our artisan laboratory at Aqua Oleum in the Cotswolds, Gloucestershire, for many years. The recipe here, however, uses the process of mimicking the hydrosol production process on a small scale.

Ingredients

1 handful of dried flowers (or 4 handfuls of fresh material), 1 litre (1.7 pints) of distilled water

Equipment

Pan with a steamer and a domed lid cover, heatproof bowl, bag of ice (optional), mini spray bottles

Method

1. Prepare the fresh flowers for the distilling process by separating the petals (or the leaves in the case of rosemary water) from the stems and washing thoroughly.
2. Prepare the dried flowers/leaves by soaking in the distilled water for at least two hours.
3. For fresh materials, place them with the water (1 part flowers to 10 parts water) into a pot.
4. For dried flowers/leaves, pour the soaked flowers with the water into a pot.
5. Place your steamer with the heatproof bowl on top of the pan and place the inverted lid on top. Leave your flowers to simmer. If you don't have a steamer, you can use an ordinary deep pan with a domed lid, and a colander with the heatproof dish inside. When the infused steam hits the inverted lid, it cools and runs down to the centre of the lid and then drips into the bowl. It is important to not let the bowl that collects your hydrosol to touch the bottom of the pot. You can use a bag of ice on top of the inverted lid to speed up the distilling process. This will make the steam convert back into liquid faster – but it is not essential. (You will also need to routinely replace the ice as it melts.) Try to make sure that the bowl is raised so that the liquid is away from the direct heat and will cool.
6. After about 30 minutes, the floral waters will be ready.
7. Once the mixture has cooled in the bowl, transfer the liquid into mini spray bottles.
8. Store in the fridge and it should last around six months without any preservative.

A Simple Distillation Technique for Making Essential Oils

It is possible to make flower waters and minute quantities of essential oils at home using an enamel kettle or a pressure cooker. You will also need a large quantity of fresh botanical material, such as rose petals, lavender flowers or rosemary leaves, to yield a small amount of essential oil.

Ingredients

Large amounts of plant material such as lavender flowers or rosemary leaves, water

Equipment

Enamel stovetop kettle or pressure cooker, rubber tubing, ice cubes in a bowl, chair, glass bowl, eye dropper or syringe, small tinted glass bottle for storage, label, pen

Method

1. Pack the plant material into the enamel kettle until it is full, then cover it with water.

2. Attach a piece of rubber tubing about 1.5m (5ft) long to the spout.
3. Pass the rubber tubing over a bowl of ice set on a chair and then place the end of the tube in a glass container on the floor.
4. Put the kettle on a heat source and slowly bring it to the boil.
5. Allow it to remain just below simmering level until the water has virtually disappeared from the kettle.
6. Repeat several times, discarding the spent plant material each time.
7. Using an eye dropper or syringe, draw off the essential oil from the top of the condensed liquid in the glass container and decant into a small tinted glass bottle, then label and date.
8. The remaining flower water can be used as a light perfume or in stillroom recipes.

Making Botanical Perfumes Using the Enfleurage and Maceration Methods

This is a lovely way to make 100 per cent pure botanical floral perfumes – although it does require some patience! Essences of lily-of-the-valley, jasmine, lilac, lily, neroli, violet and tuberose are best captured in this way as their fragrance is destroyed by heat. Always choose petals or flowers that are in good condition before using them to prepare a natural perfume. Make sure the botanical materials are completely dry before adding the oil or coconut butter.

Ingredients

Large quantity of scented petals or flowers such as jasmine or rose, jojoba oil/coconut butter.

Equipment

100ml (3.5fl oz) tinted glass jar with lid, glass funnel, muslin cloth, glass stirring rod, small decorative glass bottle, label, pen

Method

1. Pack a 100ml (3.5fl oz) tinted glass jar with fresh flower material, such as jasmine blossom.
2. Fill up the jar with jojoba oil and allow to stand for 24 hours.
3. Scoop the plant material into a muslin bag and squeeze the scented oil back into the jar.
4. Repeat the process using fresh plant material every day for at least one week.
5. Eventually this will produce a concentrated enfleurage-style perfume.
6. Decant into a small decorative glass bottle, label and store away from direct sunlight.

An alternative method, which is quicker but does not preserve the true scent in quite the same way, is to use an oil maceration process.

Ingredients
Coconut butter, large quantity of scented petals or flowers such as jasmine

Equipment
Enamel pan, spoon, sieve, small jar or pot with a lid

Method
1. Put a quantity of coconut butter in an enamel pan and place on a low heat so that it turns to liquid.
2. Place the fresh flower material in the enamel pan together with the melted coconut butter and stir gently for about half an hour.
3. Strain the coconut oil and plant matter quickly through a sieve and allow to cool.
4. Repeat if a stronger scent is required.
5. Decant into a small jar or pot with a lid, before it cools entirely.
6. The resulting coconut butter can be used as an unguent-style solid perfume as it will be saturated with the fragrance of the flowers used.

Making Herbal Culinary Oils
Age-old methods for preparing herbal-infused oils can be found in numerous ancient documents, including the Bible. Many of the most useful plants for making infused oils can be grown at home, while others can be gathered wild. This recipe uses the most traditional technique – the slow infusion method – for preparing herbal-infused oil, and although it takes some time, it remains my personal favourite.

Almost all culinary herbs can be used to add flavour to oils in the kitchen, such as a good-quality virgin olive oil. This has been done for centuries, particularly in Mediterranean countries. For steeping in oil, the best herbs to use are basil, bay, chervil, dill, fennel, garlic, juniper, lavender, lovage, marjoram, mint, parsley, rosemary, sage, savory and thyme. The aromatic oils can then be used in salad dressings, stir fries and plenty of other dishes to add an extra flavour kick. The following herbal oils are easy to prepare and make lovely gifts. Always make sure your empty jars and bottles are completely clean and dry. An easy way to sterilise all the glass jars and bottles that you plan to use is to run them through the dishwasher on a very hot setting first.

Ingredients
Dried or fresh herb material of your choice, virgin olive oil or another good-quality culinary oil

Equipment
Chopping board, sharp knife, clean dry glass jar with a tight-fitting lid, glass stirring rod or spoon, natural wax paper, cheesecloth or muslin, sieve or strainer, large jug or bowl with spout, sterilised storage jar or bottle, label, pen, sheets of newspaper or brown paper, string

Method
1. First, carefully prepare your plant material from either fresh or dried herbs, whichever you have available. Chop fresh, leafy herbs finely – it is important to cut up the herb first as it exposes more of the plant to the oil, making for a better infusion. Fresh flowers can be put in whole. Dried herbs should also be broken into small pieces before use.
2. Fill a glass jar almost to the top with the dried (or fresh) herbs and cover the herb completely with the olive oil. The ratio to use for dried herbs is approximately 30g (1oz) of dried herb to 300g (10oz) of oil but for fresh plants the ratio of the oil used can be much less.
3. Make sure the herbs are covered with at least a few centimetres of oil but allow a small space at the top of the jar so the herbs will have room to expand. If your herbs soak up all the oil, then pour more on top to ensure

that the herbs are kept well covered. Do not leave a large gap at the top of the jar as this will cause oxidation to occur.

4. Using a glass stirring rod or spoon, gently stir the mixture, making sure that all the plant material is well covered and evenly steeped with oil.
5. Cover the top of the jar with a piece of natural wax paper then screw on the lid. The wax paper will protect the infusion from any possible contamination from the inside the jar lid while it is steeping.
6. Place the jar in a warm spot (such as in an airing cupboard) but not in direct sunlight unless you are using a dark-coloured jar. Gentle heat is what helps infuse the oil, so it is important to keep it constantly warm.
7. Leave the oil steeping for three to six weeks. Be sure to check on it every few days and move it gently back and forth to help release the herbal properties and keep the plant material well covered.
8. If you see any signs of condensation appearing on the sides of the jar, remove the lid and wipe away any excess moisture arising from the plant to avoid mouldiness.
9. After three to six weeks, depending on the density of the material used, the oil will be ready to decant. Place a cheesecloth-lined sieve inside a large jug or bowl with spout. Pour the raw infusion into the strainer, then gather the ends of the cheesecloth together and squeeze out the remaining oil from the herbal mixture.
10. Pour the prepared oil into a sterilised bottle or jar and label and date the product clearly.
11. Finally store your precious herbal-infused culinary oil in a cool, dark place.

A Spicy Seed Oil – with Chilli and Garlic

This recipe uses the fast infusion method for making an exotic oil, ideal for salad dressings, stir-fries and Asian dishes. There are many suitable spices that you can use for this oil, such as coriander, fennel, dill or chervil seed – plus, garlic cloves or chilli flakes can be added if you wish.

Ingredients

2 tbs seeds (such as coriander, fennel, dill or chervil seed), Pinch of chilli flakes. For a more garlicky oil, add four cloves of garlic, peeled and crushed, 500ml (17fl oz) virgin olive oil

Equipment

Pestle and mortar, glass jar with screw top, muslin, sieve or strainer, glass funnel, decorative bottle, label, pen

Method

1. Mix the seeds in the mortar, pounding slightly.
2. Add the garlic cloves, if desired, and crush them gently.
3. Add a small amount of the oil and repeat to crush the seeds and bulbs lightly.
4. Add the seeds, garlic and chilli to a wide-necked jar and pour in the remaining oil to infuse.
5. Leave for two weeks, shaking every other day.
6. Strain the mix through a muslin sieve.
7. Pour into a decorative bottle.
8. Add a sprig of fresh coriander leaves and seal.
9. Label and date.

Culinary Herbal Vinegars

Herbal vinegars are a healthy addition to our diet, especially for supporting good gut bacteria. Some herbs are better suited to flavour vinegars, including basil, bay, chervil, chives, dill, fennel, garlic, juniper, lavender, lovage, marjoram, mint, oregano, rosemary, sage, savory, tarragon and thyme.

Ingredients

Herbs of your choice (*see* list in previous paragraph), 500ml (17fl oz) good white wine vinegar or cider vinegar

Equipment

Pestle and mortar, clean wide-necked glass jar with lid, strainer, glass funnel, decorative bottle, label, pen

Method

1. Pound a handful of your favourite herbs and bruise well with the pestle and mortar.
2. Add the vinegar and one handful of herbs in a wide-necked jar, then seal.
3. Leave for a week, then strain.
4. Repeat the process if you require a stronger flavour.
5. After the second week, strain off all the leaves and stems, and bottle the blend.
6. Finally, add a few fresh sprigs of the fresh herb for identification and a decorative effect.
7. Label and date if required.

Preparing Herbal Teas or Tisanes

Making herbal teas or tisanes is one of the easiest ways of utilising the health-giving properties of a wide range of home-grown herbs. As a general rule, use one teaspoon of dried herb or three to four teaspoons of fresh herb per cup of water. For young children or elderly people, use half the dosage. Simply place the herb in a china or enamel teapot (warmed) and allow it to steep for ten minutes before drinking. For a more concentrated tea, pour the water into an enamel pan and bring it almost to the boil. Add the herbs and retain them on the heat for ten minutes, maintaining the liquid just beneath boiling point. Drink immediately, adding honey to taste as required. As a guide:

- Peppermint is good for indigestion, to ward off colds and as a stimulating pick-me-up.
- Sage tea is a classic remedy for a sore throat, mixed with lemon and honey.
- Lime blossom and chamomile are soothing; good for encouraging restful sleep.
- Lemon verbena is refreshing and uplifting; good for lethargy and exhaustion.
- Melissa or lemon balm is the classic remedy for depression and trauma. It is known as the 'Elixir of Life' and renowned for promoting longevity.
- Fennel seed tea aids digestion and alleviates wind.
- Rosemary tisane acts as general stimulating tonic – it also makes an excellent hair rinse.

A Spicy Winter Tea

This tisane combines spices with herbs to soothe the nervous system and act as a preventative against winter chills and infections. Store in an airtight tin.

Ingredients

3 tbs whole cloves, 1 cinnamon stick, or 1 handful each of dried orange peel, dried peppermint, dried chamomile flowers, 2 handfuls of dried lemon verbena leaves, filtered water

Equipment

Pestle and mortar, glass storage jar with lid, teapot, strainer, cup

Method

1. Grind the cloves and cinnamon to a fine mixture using a pestle and mortar.
2. Add to the orange peel and mint, then combine the mixture with the chamomile flowers and lemon verbena leaves.
3. Add boiling water to the herbal mix in a teapot in the usual fashion and steep for ten minutes before straining and drinking from a cup.

A Cheering Summer Tea

This is an ancient recipe that is lovely to make due to the different colours of the ingredients. It has a refreshing taste. Keep the tea in a glass storage jar with a tight lid.

Ingredients

1 handful each of lavender flowers, marigold, lime blossom, ½ handful of fennel seeds, Pinch of poppy seeds

Equipment

Paper-lined trays or thread for hanging, glass storage jar with lid, teapot, strainer, cup

Method

1. Pick and dry all the herbs by placing them on paper-lined trays or hanging them on thread.
2. When dry, rub the petals free of the flowers and stalks and combine with the seeds. .
3. Add boiling water to the herbal mix in a teapot in the usual fashion and steep for ten minutes before straining and drinking.

Chapter 3

Botanical Home Hygiene

'The more our world functions like the natural world, the more likely we are to endure on this home that is ours, but not ours alone.'

Janine Benyus

The concept of working with nature rather than against it, diminishing our dependence on toxic chemical products and instead replacing them with environmentally friendly ones, and of protecting the delicate balance of the ecosystem of our planet by making conscious choices about our lifestyle, are all topics of vital importance today. We can all play a part individually in making the everyday changes necessary to reverse the present global trend of gross materialism by taking nature as our inspiration and our guide, now and in the future.

Today, many of us want to take the utmost care to ensure that what we use, consume and fill our homes with mutually respects the planet as well as our health and well-being. A renewed environmental respect is emerging to avoid pollutants and pesticides that can cause harm to us and our ecosystems. We are also becoming increasingly aware and cautious of the amount of toxins we are being exposed to daily, with many expressing a preference for eco-friendly products to care for the planet, as well as our own health.

A Botanical Cleaning Kit

Our cleaning cupboards can contain a surprising (or perhaps not so surprising!) number of 'VOCs' – also known as volatile organic compounds. Short-term exposure to high levels of these toxins can cause headaches, dizziness and drowsiness as well as eye and respiratory irritation. By repetitive exposure over time, they can also trigger cutaneous, respiratory, cardiovascular and neurological problems. It is now widely known that many seemingly harmless cleaning products cause allergic reactions, can disrupt our hormonal balance and worsen common conditions such as asthma or eczema, or even encourage other modern-day issues such as obesity. The best practice for anyone experiencing or seeking to avoid such symptoms would of course be to stop using the products in question.

There can be anything from hundreds to thousands of potentially harmful ingredients in an average household cleaning set. A good example of how these potentially harmful ingredients can be hidden is via the generic 'perfume' or 'parfum' term listed within the ingredients on a bottle. Chemical ingredients such as phthalates are commonly used to create synthetic fragrances in household products such as fabric softeners, but companies are not legally required to disclose what these are. A delightfully scented 'forest-inspired' scent in your bathroom cleaning spray may contain up to 1,000 phthalates. In contrast, creating, blending and crafting your own products for home hygiene is a direct way of controlling the ingredients that you and the people (and pets) you share your home with are exposed to. It is also an opportunity to create scents you love and that leave your home feeling naturally safe, tranquil and clean.

Regarding the environment, possibly the most significant direct impact of this type of chemical pollution is the toxicity of the water on our ecosystems. Wastewater containing cleaning products typically goes down the drain and while the water is purified to some degree, not all chemicals can be removed. These make their way into seas, rivers and lakes, and over time, contribute to the decline in aquatic health or the lifespan of the sea's inhabitants, as well as reducing biodiversity. Standard foam washing-up sponges, for example, shed small amounts of microplastics upon each use and these find their way into the waterways. Eco-friendly sponges or scourers made from wood pulp or loofah are plastic free, non-scratch and fully compostable. Cleaning cloths too are best made from natural fibres and can be popped in the washing machine after each use.

There may be a hesitancy when it comes to making the switch to natural cleaning products and household aids, or indeed making your own. As with any kind of change to our habits, small sustainable steps are always advisable rather than sweeping gestures. Making things feel more like a choice, rather than a chore, is always going to make any cleaning or tidying quest feel a bit more enjoyable. Whether it is starting by cutting down on the use of single-use plastics overall or simply reusing and refilling your cleaning product bottles, this is already going to positively contribute something to the amount of plastic packaging that pollutes our environment.

Within Scandinavia, the term *hygge* is used in Denmark and Norway to describe a particular quality of cosiness and comfort based on simple home pleasures that engenders a feeling of health, contentment and well-being. Also associated with relaxation, conviviality and gratitude, *hygge* has long been considered a part of the Danish national character – the ability to create a healing sanctuary through performing everyday activities. *Lagom* is another Nordic term, said to describe the basis of the Swedish national psyche by embracing moderation and simplicity through an appreciation of 'less is more' – an altogether more sustainable principle when compared to the 'more is better' slogan symptomatic of our modern-day consumer society. These Scandinavian customs evoke a peaceful, sensorial serenity and can be a helpful inspiration when it comes to clearing, cleaning and enlivening your home.

In this chapter, I have selected some *hygge*-inspired hygiene recipes to cultivate a sense of space and simplicity within your cleaning cupboard as well as to refresh your state of mind. With a little time and effort, you can easily upgrade your cleaning cupboard to be fully DIY. Not only will this reduce your environmental impact, but happily it will also be much lighter on the wallet than you might think. These are the basics I like to keep in my cupboard at home:

- distilled water
- rubbing alcohol
- vinegar
- fresh lemons and limes
- castile soap
- bicarbonate of soda
- table salt
- a wide selection of essential oils including eucalyptus, clove, lavender, lemon and rosemary
- active charcoal
- recycled or reusable containers – polyethylene terephthalate (PET) plastic, aluminium or glass bottles.

Space Clearing and Spring Cleaning

The process of space clearing is a practical exercise to help simplify and create a sense of ease within your home as well as being an ancient sacred

ritual. Over time, it is common for unnecessary objects to gradually accumulate, which impedes the flow of energy within your home – anything that you don't love or use regularly can be considered clutter. As part of a space-clearing ritual, it is good to go through each room and remove as many extraneous things as possible. For example, recycle the piles of magazines you will never read, take the clothes you have never worn to a charity shop and either mend or discard any chipped crockery. If it is hard to let go of a particular item, then give yourself some more time by putting it into a 'not quite sure' box until you are certain you want to get rid of it.

In the meantime, to make your space feel refreshed and full of vitality, shake out the rugs, clean the floors and wipe surfaces using natural botanical ingredients. Then open all the windows, allowing the fresh air to circulate inside. Actively clearing away outmoded objects and introducing refreshing energy into your home will automatically make you feel more liberated too! In fact, performing this type of space-clearing exercise regularly is one the fastest ways to transform your daily life experience while simultaneously improving your inner sense of well-being.

Purifying the energetic quality of one's environment or of an individual person is an age-old practice. Special times of the year as well as particular occasions are traditionally associated with space clearing or the ritual cleansing of a space. For example, it is common in many cultures to do a 'spring clean' at the start of the year when nature starts to wake up after the dark winter months. I find myself doing a spring clean quite instinctively once the days start to get longer and the bright sunlight begins to creep into the forgotten corners of my home! Incense or the burning of aromatic herbs is frequently used in these ceremonies. For example, in Tibetan culture, it is traditional to perform the *sang* ceremony at Losar, the Tibetan and Chinese New Year that falls in February.

Sang in Tibetan has the meaning of 'to remove, take away and purify' so a person or place is cleared, cleansed and awakened. The physical ritual involves the burning of different woods and incense, which can be mixed together with many other substances, such as ground gemstones. Juniper is a classic ingredient in the Tibetan Buddhist *sang* or smoke ritual, while across the whole Himalayan region, dried juniper needles are burnt as a purifying offering. Used since ancient times, juniper was also favoured by the ancient Greeks to combat illness or epidemics and to drive away negative forces. Likewise, juniper is one of the plants used in Scottish Gaelic rites, such as those performed at Hogmanay (New Year), where the smoke of burning juniper is used to cleanse, bless and protect the household and its inhabitants.

Herbs have also been utilised in other ways for home cleaning and purification throughout the ages. According to folklore in medieval Europe,

Strewing Herbs and Natural Insecticides

The following is a list of strewing herbs and natural insecticides:

Basil – insect repellent and air purifier
Bay – dried leaves were scattered in churches due to disinfectant properties and to repel weevils
Chamomile – insect repellent and used to stuff herb pillows
Cotton lavender – powerful insecticide
Fennel – flea repellent and dispels damp smells
Hops – used in bedrooms for its soothing effect and to stuff pillows and mattresses
Hyssop – a fragrant herb with Biblical reference to cleanliness
Lady's bedstraw – kills fleas and used to stuff mattresses
Lavender – insect repellent, for example moths, and used to stuff mattresses and pillows to induce sleep
Marjoram – used for hygiene up to the end of the seventeenth century and a favourite of Elizabeth I
Meadowsweet – a pleasing, sweet scent, a favourite of Elizabeth I
Oregano – has antiviral and antiseptic properties
Pennyroyal – kills fleas (also known as fleabane) and repels ticks
Peppermint – traditionally used for its fresh, stimulating effect and repels ants and bugs
Rose – Romans scattered petals at festivals and banquets and it was used on floors in Elizabethan times
Rosemary – strewn in churches being antiviral, anti-infectious and disinfectant, and to repel insects
Rue – insect repellent and cat deterrent
Sage – insecticide, purifying and bactericidal, and repels moths
Southernwood – known as 'lad's love', renowned as an aphrodisiac, so often used in bedrooms
Sweet flag – sweet smell with rush-like leaves
Sweet woodruff – insect repellent and popular in Elizabethan times to scent and disinfect rooms
Tansy – flea repellent
Thyme – insect repellent with bactericidal properties
Winter savory – insect repellent
Yarrow – repels insects such as moths, lice and ticks and used to scent private rooms

it was believed that adding nettle tea into bath water or floor-washing water removed any bad spells from a person or the home. Scattering nettle leaves inside or outside the home was another way to remove all negativity and drive out any evil or unwanted spirits. Strewing herbs were another category of plants that were commonly scattered or strewn over the floors of dwelling places and other buildings because of their hygienic and cleansing qualities. During the early Middle Ages, bathing had declined in England, so the use of these fragrant herbs became popular (and necessary). These natural aromatics were used in all areas of the house, including kitchens, dining halls and bedrooms, along with reeds, rushes or straw, so that their pleasant odours would be released when people walked on them. In a typical medieval English monastery, for instance, the floor of the dormitory would have been strewn with fragrant rushes that were swept and replaced once or twice a year. Both rich and poor households used strewing herbs, and royal households were no exception. Indeed, the post of 'royal herb strewer' was created in 1660 by King Charles II in England to ensure his chambers were always fresh and sweet-scented, while Elizabeth I favoured meadowsweet in her household. Such plants usually had a fragrant scent, while many also served as insecticides or disinfectants. Certain plants could also help keep pests, weevils or fleas at bay, and the use of these natural botanical hygiene agents was widespread throughout Europe right up to the eighteenth century.

House plants that Purify the Air Naturally

House plants always add an extra sense of vitality to any space, but did you know that certain plants can also help purify the air and keep our homes clean and fresh by removing toxic gases from the atmosphere? It has even been said that house plants will be the technology of choice for improving indoor air quality in the future! All plants take in carbon dioxide and release oxygen into the air to improve air quality overall and act as natural air conditioners by releasing moisture into the atmosphere. They can also help filter cigarette smoke, eliminate toxic off-gassing from synthetic paints and furnishings and even help reduce airborne mould spores and bacteria within damp environments, such as in bathrooms or basements.

In 1989, NASA conducted a research study to see if certain plants could be used to specifically filter the air in sealed environments, such as in a spaceship. The results of their scientific study showed that the leaves, roots and associated micro-organisms of some plants could reduce concentrations of common toxins in the air considerably within an enclosed space. These include benzene, which is found in many household paints and detergents; trichlorethylene, an irritant found in many standard solvents and cleaners; and formaldehyde, a residue left behind by cigarette smoke and some building materials.

The weeping fig (*Ficus benjamina*), for example, which has been a favourite house plant since Victorian times, was found to remove 47 per cent of formaldehyde and 30 per cent of benzene from the air, making it a good plant for places like bars, where cigarette smoke tends to linger. Snake plants of the *Dracaena* family – meaning 'female dragon' – were found to remove 79 per cent of benzene and 18 per cent of trichlorethylene from a room per day – this plant is therefore a great air purifier for homes that have been newly painted. The species 'mother-in-law's tongue' (*Dracaena trifascianta*) is one of the few plants that can also convert carbon dioxide into oxygen overnight, making it ideal for bedrooms to keep the air fresh and improve sleep quality. In feng shui, snake plants are also believed to bring good fortune and attract positive energy into a space.

Aloe vera (*Aloe barbadensis*) is another plant that emits oxygen throughout the night, simultaneously taking in carbon dioxide, leading to cleaner air

within the home. Aloe vera was also found to absorb both benzene and formaldehyde, and since its fresh gel can also be used to treat burns and wounds, it is an excellent plant to keep on a sunny kitchen windowsill. English ivy (*Hedera helix*) is also a valuable house plant, filtering out 90 per cent of benzene and 11 per cent of trichlorethylene from the air; it also helps to counter airborne mould spores, making it the ideal plant for bathrooms or damp basements.

For an unusual scent and a trailing habit, 'string of beads' (*Senecio herreianus*), which has masses of round pea-sized leaves, is a good air purifier and perfect for hanging baskets. It also produces clusters of small white flowers that smell like cinnamon throughout the summer. It only needs a few hours of sunlight a day and can tolerate infrequent watering so it is perfect for those who are regularly away from home. With their curling green fronds and trailing tendrils, the humidity-loving fern family, such as Boston 'green lady' (*Nephrolepis exaltata*), are also some of the best air-purifying plants available and can tolerate shady locations. Another of NASA's top favourites is philodendrons, which have large leaves that are bursting with the detoxifying substance chlorophyll. As tropical plants, they love moisture and warmth and will also increase the humidity levels in any room, so make lovely conservatory plants. The ability of rubber plants (*Ficus elastica*) to filter the air is well documented – formaldehyde, benzene and carbon monoxide are all prevalent indoor contaminants that can be absorbed by rubber plants. Additionally, since this plant can also eliminate airborne bacteria and mould spores, it is one the most effective all-around air-purifying plants to grow indoors.

Another completely natural and highly effective air purifier is charcoal, a familiar, 100 per cent plant-based material. Also known as activated carbon, charcoal is a versatile, organic, non-toxic, fragrance-free 'of the earth' material. The term charcoal is used to describe the substance that remains after incomplete combustion occurs – the carbon residue formed from burning wood. Like many of the best modern innovations, the first instances of charcoal being used for filtration purposes can be traced back to 2000 BCE, when ancient Sanskrit texts referenced filtering water through charcoal. In 400 BCE, Egyptians began replacing their rotten wooden docks with charred wood after accidentally discovering charcoal's antiseptic and preservative properties. Today, activated carbon is chiefly used in sophisticated water filtration systems and machines used to filter out mercury, chlorine and other organic compounds from our drinking water.

In Praise of Lemon

Lemon (*Citrus limonum*) is a small evergreen tree that can reach a height of 5–6m (16–20ft) and is one of the sixteen recognised species of the citrus family. Besides the fruit, which is the most commonly used, the lemon tree also produces fragrant flowers, and this blossom can make a beautifully fragrant herbal tisane or tea. Its healing qualities have been widely documented, being most prevalent in Ayurvedic and Chinese traditional medicine, as well as in European folk medicine. The name 'lemon' was coined sometime around 1300–1450 CE, most likely derived from the French limon and Italian limone – themselves likely newer adaptations of the Arabic laymun and the Persian leemoo.

This sunshine-coloured citrus fruit has a rich, vibrant history, acclaimed within each passing century for its bright uplifting scent, as well as for its humble yet highly praised ability to remedy a diverse range of health concerns – not to mention a preferred ingredient or standalone component in all matter of cleaning and household aids. Documented uses of the lemon range from curing disease to casting love spells and everything in between. For the Greeks and Romans, it was a revered and prized source of medicine used to remedy poisons and venom. In India, lemons were often hung outside the home together with

Six Ways to Use Charcoal at Home

Charcoal is an inexpensive and easy way to filter air and water, as well as facilitate the removal of harmful particles that lead to indoor air pollution and prevent the growth of harmful bacteria or mildew.

1. Water Filtration

Charcoal can be purchased in sticks to place inside water bottles and jugs to purify water for drinking, then stored in the fridge or at room temperature. It is an effective way to remove toxins without stripping the water of valuable salts and minerals. Replace the charcoal filter every twelve months or so.

2. Purifying the Air

Charcoal is a helpful tonic for respiratory conditions like asthma and long COVID, and a much healthier alternative to any commercial fragranced product. You can purchase bamboo charcoal bags or experiment with making sacs with powdered charcoal, which can get a little messy! These are excellent for placing around the home – in basements and poorly ventilated spaces to remove unpleasant smells, as well as inside cars or by the bed to keep the air clean and fresh. The bags should be regularly refreshed in sunlight once a month and can last up to two years.

3. Absorbing Household Odours

Cover a handful or block of charcoal in cheesecloth or place in a lightweight cloth bag and pop in the fridge, freezer or behind the toilet to absorb unwanted odours. As a natural deodorant, it can also be kept inside boots or trainers to neutralise any foot odour.

4. Keeping Your Cut Flowers Fresh

Like our drinking water, flowers can benefit from charcoal-filtered water. Place a small block or two beneath cut stems in a vase to keep the water fresh and keep your beautiful flowers thriving for longer.

5. Temporary Cosmetic Furniture Fix

Charcoal is an easy and effective natural stain for dark wooden floors and furniture until you have time for a proper repair job. Rub charcoal into any scratches on dark wood to temporarily stain it, then follow up with some linseed oil.

6. Composting

Charcoal is 100 per cent biodegradable – but go easy with it. Charcoal should not be composted regularly, but a little here and there will add carbon, a vital piece in the composting process. A handful every few weeks is ample.

Lemon Cleaning Tips

The fruit of the lemon tree is a botanical treasure that can truly claim its prize for being a versatile, natural, powerful cleaning product. It is naturally antiseptic and antibacterial, rich in neutralising and reactive citric acid – it will impart the most enlivening and uplifting fresh fragrance to household items.

Chopping Board Cleaner

After chopping onions, garlic and spices, use half a lemon to wipe down before rinsing with hot water. The juice is also a good way to neutralise the scent of these on your hands after cooking.

Stain Removal

Lemon is the perfect ally for stain removal, particularly on white clothing. Squeeze the juice of half or a whole lemon directly onto the stain, then pour kitchen salt over the stain. Using your fingers, rub the lemon juice and salt into the stain, then rinse with warm water.

Microwave Wash and Deodoriser

Cut a lemon into slices, place in a microwave-friendly bowl and cover it two thirds full with water. Heat for three to five minutes on the highest setting then leave the bowl inside for ten minutes before opening the door, allowing the inside door to steam up. Use a soft cloth to wipe down.

Limescale Descaler

Lemon can help with limescale build-up on taps, inside kettles and on other household appliances that are in contact with tap water. Simply cut a lemon in half and wipe over the sink and taps, leave for a few minutes, then rinse off. To descale a kettle, place some lemon halves (fresh or previously used) inside the kettle and fill with water; boil, leave overnight and repeat two or three times

Applying Fresh Lemon Magic to Leather

You can also use fresh lemon juice on leather shoes or bags to freshen them up.

Lemon essential oil tips

Citrus-scented Fridge Refresher

In the last stage of cleaning the fridge, dampen a clean eco-cloth in hot water and add 3 drops of lemon essential oil to it before a final wipe around.

Antimicrobial Air Freshener

There's nothing like the fresh citrus zing of lemon oil to clear away cobwebs! Add 5–7 drops of the oil to a room vaporiser to purify the air and dispel germs and any airborne viruses.

Surface Grease Remover

Add 500ml (17fl oz) hot water, 75g (2.6oz) black liquid soap and 15 drops of lemon oil to a spray bottle. Shake well and apply to baking trays, oven hobs and so on, etc., then wipe clean using an eco-sponge or scourer.

Natural Floor Disinfectant

Mix 1 tbs black liquid soap and 5 drops of lemon oil to a bucket of hot water. Use a microfibre mop to clean surfaces, leaving a lovely, fresh, purifying fragrance.

Waste Bin Refresher

Soak a piece of kitchen towel with a few drops of lemon oil. Place in a waste bin before inserting the bag to combat germs and unpleasant smells.

Kitchen Surface Spritz

Simply blend 20 drops each of lemon, grapefruit and geranium essential oils in 100ml (3.5fl oz) water, then add the mixture to a spray bottle. Shake well before each use and spritz onto surfaces as a light surface cleaner around the room.

LEMON
CITRON
aqua
oleum

charcoal and chillies, called a *nimbu mirchi*, to protect against misery and poverty.

The first recorded medicinal lemon recipe appeared in a twelfth-century Egyptian treatise from Ibn Jumay, a Jewish physician in the court of Saladin. Titled *On Lemon, its Drinking and Use*, this was a medical cookbook of sorts, recommending various parts and preparations of lemon for restoring health and vitality. This is also widely considered the first recorded recipe of preserving lemons, which many chefs and restaurants have adapted since. Lemon juice with honey and/or ginger has been taken as a remedy for seasonal chills far and wide across the world as far back as we can tell.

Lemon provides us with the ultimate comforting, clean and fresh scent. Perhaps the most widely known and versatile of all the citrus fruits, lemon is a valuable component in a wide range of cleaning products and consumables – indeed lemon is one of the most commercially important citrus fruits in the world today. The Mediterranean region produces almost all the lemons we find in the products used today, with any wastage from the plant being minimal, due to the fact almost all the fruit is used for something. Whole lemons – the juice, rind, pip and essential oil – are all extracted for use in all kinds of consumer products, one of the most prevalent being cleaning products. Lemon is a common ingredient, but it is also a simple, everyday inexpensive fruit that we all have readily available to us, which can work wonders in keeping our home clean, healthy and hygienic.

From witchcraft to well-being, the unequivocal natural potential that lemons offer is attracting lots of attention today. For many of us, it is common to keep a couple of lemons at home on an everyday basis, due to their culinary and practical value, which may in addition include their cleaning and purifying properties. We can find numerous references to lemon in inherited traditional family recipes as well as in modern lists of well-being recommendations from trendy influencers utilising the juice, the rind or even the leaves of the lemon tree. Health enthusiasts drink it first thing in the morning to support the body's natural detoxification, aid digestion and alkalise the body, while more esoteric practices extend to using lemons in spells for attraction or banishment, as well as a healing tool for aura cleansing and unblocking the chakras. A 2005 study assessed how the virtues of the lemon species in ancient and medieval texts were compared to those known to modern science and concluded that a much broader spectrum of pharmacological properties was recorded by these early writers than one might expect.

Note: Like many citrus oils, lemon essential oil is a mild photosensitiser (light absorber) and should never be used neat on the skin, or even applied diluted, before exposure to direct sunlight or UV sunbeds, as it can cause discoloration.

Recipes & Crafts

There are many simple ways to introduce natural hygiene effects into the home and workplace – for example, by just adding a few drops of a bactericidal essential oil, such as lemon or eucalyptus, to the water used for washing floors. Other easy solutions include: using essential oils, such as lavender, to scent linen for its soothing effect in the bedroom; using peppermint or spearmint oil to prevent travel sickness in the car; peppermint or citronella oil to keep ants and insects away at home; or employing antiviral oils such as rosemary in the workplace to prevent the spread of airborne infections. The recipes here combine several ingredients in eco-cleaning solutions and can be pre-prepared and kept in your DIY cleaning cupboard in place of commercial products.

Household Multipurpose Cleaners

Refreshing Citrus Disinfectant Spritz

This recipe utilises fresh lemon peels and takes three to four weeks to marinate. You can of course combine other citrus fruits like grapefruit, lime and orange if you wish. Alongside citrus, I suggest employing the antibacterial benefits of herbs like lavender, sage and thyme for their powerful disinfectant effects. Use this multipurpose cleaner for surfaces in the kitchen and bathroom, around the home and in the workplace to keep things naturally hygienic, spotless and fresh.

Ingredients

75g (2.6oz) lemon peels (or other citrus fruits such as orange, lime or grapefruit), 20g (0.7oz) dried herbs (such as lemon balm, lavender,

thyme, sage or rosemary), 500ml (17fl oz) white vinegar, 500ml (17fl oz) distilled water, 20–30 drops essential oils of lemon or lavender (optional)

Equipment

Large Kilner jar, wax paper, fine-mesh sieve, cheesecloth or a clean coffee filter, 500ml (17fl oz) atomiser bottle with a large nozzle (for ease of use; you could also use several smaller-sized atomiser bottles), eco-cloth

Method

1. Finely chop your citrus peels and herb sprigs.
2. Combine the citrus peels and herbs into a 1-litre Kilner jar.
3. Pour 500ml (17fl oz) of white vinegar on top.
4. Place a piece of wax paper between the lid and the jar then seal.
5. Let ingredients steep for two to four weeks in a dark place, shaking every couple of days.
6. After two to four weeks, strain the plant material from the vinegar using a fine-mesh sieve, cheesecloth or a clean coffee filter.
7. Add 500ml (17fl oz) of distilled water to your 500ml (17fl oz) of strained herbal-infused vinegar and decant into a suitably sized or several smaller-sized atomiser bottles.
8. If desired, add 20–30 drops total of essential oils such as lavender or lemon.
9. Shake well before use.
10. Spray the surface you want to clean with the solution and wipe with a clean eco-cloth.

Simple Surface Cleaner

In this easy recipe, the benefits of lemon are combined with the versatile eco-cleaner, castile soap. Castile soap is a multipurpose product everyone should have at home. It is a non-toxic hard or liquid soap made from 100 per cent vegetable oil instead of animal fats or synthetic substances. It was historically and traditionally first produced using local olive oil and laurel oil. It removes grease effectively and is an ideal ingredient for making all kinds of household cleaning products. Castile is not a brand or trademarked name but simply named after the Castile region of Spain, where it originated.

Adding an element of citrus imbues not only a gorgeous scent, but a myriad of fresh, antibacterial benefits. Lemon has acquired the title 'master cleanser' – but you can choose from lemon, lime, orange, grapefruit, bergamot or lemongrass essential oil or combine a few together here to suit your preferences. Clove oil is also added here – in Asia, cloves are nicknamed 'flowers of the gods' due to their medicinal value. Their major constituent is eugenol, having excellent antibacterial, anti-fungal and antioxidant properties.

Ingredients

2 tbs unscented castile soap, 10 drops of clove essential oil, 20 drops (in total) of lemon, lemongrass, bergamot or assorted citrus essential oils, 500ml (17fl oz) distilled water

Equipment
500ml (17fl oz) atomiser bottle with a large nozzle (for ease of use), glass funnel, eco-cloth

Method
1. Combine all ingredients into a 500ml (17fl oz) atomiser. A funnel may be useful for pouring the soap or use a pouring jug for ease.
2. Shake vigorously before use each time.
3. To use, spray onto an eco-cloth or fabric and use it to clean around the home, such as on countertops, desks, bookshelves.

Tip: Best suited to plastic, tiles and wooden surfaces.

Easy Floor Wash
Castile soap is the perfect floor cleaner for wood, laminate and marble-tiled floors. Lavender essential oil – from the Latin *lavere*, to wash – has a classic, fresh, purifying action, and here sweet orange oil is also added for a touch of warmth.

Ingredients
2–3 tsp castile soap, warm water, 3 drops each of lavender and orange essential oils

Equipment
Bucket, mop

Method
1. Add 2–3 tsp of castile soap to a bucket of warm water.
2. Add 3 drops of lavender and 3 drops of sweet orange essential oil to the water and stir well.
3. Mop the floor with the aromatic water for a lovely, natural, hygienic effect.

Vinegar Streak-Free Glass Cleaner
Vinegar and water are all you need for streak-free mirrors and windows. The addition of an essential oil can add an uplifting scent – but this is optional.

Ingredients
Modify the following quantities to suit the size of your bottle: 250ml (8.8fl oz) distilled water, 200ml (7fl oz) white vinegar, 25 drops total of essential oils such as lemon, grapefruit or bergamot

Equipment
500ml (17fl oz) atomiser bottle (with a large nozzle for ease of use), eco-cloth, a lint-free towel or some scrunched-up newspaper or paper towel

Method
1. Combine all ingredients into the bottle and shake vigorously before each use.
2. Spray onto an eco-cloth or fabric and use it to clean windows, mirrors and glass surfaces – it is best to start at the top and work down.
3. A lint-free towel or simply some scrunched-up newspaper or paper towel is also helpful in removing any remaining solution, and then polishing it up to leave it shiny and sparkling.

> **Tip:** A squeegee can also be a useful tool for getting your windows, shower screens and mirrors super clean.

Kitchen and Utility Room

DIY Dishwasher Liquid

Dishwashers are a modern invention that many of us could not bear to live without. Commercial dishwasher products typically contain phosphates that can become hazardous to waterways. Once it has cleaned our dishes, it ends up in our rivers and oceans and contributes to the rising amounts of algae and phytoplankton. This recipe is a cheap and easy alternative; having these common staples to hand ensures you will not be caught short running out of dishwater tablets either. Recycling an empty bottle with a squeezy lid is perfect – you can shake and squirt it directly into the dishwasher.

Ingredients

125ml (4fl oz) water, 125ml (4fl oz) unscented castile soap, 70ml (2.5fl oz) white vinegar, 1 tbsp lemon juice, 3 drops of lemon or lime essential oil

Equipment

Recycled empty bottle with a squeezy lid

Method

1. Add all ingredients to a reusable bottle and shake. The ingredients may look a little strange and seem to curdle but don't worry about this look.
2. Add solution to the dishwasher in place of tablets and use on regular settings.

Eco-Friendly Washing-Up Liquid

This eco-alternative to standard washing-up liquid, which is gentle yet effective and can be used as normal with scourers made from natural fibres, is based on castile soap.

Ingredients
125ml (4fl oz) castile soap, 6 drops (in total) of essential oils, such as lime or lemon

Equipment
Recycled empty bottle with a squeezy lid, eco-sponge or reusable cloth

Method
1. Combine 125ml (4fl oz) of castile soap with 6 drops of citrus essential oils such as lemon or lime.
2. Add warm washing-up water as usual, using an eco-sponge or reusable cloth.

Note: Castile soap will not foam like commercial washing-up liquid, but it works just as well.

Natural Washing-Machine Detergent and Fabric Softener

Scented fabric softeners are usually complex synthetic blends and are one of the main culprits for causing allergic skin reactions. This is a natural environmentally friendly alternative.

Ingredients
125ml (4fl oz) castile soap, 6 drops (in total) of essential oils, such as lavender, lemongrass or geranium, 63g (2.2oz) baking soda (optional)

Equipment
Scoop

Method
1. Use a scoop to half-fill the tray in your washing machine with castile soap, for a normal load of washing.
2. Add 6 drops of essential oil (in total) such as lemongrass, lavender or geranium to the tray.
3. If the load is particularly soiled, you can also add 63g (2.2oz) of baking soda.
4. Use wash settings as normal.

Note: Soap nuts are also a natural washing-machine detergent that literally grow on trees. The shells contain saponins, which, on contact with water, release mild suds and can be used as a naturally sourced alternative to chemical-based laundry detergents and leave your clothes feeling soft.

Fragrant Clothes Drying

Although it is more economical and ecological – as well as more pleasingly fresh – to dry linens and clothes outdoors – this is not always possible, unfortunately. This is a way of giving tumble-dried clothes a fresh scent naturally using your favourite essential oils.

Ingredients
A few drops (in total) of your choice of essential oils such as lavender or lemon, clean eco-cloth

Method
Simply add a few drops of lavender essential oil (or the essential oil of your choice) to a clean eco-cloth and pop it into the drier before use.

Bathroom

Aromatic Bathroom Cleaning Spray

This is a quick recipe to create a cleaning spray within minutes that you can use immediately. The pairing of vinegar and naturally antibacterial and antiviral essential oils is a simple and easy first step to removing unnecessary chemicals from your home. This is no 'old wives' tale – vinegar really is a hero ingredient of the cleaning cupboard, thanks to its acetic acid content, which helps combat germs and mould, loosens mineral deposits and dissolves soap scum. In this recipe, it is combined with naturally antibacterial, antiviral essential oils that have the bonus of smelling delightful.

Cypress adds a green, herbaceous accord, paired with the woody base notes of cedar to create a delightfully pleasing forest aroma, and the citrus element imparts a sunshine note. For extra cleaning power in the bathtub or toilet, sprinkle a little baking powder or bicarbonate of soda on surfaces first to make a paste, before spritzing with this solution and then scrubbing off with an eco-sponge or brush.

Ingredients

325ml (11.4fl oz) white vinegar, 175ml (6.1fl oz) purified water, 10 drops each of lemon, cedarwood and cypress essential oils

Equipment

500ml (17fl oz) large nozzle spray bottle – glass or recycled plastic.

Method

1. Pour the vinegar and water into your 500ml (17fl oz) spray bottle – a glass spray bottle is ideal, or recycle a clean plastic one.
2. Add 30 drops of essential oils (in total).
3. Shake gently to combine all ingredients.
4. Spray and use around the home to clean surfaces, avoiding granite and marble.

Tip: This handy solution can also be used to clean glass or mirrors with a soft eco-cloth, or as a deodorising air freshener in the bathroom.

Fizzy Toilet Tabs

These tabs are fun to make and a great way to get children involved in keeping the house clean too! You can make these in batches and use one or two fizzes per week or as desired. The trio of antibacterial citrus – lemongrass, grapefruit and lime – are zesty, uplifting and refreshing, but feel free to experiment with your different combinations or use what you have to hand.

Ingredients

125g (4.4oz) bicarbonate of soda, 60ml (2fl oz) of citric acid, 20 drops each of grapefruit, lemongrass and cypress essential oils

Equipment

Spoon, ceramic mixing bowl, spray bottle filled with tap water, silicone moulds or an ice cube tray, knife or flat tool, airtight storage jar

Method

1. Use the spoon to combine the bicarbonate of soda and citric acid in the mixing bowl.
2. Add the essential oils and stir well to combine.
3. Spritz the mix with the water slowly to combine but don't overwater as it will fizz too soon – just spray around 20 times.
4. Spoon the mixture into your silicone mould or ice cube tray and press down so it has a flat and smooth edge.
5. Leave overnight or for 12–14 hours in a dry place and out of direct sunlight.
6. Remove the fizzy toilet tabs from their casing using a knife or flat tool if needed.
7. Add to the toilet bowl as needed.
8. Store the rest in an airtight jar for future use.

Perfumed Wash Balls

For centuries, botanicals have been used to perfume toiletries. Lavender has been used for its clean, fresh fragrance since Roman times, while the herb soapwort provided an early form of soap. As a sign of respect, rosewater was used in the East to bathe the hands and feet of visitors after a long journey. In medieval Europe, it was customary at major feasts to place great bowls of herbal water at the table for guests to wash their hands. Later, scented wash balls made from castile soap and blended with rosewater and other herbs, such as lavender, cypress or rosemary, were prepared in the stillroom. This modern version also makes a delightful gift.

Ingredients

120g (4oz) grated unscented olive oil soap (or

Bathroom Hygiene
– Four Ways with Eucalyptus

Eucalyptus is a species of flowering plant in the botanical family Myrtaceae, related to the Melaleuca or tea tree genus. The essential oil is extracted from the leaves of the trees, native to Australia but now grown worldwide. There are over 700 species of eucalyptus and because of their medicinal value, ongoing research is being carried out into the different constituents of each oil, which can roughly be divided into three categories: camphoraceous oils, such as blue gum (*Eucalyptus globulus var globulus*), containing large amounts of 1,8-cineole; mint species, such as peppermint eucalyptus (*E. piperita*), containing mainly piperitone; citrus-scented varieties, such as the lemon-scented eucalyptus (*E. citriodora*), containing mainly citronellal.

All these types of eucalyptus oil have a variety of home uses, although perhaps the blue gum variety has the most evidence of its abilities is in its capacity as a powerful purifying agent for spaces and places. This is one I always keep in my DIY cupboard.

1. Fresh Eucalyptus Posy

Tie a bunch of fresh eucalyptus leaves under the shower head, so that each time you have a shower the steam releases some of the fragrant essential oils, creating a sauna-like atmosphere at home.

2. Eucalyptus Steam Shower

Alternatively, you can use 3 drops of eucalyptus essential oil on the floor of the shower tray to create a refreshing, invigorating aroma that will have a fresh and clearing effect while also purifying the air.

3. Toilet Freshener

Keep a bottle of eucalyptus essential oil in the bathroom and simply add 3–5 drops after using the toilet to refresh the scent as necessary between uses.

4. Clean Towels and Linen

Add 10 drops of eucalyptus essential oil to the detergent drawer of the washing machine to ensure your towels are hygienic and clean-scented. This has also been shown to be particularly effective for bed linen to get rid of dust mites.

assorted recycled soap ends), 150ml (5.2fl oz) rosewater, 5 drops each of lavender and petitgrain essential oils, natural food colouring (optional), loose lavender flower heads

Equipment

Glass bowl, fine grater, bain-marie, saucepan, spoon, pestle and mortar, mixing bowl, tissue paper and narrow ribbon (optional).

Method

1. Grate the soap into a glass bowl using a fine grater and add the rosewater.
2. Put the mixture in a bain-marie and heat gently until the mixture thickens.
3. Take off the heat.
4. Add the essential oils and stir (with some natural food colouring if desired).
5. Blend in a bowl or using a large pestle and mortar.
6. Let the mixture dry out slightly, then take a small handful of the paste and roll it into a neat ball.
7. Repeat, making several balls until the soap mixture is used up.
8. Before the balls harden, wet your hands with some rosewater and polish the balls to a smooth finish.
9. Decorate with the loose lavender flowers and wrap the balls in coloured tissue paper and ribbon for a professional finish.

Living Spaces and Furniture

Nourishing Wood Polish

Pine and cedarwood essential oils create a beautiful clean, green, tree-like aroma that is naturally antiviral, deterring moths as well as airborne bacteria. Beeswax is a versatile, highly protective natural wax that contains natural protective qualities that replenish and lock in moisture – be it for wood furniture or skin! There is something lovely about having ingredients at home that can be used universally both for the health and well-being of our home as well as our body.

Olive oil is another excellent multipurpose ingredient that almost all of us have in the kitchen. It is not just great for furniture but skin and hair too, thanks to its high content of natural fats and minerals that act as a conditioner and emollient to both furniture and fingernails alike. The combination of cedar, beeswax and olive oil creates a natural colouring that resembles and enhances a natural wood hue, so can often make faded furniture look fresh and vibrant. Use on any wooden furniture to naturally clean, buff and polish.

Ingredients

40ml (1.4fl oz) olive oil, 10g (0.3oz) beeswax, 15 drops each of cedarwood and pine essential oils

Equipment

Bain-marie, recycled or reusable metal, aluminium or glass jar with lid, eco-cloth, old piece of fabric or tea towel

Method

1. Melt the beeswax and olive oil in a bain-marie over medium heat and stir to combine.
2. Remove from the heat and leave to cool for one minute, then add the essential oils and stir to combine again.
3. Pour into your jar and let cool completely.
4. It will be ready to use within five minutes or you can store it until you need it. Apply to wooden furniture using an eco-cloth, old piece of fabric or tea towel and 'buff' using circular motions.

Vacuum Refresher

This is an easy way to make your home smell incredible as you vacuum – a multitasker at its simplest. All you need is some cotton wool and essential oils. The combination of vetiver and palmarosa paired with the comforting, fresh scent of mandarin evokes a cosy, clean and uplifting scent, but you can experiment with your favourites or use whatever essential oils are available to you, such as rosemary, fragonia, lemon or lavender oil.

Ingredients

30 drops (total) of vetiver, palmarosa and mandarin essential oils or your choice of essential oils

Equipment

Cotton wool balls, vacuum with a hose

Method

1. Place 10 drops of each essential oil (30 in total) onto one or two cotton wool balls.
2. Hoover up the cotton wool balls and continue to vacuum the room as normal.
3. Repeat as necessary.

Carpet and Rug Deodoriser

Especially for households with pets, carpets and rugs can end up containing a lot of unwanted odours, hair and dirt. This mixture is best used after first hoovering a room, and for optimum results, leave the mixture on for six to eight hours to fully absorb, then give it another vacuum to remove the residue. The hero ingredient here is bicarbonate soda, which lifts dirt, stains and odours from your carpets and rugs with ease. This can be used by itself, but the addition of rosemary and lemon helps to impart a beautiful aroma reminiscent of a Mediterranean garden. This can be done once a month or as often as required.

Ingredients

120g (4.2oz) bicarbonate of soda, 5–15 drops each of rosemary and lemon essential oils (or oils of your choice)

Equipment

Mixing bowl, wooden spoon, small sieve

Method

1. Pour the bicarbonate of soda into the mixing bowl.
2. Add 10–30 drops of essential oils.
3. Use the wooden spoon to combine the essential oils and soda.
4. Sprinkle the mixture onto a hoovered carpet, using a spoon or a small sieve if preferred.
5. Allow the carpet freshener to sit for at least 30 minutes, but ideally six to eight hours.
6. After allowing the carpet deodoriser mixture to absorb, vacuum it up to get rid of any remaining mixture.

Tip: For a lighter scent, add 5 drops of each essential oil, and for a strong scent, use a maximum of 30 drops.

Chapter 4

Incense, Perfumes and Room Fragrances

'Perfume is a story in odour, sometimes poetry in memory.'

Jean-Claude Ellena

The use of incense and the practice of scenting the spaces and places we inhabit has played an intrinsic role in our daily lives, stretching right back to the rituals of ancient civilisations. The word 'perfume' literally means 'through the smoke', from the Latin *per fumare*.

Consider how the aroma of an outdoor fire, barbecue or cigarette smoke can seep into the fabric of our clothes and linger in our skin and hair, even days later. Smoke has undeniable staying power! The original smoke-based scents came from burning fragrant plants and woods as incense and for fumigation – these were the earliest types of perfume in existence. Incense and homemade scents made of aromatic botanical ingredients from spices, trees and flowers have been used in religious rites, for the maintenance of health and hygiene, as well as for sensual pleasure, since the earliest times. In Europe, for example, scented woods and herbs were burnt to prevent the spread of infection but also to help cover unpleasant odours or get rid of musty smells. The Deanery of St Paul's was fumigated twice a week with aromatics such as rue or angelica root during the Great Plague of London during 1665.

The term 'incense' originates from the Latin *incendere*, meaning 'to burn' – a broad term used for materials bound or crushed together in bundles that must be set on fire to release their scent as smoke. Records suggest that the earliest incense was found in the East, especially in India, China and Japan. The *kōdō* ceremony – the 'way of incense' – in Japan is considered one of the three traditional Japanese arts, alongside the flower ceremony, *kado*, and the tea ceremony, *chado*. Involving centuries of practice, *kōdō* is widely considered to have been formalised around the sixteenth century.

The Story of Incense

Since ancient times, natural aromatics and incense have universally been used to alter states of consciousness and to lift the spirits, as well as to drive out evil influences in cases of mental illness and physical disease when performed within a ritual context. Incense was highly valued both as a tonic for humans and a messenger to commune with the higher realms, possessing a duality of being simultaneously utilitarian and mystical. Aromatics were seen above all as a means of communicating with the divine and a means of transcending mundane reality. In fact, incense has been used to influence the deeper recesses of the mind and psyche for thousands of years, especially in the context of religious and spiritual practices.

Our sense of smell is intimately connected

with mood and memory as it is processed by our limbic system in our 'primitive' brain – unlike visual stimuli, which are processed by our cerebral cortex – so it can profoundly inform and influence us on a subliminal level, even if we are unaware of it. It is therefore not surprising that incense held such an esteemed position in an age when ritual was an intrinsic part of everyday life.

The origin of the numerous magical beliefs and rites surrounding aromatics, incense and herbs is based on long-standing cultural traditions alongside their inherent healing properties. One of the most famous women in the early European herbal tradition was Hildegard of Bingen, a twelfth-century Benedictine nun, who wrote a medical text called *Causae et Curae*. In this visionary text, astrology, magic, religion and herbal lore were combined into a complete philosophical system where humanity was perceived as divine and at one with nature itself. Her view virtually mirrored the pagan beliefs of the ancient Celtic tribes of Ireland, Scotland and Wales, and other parts of pre-Christian Europe, who were deeply connected to the natural world and believed that all things like the wind, trees and mountains had divine spirits. However, under the spreading influence of Christianity, early pagan rites were amalgamated into Christian rituals, while herbal knowledge was condemned, and its practitioners systematically hunted down if they did not wish to follow the new religion.

Perhaps the best-known botanical aromatic still used in this kind of religious and ritualistic manner in the West today is frankincense, which is traditionally used in the Roman Catholic Mass. However, in ancient times, it was the focus of an entire incense trade route that ran from East to West. Frankincense, a resin derived from the Boswellia tree, once played a vital ritualistic and religious role in the practices of ancient Egypt and Persia; the rites performed for the Greek and Roman gods; as well as having many ceremonial references in the Bible. It is one of the oldest commodities, being traded for over 5,000 years. Often nicknamed the King of Aromatics or 'liquid gold', this prized possession has at times demanded a price higher than gold itself! Also known as olibanum and locally as *luban*, this rich and fragrant incense resin has long been associated with stories of magic, mystery, medicine and myth – as in the legends surrounding Cleopatra. The English name frankincense is derived from the old French expression *franc encens*, meaning 'quality incense', and it is a scent many of us still associate with worship, meditation and prayer. German research in the 1980s demonstrated that it contains a substance called trahydro-cannabinole, which directly affects the imagination.

Traditional Incense and Perfume Recipes

Fumigating Pastils: A Way of Incense

Coarsely powder and mix together 1lb each of gum benzoin and frankincense, a ¼lb each of cascarilla and gum myrrh, and ½oz of cinnamon.

To Make Fumigating Pastils

Mix the following ingredients, all having been separately powdered: 2lb of charcoal, 1lb each of frankincense and gum benzoin, and ½lb of gum storax. Add to the mixed powders: 4oz of syrup, 6oz of tincture of benzoin, 2oz each of oil of almonds and essence of ambergris, and 1oz of essence of musk. Make the resultant paste into cones, adding a little warm water if required.

To Make Aromatic Cones

Mix 125 parts gum benzoin, 25 parts balsam of tolu, 100 parts powdered sandalwood and 1 part each of nitre (saltpetre), oil of sandalwood, cinnamon and cloves. Make into a paste with a solution of gum tragacanth (made by pouring 6 parts warm water over 1 part gum tragacanth, letting it stand a few days and then straining), and form into cones.

To Make Aromatic Pastils

Mix 125 parts charcoal, 25 parts each of cascarilla bark and gum benzoin, 12 parts nitre (saltpetre), 10 parts myrrh and 5 parts each of oil of cloves and oil of nutmeg. Make into a paste with a solution of gum tragacanth.

Burning Oleo-Gum Resins

Mix together granules of aromatic oleo-resins such as frankincense, myrrh, elemi, or copaiba (or use individually), and place them on a charcoal tablet base in an incense burner or heat-proof bowl.

'Fragrant twirls of frankincense
Rise dreamily, intoxicating my senses,
Its warm and musky embrace,
Enticing and mesmerising me –
And I feel I could touch the heavens!'

'Frankincense' by Pragya Deb Burman

Most of the frankincense material supplied across the globe is cultivated in the Red Sea region and there are five primary species of *Boswellia carterii trees: B. sacra, B. frereana, B. serrata, B. thurifera and B. papyrifera.* Almost the entire tree has been utilised for traditional remedies – bark, resin, pollen, fruits and even the ashes are all valuable. Harvesting frankincense is a delicate procedure and its process has not changed much in thousands of years. Incisions are made in the bark of the trunk or branches, where the secretory tissues occur, then the slowly exuded resin is collected when it has hardened sufficiently. As it is such a sacred tree, it deserves to be treated with reverence, rather than being over-exploited as has been the case with *Boswellia sacra* and *B. serrata*, which both face a variety of pressures from overharvesting as well as from natural environmental threats.

The Magic of Aromatics

Herbal lore and the unique qualities of each ingredient used in a specific recipe were traditionally passed down from one generation to another verbally, and at one time it was common knowledge for many country folk to know how to use a wide range of plants. Our ancestors knew which herb could be used as a protection against evil, what plant produced prophetic dreams, or the botanicals employed in making a love charm.

Over time, a body of magical knowledge accumulated surrounding the use of herbs, both as 'simples' to remedy common complaints, such as colds or aching joints, and as 'charms' for a range of purposes. These qualities were identified based on their ancient herbal usage, direct experimentation, observation about the way they grew, plus their verified healing actions. Women especially played an important role in the passing down of herbal knowledge, including their medicinal benefits – and it was these same women who were ruthlessly persecuted from the early decades of the fourteenth century until the mid-seventeenth century right across continental Europe. During a period of about 300 years, over 200,000 witches were executed, 85 per cent or more of whom were women. Yet it is ironic that the origin of the broomstick favoured by witches in fairy tales was most likely based on the fact these women were aware that cleanliness and home hygiene were vital for keeping illness at bay, while their familiar cat companion was essential for keeping vermin and rats away – rats being the main carriers of plague and infection.

In England, an anti-lightning charm for the home consisted of some twigs of bay laurel, mistletoe and hawthorn bound together using silver or white thread, then hung inside the chimney or from the highest point on the roof to provide protection. Garlic was another of the most powerful protective charms and was once placed beneath the pillows of sleeping children to protect them at night; of course, this was also one of the main defences against vampires. A necklace of cloves was hung around the necks of babies or were strung from their crib as a safeguard against disease and all kinds of ills. A sprig of rosemary placed under the pillow was thought to protect the sleeper from nightmares, whereas a bunch of mugwort brought clairvoyant dreams.

Many aromatic herbs were commonly used to make sachets and protective amulets, including angelica, basil, bay, fennel, garlic, mugwort, rosemary, St John's Wort and tarragon. For example, a practice that goes back to Babylonian times, and which was later commonly employed in Britain and on the Continent, was to bind the stems of a number of these protective herbs together with red thread, then to hang the posy

above the doorstep or outside the front entrance of the house to protect all those who lived within. St John's Wort was believed to drive away evil spirits and it became a common custom to hang a sprig of this herb above the doors of houses and churches on the Eve of St John's at the summer solstice, an important pagan festival.

Modern scientific studies have largely de-mythologised the former magical status of herbs by expanding our understanding of how they work based on pharmacology. Very often, newly emerging medical research validates ancient folk knowledge and practices, although this is not always the case, as superstition was also rife in many early cultures. Yet in many parts of the world, we can still see the effectiveness of shamanic-type approaches to healing where the use of certain herbs and the power of suggestion are inextricably entwined. The overall effectiveness of this type of practice depends largely on what would be called the placebo effect from a contemporary scientific point of view, while today the psychosomatic foundations of many types of disease are also being recognised. It is now acknowledged that the fundamental cause of many illnesses can be traced back to a person's negative outlook or underlying fears since emotional distress eventually has a degenerative effect on our entire organism. It is apparent that mental states such as anxiety, irritation or anger can also cause physical changes in our body, including an increase in heart rate, breathing and muscle tone. Complaints such as asthma, stress and hypertension are often directly related to underlying mental disturbances or discomfort, which are at the root of so much of our twenty-first-century disease.

In fact, plants have formed the basis for all forms of medical practices since the birth of civilisation and it is often just the language and their manner of preparation that have changed over the centuries. Today, a certain plant that might have once been used to make a protective amulet or magical charm is instead said to have good prophylactic properties or display powerful bactericidal and antiviral activity. In Scandinavia, for example, it was common until recently to carry a lump of crude camphor as a protective measure during times of infectious illness, based on knowledge of its prophylactic powers. Camphor was also one of the main ingredients in the miraculous antidote carried by the corpse robbers of London during the Black Death, which effectively shielded them from infection, as exemplified by the 'Story of the Four Thieves':

> When this fast-spreading plague hit England in the fourteenth century, no one knew how to protect themselves from this deadly new disease. Taking advantage of this horrific epidemic for their own benefit, a group of spice merchants who were well versed in the use of natural aromatics gained a reputation in London as fearless corpse robbers. When the king heard about the thieves, he wanted to know how they were able to survive the plague and even touch the dead bodies without becoming infected themselves. Four of the thieves were caught and questioned. The king gave them a choice of sharing their secret formula or being executed – they chose to share their secret! Their recipe consisted of a combination of camphor, cinnamon, cloves, eucalyptus, rosemary and lemon.

All these essential oils were subsequently tested at Weber State University, Utah, USA, in 1997 and found to have 99.96 per cent effectiveness against airborne bacteria due to their outstanding antimicrobial and antiviral properties.

Botanical Perfumes

All early perfumes were made wholly from natural ingredients, using fragrant petals, seeds, roots or bark, together with scented gums and resins, as well as a small number of products derived from animals, such as musk. The first body perfumes were called unguents and were a type of ointment made by simply immersing the aromatic material in an oily or fatty base – a process called enfleurage (*see* Chapter 2). Later, fragrant essential oils were extracted from the raw material in a variety of ways – by simple pressure (as is the case with most citrus oils) or by steam distillation.

Since antiquity, scent has formed a vital element in our spiritual, self-care and amorous rituals – the art of making fragrant elixirs and potent love potions is a tried and tested practice. The Egyptians were renowned for their perfumery expertise, but one of the first aromatic alchemists on record was a Mesopotamian woman named Tapputi Belatikallim – a title that roughly translates as 'female palace overseer'. Her perfume-making methodologies were found on cuneiform tablets and are thought to be the first documented records of the process involving a primitive type of distillation using botanicals. Clay pots used for distilling essential oils from plants dating back to 3,500 BCE have also been unearthed during excavations in Mesopotamia.

The Arab world and East Asia likewise enjoyed a passion for scent, although they had different ingredients at their disposal. Perfume materials such as sandalwood, cedar and jasmine, together with a whole array of spices such as cardamom, ginger and clove, gave East Asian products a rich and sensual allure. These aromatic raw materials of perfumery, being both costly and in great demand, were among the first items to be traded between East and West. However, it was not until the eleventh century CE, under the Arab physician Avicenna, that the art of distillation was perfected for producing pure essential oils and aromatic waters. This new process of steam distillation was critical to the development of perfumery as a whole and it was from Arabia that knowledge of botanical aromatics and perfume-making were first brought to medieval Europe. The Greeks and Romans favoured personally scented items so aromatic oils were used extensively, and they had a considerable understanding of their psycho-therapeutic properties. The physician Marestheus maintained that certain scents, such as rose or hyacinth, had uplifting and euphoric qualities while Hippocrates recommended a daily bath and massage with aromatic oils to promote a healthy body and mind, and to prolong life.

The first books explaining perfumery techniques began to appear at the beginning of the early sixteenth century in Europe and it became common for women to prepare their own perfumes in a special stillroom. This was also around the time that Elizabeth I is said to have issued an order for all public spaces in England to be scented, and it was reported that she was particularly fond of the sweet aroma of meadowsweet (*Filipendula ulmaria*) as a strewing herb for her own chambers. A whole range of fragrant toiletries and perfumed household items were also in high demand during this period, including the use of smelling salts. As the formulation and production of perfumes became more sophisticated, they took on a whole range of different forms, including scented powders, flower waters, aromatic infusions and room fresheners, as well as concentrated essences. Then with the discovery of the alcoholic extraction process in the fourteenth century, the art of perfumery assumed a new finesse. Perfumed gloves became popular in France and, in 1656, the guild of glove and perfume-makers was established. Then in the early eighteenth century, the Italian perfumer Johann Maria Farina made the first eau de cologne, named after the town in Germany where he was residing. He wrote in a letter to his brother in 1708: 'I have discovered a scent that reminds me of a spring morning in Italy, of mountain narcissus, orange blossom just after the rain. It gives me great refreshment, strengthens my senses and imagination.'

Indeed, over the following centuries, right across Europe, home-grown aromatic plants and herbs were used to make a wide range of different

Traditional Herb and Spice Pomander Recipe

One ancient type of home perfume and a highly effective medicinal air purifier is the pomander, traditionally employed as a means of protection against negative spirits and demons of disease or misfortune. A modern adaptation of a pomander is easy to make and can be tailored to suit your ingredient preferences. It will help to purify the air in your home, absorb unpleasant odours and will also look lovely as part of a decorative display. You can also keep pomanders inside cupboards to keep clothes smelling fresh and deter moths from cashmere, silk and wool – *see* recipe in Chapter 4.

One of the earliest aromatic herb-based recipes for a pomander paste – to chase away poisons – can be found in a verse of by German Meistersinger Hanz Folz (c.1450–1515) called '*Die Reimpaarsprüche Pestregimen in Versen*':

Therefore, we need to know now
What withstands these poisons.
That is: to temper the air, strengthen the stomach, heart and brain,
Taste and savour aromatic things,
(To chase away these forces)
One could wear a pomander
Prepared as the recipes say:
With frankincense, aloes, amber,
Camphor, cloves, oil-of-Ben, dried ginger root,
Mace, lemon zest,
Ground mint, nutmeg,
Aromatic reeds,
Stem of valerian,
Roses, gum, sandalwood,
Java pepper, cinnamon,
White turmeric, bugloss, laudanum,
Marjoram and bone charcoal.
Two types of apple are made of this
For Summer and for Wintertime.
But whoever has the illness now
Taste it quickly, is my advice.'

perfume materials, and this practice did not change until the mid-nineteenth century, with the birth of modern perfumery. France ultimately established itself as the perfume capital of the world, with Grasse considered the place to study and finesse the art of perfumery, as well as a place to see and be seen within the industry. Many of the most famous and highly regarded 'noses' are still based, or spent years honing their craft, in Grasse. This city has such an affinity with the production of fragrance, even featuring as the backdrop in the last chapter of Patrick Süskind's best-selling book, later adapted into a film, *Perfume: The Story of a Murderer.* While fragrances from natural compounds made up a well-documented and traditional inventory used for thousands of years, synthetic scents, which only emerged 150 years ago, were suddenly able to provide a limitless source of cheaper and stable notes or fragrances.

Today, there is a shift of emphasis back towards a more natural type of perfumery. The psychological allure and mood-elevating experience of pure botanicals is something we can all resonate with. The ever-increasing interest in the field of aromatherapy is having a notable effect on the perfumery world, with many cosmetic and perfumery houses moving towards a more naturalistic emphasis. All perfumes are described in botanical terms, such as 'floral', 'mossy' or 'woody', and many cosmetic products are described as containing pure rose oil or lavender essential oil, for example. Meanwhile, the aromatherapy industry itself is moving in the direction of mainstream perfumery by becoming more sophisticated and far-reaching in its impact, thus producing a merging of the two disciplines.

By having a direct pathway to our emotional centre, the scent of certain essential oils can help combat conditions such as insomnia, anxiety, depression or grief, which are so often the result of today's stressful lifestyle, while helping to promote feelings of optimism and well-being. Essential oils are effective for both physical and emotional complaints, the two being intimately related. Introducing natural aromatics back into the home is therefore a healthy and enjoyable substitute for the numerous synthetic fragrances with which we are now surrounded, many of which can cause allergic reactions, respiratory irritations and headaches.

The Psychology of Scent

Perhaps what makes the psychology of scent and how it works so fascinating is that each aroma is unique to us as an individual, based on our own lived experiences and our own associations. The French verb *sentir* means both 'to feel' and 'to smell', which is an accurate way of describing how scent effects our brain as well as the power it can have over our feelings and its ability to transform our state of mind.

Smell is the first sense we gain *in utero* – the nose and olfactory receptors develop in the first trimester of pregnancy. At the time of birth, our sense of smell is a baby's most advanced sense and typically within the first hours and days of being born, they will demonstrate a preference for the scent of their mother. A human nose has around 400 scent receptors, and we have the capability to detect over one trillion different odours. With all these odours available to us, however, our linguistic capabilities only seem to get us so far. We commonly struggle with defining or explaining what a smell is like because our vocabulary is often too limited for the intricacies in the scents that our brain is detecting. Our taste buds by comparison can only distinguish four main flavours – sweet, salty, sour and spicy – so it is actually our sense of smell that allows us to perceive all the delicate nuances of scent that we enjoy while eating and drinking.

In various quests to get closer to defining, explaining and categorising scent, there have been many attempts throughout the centuries to take inspiration from classification systems based on sound, colour or taste and then apply them to scent.

To define sound, we can measure their wavelength and frequency. Consider the well-known perfumery terms of top, middle and base notes. This system stemmed from an idea of a nineteenth-century perfumer called Septimus Piesse who attempted to relate each type of fragrance to a musical chord. His system ultimately failed, but ironically the terminology stuck and is popular as a marketing technique and as an easy way to illustrate the symphony of a scent. It is a bit misleading, however, because aromatic notes do not come and go – they are all present at once in a fragrance, then evaporate at their own pace according to their unique and specific vapour pressure. As we will explore further in the recipes of this chapter, it is a marketing myth that a beautiful scent requires a balance of top, middle and base notes, as much as the industry wants us to think otherwise.

With colour analysis, the creation of tools such as the colour wheel can help us to understand colour theory by showing the relationship between colours and the spectrum of light rays. Through an extended application, the colour wheel formed the inspiration for the fragrance wheel. There are various versions and evolutions of this wheel depending on the source, but its inception was most likely in 1983 made by Michael Edwards, the so-called 'perfume experts' expert', who published an impartial and independent perfumery guide named *Fragrances of the World*. He originally developed the fragrance classification chart in wheel form, placing fragrances into four main groups: floral, 'oriental', woody and fresh. This fragrance wheel later became a kind of modern map by which to explore and explain the relationship between the ever-increasing sub-categories of fragrance families.

Our individual responses to smells can be both pleasurable and painful. Consider the scent of your favourite place in nature, the aromas of your favourite meal in childhood, smelling clothes belonging to a loved one or being taken aback by the familiarity of a stranger's perfume reminding you of an ex-lover. Scent can be, in its most expansive terms, so much more than just a product. It is an olfactory déjà vu, a nostalgic contemplation – a connection and gateway to our deepest memories and most vulnerable emotions.

> *'Smell is a potent wizard that transports you across thousands of miles and all the years you have lived. The odours of fruits waft me to my southern home, to my childhood frolics in the peach orchard. Other odours, instantaneous and fleeting, cause my heart to dilate joyously or contract with remembered grief.'*
>
> **Helen Keller**

For me, the sweet heady scent of lily-of-the-valley always reminds me of my mother, as it was her favourite scent as well as being the national flower of Finland. The role and power of scent continues to be explored as a medium of influencing and enhancing everyday living, whether for the individual or a group. Records show olfactive experiences being trialled as part of entertainment in live theatre as early as 1868, while 'Smell-O-Vision' launched in cinema in 1959 to pull viewers deeper into the story. Hoteliers and spas often like to have a 'signature' scent for their properties to enhance their guests' experience and create a sense of comfort and feeling at home. In my book, *Aromatherapy and the Mind,* all these themes are explored at length – it has even been said that the twenty-first century will be the 'Era of Scent' as its multi-dimensional effects are researched and understood more fully. As Maurice Rogers of Dior says: 'Scent, even in hard materialistic times like these, still offers a direct route to the unconscious… Perfume is one of the last territories of the irrational. The deep aim of perfumery is to find ingredients that will open new doors.'

Formulating Modern Room Fragrances

While all scents have an innate ability to influence our emotional state and contribute to our sense of happiness, working with plant-based, natural ingredients has infinite potential and power when it comes to improving our health and sense of well-being. The beauty of having our own alchemical kit means we are free to experiment and enjoy countless variations and adaptations of our own formulations. While some ingredients can be costly, in crafting our own home fragrances and scents from potent and precious natural aromatics, we can create products that are affordable compared to their off-the-shelf counterparts, which are typically always synthetic. Many botanical ingredients can be cultivated easily and thrive quite happily in many climates and conditions. A lot of the herbs you might grow yourself, for example, lavender, rosemary or peppermint, are also all relatively inexpensive

to purchase as an essential oil. The more delicate plants, especially those native to warmer climates, and those that require a more complicated extraction procedure, such as frankincense, myrrh, rose, sandalwood or orange blossom, will of course be pricier as a result.

Starting your home fragrance exploration is easy as you can create a simple air freshener spray in a matter of minutes or make a blend of essential oils for use in a room diffuser that can immediately elevate the atmosphere in your home. As mentioned in Chapter 3, citrus oils such as grapefruit, lemon or lime are excellent choices for use in a home diffuser or vaporiser to purify the air, as they create a fresh, uplifting feeling, while disinfecting the environment naturally. Research suggests the citral and citronellal content of these oils exhibit good antimicrobial activity, as well as in other citrus-scented oils such as lemon eucalyptus, may chang and lemongrass.

Citrus oils also tend to possess a duality of being antidepressant and supportive to the nervous system, as well as purifying and protective for the immune system. This is particularly true of bergamot, since it possesses a unique ability to sedate and regulate the nervous system while encouraging a cheerful, optimistic perspective and outlook. This is due to the specific constituents found within the essential oil, including linalool and linalyl acetate, widely researched for their uplifting effects and noted for their sedative, anti-inflammatory and calming influence. Clinical trials and research by Italian professor, Paolo Rovesti of Milan University, continue to monitor and observe bergamot as a valuable remedy for alleviating depression, nervous tension and stress.

Camphoraceous essential oils that have valuable antibacterial properties for the home or workplace include all types of eucalyptus, tea tree, rosemary, ravintsara, ravensara, cajeput and niaouli. Spice oils, clove in particular, also have excellent antimicrobial, antioxidant and antiviral activity, making them a third category of oils well suited to room vaporisation for purifying the environment of airborne germs. Diffusing a selection of essential oils around your home, or making personalised blends to enhance the spaces and places where you spend your time, is also a pleasurable way to experience their mood-enhancing capabilities.

Intuitively, we may be drawn to picking oils from the same category or family, such as combining different types of citrus oils into a blend for a powerful refreshing effect. Alternatively, we may be drawn to selecting plants from different families, for example combining a citrus oil (lemon) with a herbal oil (peppermint) and a spice oil (clove), as this may be something we have combined in the kitchen for culinary purposes, for example. However, the same principles can be applied when it comes to blending household formulations for scenting spaces and perfuming the home – simply by using our experience and creativity. In this way, it is possible to create unique and personalised scents to suit our personal preferences and mood, without having to follow the so-called rules of blending based on using a balance of notes. This straightforward method of combining three essential oils from different botanical families is a good starting point for creating interesting aromatic room fragrances with a unique character – for example, grapefruit, thyme and black pepper or lemon, rosemary and ginger.

Essential oil room vaporisers come in many different shapes and sizes, with one to suit every style or design scheme. It is ideal to avoid excessive plastic wherever possible, and opt for a diffuser that incorporates ceramic, glass or wooden design. Modern electronic room diffusers use ultrasonic technology or heat to disperse essential oils or fragrances into the air. Often these double up as an atmospheric lamp and as a humidifier as well as scenting a space. Typically, this style of diffuser will stream an extra fine mist into the air and often includes an incorporated interval mode option, so you can have an hour on, then an hour off, for example. These come in many sizes, with 100ml (3.5fl oz) being an industry standard. These are perfect for larger spaces such as living or dining areas or home offices. With natural home fragrances becoming more mainstream, there are now plenty of multifunctioning and minimally designed machines to suit all budgets and scent spaces of various sizes.

The original oil burner or candle-lit diffuser still has a romantic and alluring appeal, as they often omit a warm glow and create a cosy and relaxed ambience in smaller spaces such as bathrooms and by the bed before unwinding in the evening. Today, there are an array of handmade options, beautifully crafted and created by ceramicists to make them look more stylish, or simply designed to make them efficient and easy to clean, with a removable top. This type of essential oil burner, which has been around for hundreds of years, requires no electricity and is still popular. Safety is of course a priority with this type of diffuser to ensure it is not placed near a curtain or where young children can reach it, or left burning unattended if we fall asleep, for example. There are also continuous innovations and reinventions for different essential oil vaporisation methods, such as on-the-go diffusers, aroma stones, USB sticks and more.

Recipes & Crafts

Citrus Pomander Air Purifier

A traditional pomander is a lovely decorative item for children to craft and enjoy the sensory process of using all the aromatic ingredients, especially around Christmas. There are many ways to decorate or personalise your pomander with coloured ribbons or strings, and you can experiment with your own versions of the spice mix too. Your creativity can spark both the style of the design as well as new ways of using or displaying your pomander around the home.

Using an Ayurveda-inspired spice mixture will act as a natural preservative to extend the shelf life of your pomander for several months or potentially even up to a year. Orris root can be considered as a medieval glue of sorts – it is useful as a fixative and binder for ensuring the spice mix sticks to the orange.

Ingredients

Citrus fruits, such as clementine, orange or blood orange, jar full of cloves, approximately 25g (0.8oz) of a selection of your choice of dried spices such as clove, cardamon, nutmeg, black pepper and turmeric (or simply use a ready bought spice mix), 5g (0.2oz) orris root powder (optional)

Equipment

Piercing tool, such as a metal skewer, sewing needle or strong cocktail stick, coloured ribbon or string for hanging, masking tape, any creative extras you fancy

Method

1. Use your sharp implement to pierce a few starter holes into the citrus.
2. Insert whole cloves into each hole. Cover the citrus in cloves as little or as much as you like. You can do it in sections or patterns, using the masking tape as a divider, or freestyle it.
3. Once you are satisfied with your clove placement, cure your pomander in the Ayurvedic spice blend: mix the spices altogether in a bowl and combine with (optional) orris root powder in a large bowl; fully cover each pomander in the spice mix and leave in the spice bowl for up to 24 hours, turning the pomander every so often to recoat it with the spice mix.
4. Once ready, display in a bowl, add to a tablescape or hang using string to decorate the home.

Tip: Leave some space between each clove as they will end up closer together as the orange dehydrates and shrinks over time.

Aromatherapy Spritz Air Fresheners – with Seasonal Suggestions

You can make a simple room fragrance product with just water and essential oils – but the addition of a little witch hazel (or alcohol) will help to prolong its shelf life to help it last for a year or so. These lightweight air fresheners can be enjoyed in any room – sprayed onto cushions, rugs, fabrics and clothes – but are best avoided on silk or delicate items. These products are not designed for use on skin so avoid contact with the face and body. An aromatic room spray will instantly impart a transformative effect on your environment – a particularly lovely thing to do to mark the start or end of the working day. They can also be used as a sensory pick-me-up at any time, as part of a relaxation ritual, or for setting the space for breathwork, yoga, meditation or movement practice. In addition, they are ideal for festive occasions.

Ingredients

1 tsp witch hazel (or ½ tsp vodka or another pure fragrance-free alcohol), 95ml (3.2fl oz) purified water, 50 drops (in total) of essential oils to suit your preference – *see* the seasonal suggestions at the end of this section.

Equipment

100ml (3.5fl oz) tinted glass bottle with atomiser spray cap

Method

1. Pour the witch hazel (or ½ tsp alcohol) into your bottle.
2. Add 50 drops of essential oils.
3. Fill the bottle up with purified water.
4. Place the cap on and shake vigorously to combine, then shake before each use.
5. It is now ready to spritz liberally around the home or for use as an air freshener.

Seasonal Suggestions

Spring Blend

15 drops of peppermint
15 drops of lemongrass
10 drops of sweet fennel
10 drops of petitgrain

Summer Blend

15 drops of geranium
15 drops of rosemary
10 drops of palmarosa
10 drops of lavender

Autumn Blend

15 drops of sweet orange
15 drops of cypress
10 drops of black pepper
10 drops of nutmeg

Winter Blend

15 drops of juniper berry
15 drops of mandarin
10 drops of frankincense
10 drops of clove

Tip: Alternatively, simply add 60 drops of selected essential oils into 100ml (3.5fl oz) purified water and shake well before each use.

Reed Diffuser Recipes for Different Rooms

Reed diffusers are perfect for scenting small spaces such as a bathroom, the hallway, above the toilet, by the bed or next to the cooker. They are effective for any site where you want to make a pleasing atmospheric impact without leaving a candle burning unattended – and of course they are always 'on', diffusing a delicate aroma day and night. This type of method works by drawing a blend of essential oils up through thin rattan reeds, to suffuse the air with your aromas of choice. The beauty of making your own reed diffuser blend

is that you can create bespoke perfumes and try out new combinations for different spaces in the home.

Ingredients

Base oil such as sweet almond or grapeseed oil (enough to half-fill your vessel – in this case, 50ml (1.75fl oz)), 30 drops (in total) of essential oils – *see* suggestions at the end of this section, 1 tsp of alcohol such as ethanol, vodka or perfumer's alcohol

Equipment

100ml (3.5fl oz) clean glass empty vessel – either re-use an existing reed diffuser base or upcycle a small glass or ceramic vessel with a narrow neck, glass stirring rod, 5–8 rattan reeds depending on size of vessel

Method

1. First pour your base oil into the vessel so it is half full.
2. Create your scent by adding your essential oils together (in this recipe, use 30 drops in total).
3. Add 1 tsp of alcohol to the mixture and stir well using the glass stirring rod.
4. Place the reeds into the neck of the bottle so they point upwards.
5. Turn the reeds every few days so that the oil permeates them fully.
6. Replace the reed sticks as needed – when completely saturated and the scent starts to disappear.

Kitchen Purifier
10 drops of lemongrass
10 drops of thyme
10 drops of grapefruit

Bathroom Refresher
10 drops of eucalyptus
10 drops of sweet orange
10 drops of clove

Bedroom Soother
10 drops of chamomile
10 drops of clary sage
10 drops of vetiver

Making Incense with Makko Powder

Incense is made from aromatic, botanical material that produces fragrant smoke when burnt. As already touched upon, it was historically favoured to create ambience or for creating a sacred space for meditation, prayer and worship. It is said that the burning down of incense was once used as a measurement of time.

Popular with healers, spiritual and religious leaders, it also found favour with scholars and the aristocracy, who used it while composing poetry, playing musical instruments or hosting parties. It can be used for similar purposes in our modern lives, and it is relatively easy to make your own, using your desired *Materia aromatica*.

The basic formula is base + binder + aromatic + water = incense. Incense will always require a binder and water, which act as a glue to keep the incense materials together. While the aromatics create the scent, the base ensures a steady, clean burn. Makko powder, made from the bark of the Machillus tree, is commonly used in the process of making incense, as it doubles up as both a base and a binder, making things a little easier. If you cannot get hold of makko powder, powdered charcoal can work in its place, but it is easier to use makko.

All manner of herbs, resins and woods have wonderful aromatic properties for incense, and there are limitless possibilities! Gum resins,, such as frankincense, myrrh or copaiba, and powdered woods, such as sandalwood or cedar, are classic incense materials. You will need to multiply the quantities used here if you wish to make a larger batch at one time.

Ingredients

Per single incense cone: 2 tsp crushed herb material such as juniper, cypress or rosemary, 1 tsp powdered resins or woods, 1 tsp makko powder, a few small drops of purified water to create a paste

Equipment

Pestle and mortar (or kitchen blender), parchment (or kitchen paper), matches, heatproof bowl

Method

1. Crush the plant material with a pestle and mortar or in a blender.
2. Combine the dried herbs and makko powder with a few drops of distilled water to make a doughy paste. When the ingredients are sticking together easily, you have the right consistency.
3. Use your hands to shape the dough into cone shapes, roughly 2.5cm (1in) in height.
4. Place the cones onto parchment paper and let them dry overnight or for eight to twelve hours. You can flip the cones halfway through if desired.
5. Now your cones are ready to use. Place inside a heatproof bowl and light the tip of the cone.
6. After a few seconds, blow out the flame. The cone will continue to emit smoke plus a lovely aroma until there is nothing left but ash.

Caution: Pour cold water over any incense remnants to extinguish any lingering embers before putting it in the bin.

Foraged Smoke-Cleanse Sticks

Smudging is an ancient custom originating in indigenous tribes in North America. Using local herbs such as white sage, cedar and sweetgrass, the ritual involved tying these into a smudging stick and setting it alight to purify the air, clear any negative energy and invite renewal and prosperity into the space.

To honour the reverence and integrity of this practice, it is best to create your own home-grown or locally foraged versions of a smoke cleanse at home. This is a lovely practice to perform upon moving house or to reinvigorate or purify a space before any new initiative.

Suggestions for which plants to use include any herbs you have growing in the garden, such as common sage, rosemary, thyme, lavender and lemon balm, or any you can find in the hedgerows and surrounding green spaces, such as juniper or mugwort. Mugwort is known as the 'dream weed' due to its ability to stimulate dreams, and has a particular affinity with the summer solstice. *Artemisia*, its genus name, suggests a connection with Artemis, the Greek moon goddess, protector of young women and children.

Ingredients

At least 15–20 sprigs of fresh plant materials that are free of any moisture – I like to use mainly common sage, but rosemary, juniper, lavender and so on are also traditional 'burning' herbs.

Equipment

Hemp or natural string, scissors, matches/lighter, heat-resistant bowl, some stones or some sand

Method

1. Gather the herbs together, snip them to a similar length and tie them tightly at the bottom.
2. Begin to tie the bundle together by wrapping the string around the herbs in a criss-cross or zig-zag formation to ensure the herbs stay in place, so the bundle is approximately 4cm (1½in) in diameter, securing with a knot at the bottom.
3. Cut off any excess string.
4. Leave to dry out fully by hanging in a cool place – previously dried herbs would be too brittle to bind together.

5. When setting it alight, leave your stick to burn for a couple of seconds before blowing out the flame.
6. Now use the smoke from the stick to cleanse the air and space around you.
7. Once you have done your smoke cleanse, use a heat-resistant bowl, some stones or some sand to stub the stick out carefully.

Tip: If prepared in the manner described here, your smudge stick should last up to two years.

Aromatic Wax Melts

These mini aromatic cubes create a sense of simple luxury at home and are a lovely way to scent a room using a traditional oil burner. They are also fun to make! Essential oils that have good staying power – such as lemon, grapefruit, lavender, geranium or rosemary – are best used when making aromatic candles and wax melts. Resinous and balsamic oils such as myrrh, benzoin, frankincense or amyris also work well combined in this recipe due to their tenacious quality.

Ingredients

200g (7oz) soy or vegetable wax flakes, 30 drops of essential oils of your choice, dried rose petals (optional)

Equipment

Heatproof jug, saucepan of water, silicon tray (or ice cube container), glass stirring rod, traditional oil burner (with nightlight), matches/lighter, airtight tin

Method

1. Put the wax flakes into the heatproof jug and place in a saucepan of water.
2. Simmer over a low heat until the wax has melted completely and it is hot.
3. Add the 30 drops of essential oils (*see* suggestions at the start of this section) and stir well with the glass stirring rod.
4. Prepare the moulds by scattering a few rose petals into the base of the silicon tray or ice cube container (optional).
5. Carefully pour the aromatic wax into the moulds and set aside to cool.
6. Once hardened, gently remove the cubes from the tray.
7. To use, place one wax melt into the upper bowl of an oil burner, light the candle and allow the wax to melt, infusing the room with its scent, which can last for up to twelve hours.
8. Store any remaining melts in an airtight tin (or jar) and they will be good for up to two years.

Chapter 5

Elemental Healing and the Value of Ritual

'In wilderness is the salvation of the world.'

Henry David Thoreau

The home as a botanical sanctuary is a place of refuge in which to retreat from the world. We can then re-emerge feeling renewed and regenerated. By embracing nature, it can also become a source of elemental healing where we feel nourished and safe: a sacred space that nurtures our soul. In symbolic language, according to the psychoanalyst Carl Jung, our house represents our psyche. Seen in this context, our home, like the human psyche, has two components: a facade and an interior, one corresponding to the public self and the other to the private self. For Jung, homemaking is the perfect metaphor for the integration of the personality, to bring our outer lives into harmony with our innermost desires.

Since our home is a representation of our inner psyche as well as an outer expression of our personality, it is important that we also feel comfortable and at ease within our personal dwelling. The way we furnish our homes, our design decisions about the materials we use and the colours on our walls are all artistic representations of the way we interact with the world around us. It is also an expression of our personality, for example, if we select items that are ecologically sourced and sustainable, such as environmentally friendly cleaning products, natural-fibre fabrics, non-toxic paints and second-hand pieces of furniture that can be upgraded to suit our individual style. Our homes are an expression of our creativity, and nature can be an inspiration for our art, making it possible to live within our unique creation.

In recent years, the Nordic art of ensuring that our home is not only harmonious, artistic and comfortable but also conducive to our sense of well-being has become popularised. This is also true of Finland, since the Finnish people are very health-conscious and fully appreciate their pristine environment, often opting to spend their weekends in a wooden hut beside a lake enjoying an elemental sauna experience. In Scandinavian design, light, space and the use of natural materials, together with the warmth of an open fire and being surrounded by plants, all help to create an atmosphere of cosy relaxation. This way of seeing the home also incorporates the principles of pleasure, gratitude and togetherness as well as our basic need for shelter.

By surrounding ourselves with elements from nature in our homes, we are simultaneously elevating our senses and soothing our souls at a primal level. Recognising and honouring our interdependence with the natural world is also a key to establishing a meaningful relationship with ourselves, our family and our environment. Ritual is also a key part of home life, whether this is an everyday activity such as bathing or a ceremonial custom that is only associated with certain times of the year. Whatever the case, ritual is always directed at enriching and elevating our experience of our daily life.

Nature Therapy

Making a connection between inner and outer spaces, with views of a garden or some area of greenery, also contributes to a sense of serenity within the home. Nature therapy or 'ecotherapy' is an emerging form of psychotherapy based on the idea that we are all connected to and impacted by the natural environment. A growing body of scientific research supports the benefits of feeling connected with nature and its positive effects on our mental and physical well-being. In one study, conducted by Mind, a mental health organisation in the UK, just taking a walk in a natural environment reduced symptoms of depression by 71 per cent of participants. Research has also shown that the beneficial effects of spending time in nature are especially pronounced when they are experienced through all five senses. For example, in another study, participants recovered more quickly from symptoms of psychological stress when they were also exposed to the natural sounds of flowing water and birdsong than when they were exposed to road traffic noise.

While direct contact with nature has many benefits through walking, gardening, exercising or meditating outdoors, individuals need not necessarily have to spend time within a green environment to experience the positive effects of nature. Several studies have found that just seeing greenery within the home or from a window can improve people's overall mood, mental health and life satisfaction. For example, one recent study found that office workers who had a view of nature from their window reported higher job and life satisfaction than those who did not enjoy such a view. Studies have also shown that children who live in buildings with a nearby green space to play in generally have a greater capacity for paying attention and an increased ability at school than children who live in buildings surrounded by concrete. Even the simple process of tending to house plants and creating a green environment within the home can help to encourage a sense of well-being.

Our bodies have adapted to live with nature for millions of years, and even though we may try our best to ignore it, the demands of our modern society can often put our bodies into a permanent condition of overload. Today, over 50 per cent of the world's population live in urban areas, and with the increased emphasis on modern technology, this state of stress has only increased. In our modern society, especially with the effects of social media, we can feel like we are on call twenty-four seven. Having contact with plants and greenery can therefore bring us closer to our original relationship with the natural world, as well as help to induce greater peace of mind.

Since stress-related diseases have proliferated in society today, attention is gradually turning back to many of the more traditional forms of therapy and to nature itself as a resource. The basic concept behind nature therapy is to increase physiological relaxation and use it as a preventative medicine by improving our body's natural resistance to disease, which is suppressed under conditions of stress. The practice of 'forest medicine', which simply involves spending time walking in woods and observing nature close up, is now being carried out in several established centres in England, Scotland, Scandinavia, Japan and the US.

Several research studies have shown that spending time immersed in nature can help reduce stress levels and blood pressure, improve weakened immunity and increase our overall sense of well-being. In one study, it was shown that breathing in the aroma of pine and cypress significantly calmed pre-frontal brain activity and boosted the parasympathetic nerve activity that

increases during relaxation. Such studies also illustrated that it is important for an individual to enjoy the scent of a particular plant or aromatic oil for this increased sense of ease and relaxation to be triggered.

> *'Nature in our daily life should be thought of as part of our biological need.'*
>
> **Christopher Alexander, *A Pattern Language***

Studies have shown that spending just one hour in nature can help reduce anxiety and excessive worry about the past and future plus increase our ability to have a positive outlook on life. It also provides a sense of relief by having a break from our daily concerns, a bit like having a mini holiday. Noticing the beauty of seasonal changes in the leaves, flowers, fruits and seeds, and the habits of any local wildlife, such as the birds in the woods or in your garden, is an enriching experience. It can also help us to slow down. If we are always in a hurry, we can miss out on the joy of simply being. The world we live in today moves at a fast pace, but nature is never in a rush. In this way, we can start to become more aware of the natural world and slowly begin to become more attuned to our environment, reading the signs that are all around us, such as recognising different animal tracks or variations in birdsong.

Healing through the Senses

Being close to the natural world is inherently healing. Like when an injured animal retreats into the forest to lick its wounds, nature can also help us to recover from injury, grief or the stresses of modern life. The rhythms of nature can provide a soothing balm for many ailments: it is for a good reason that most indigenous cultures from around the world traditionally spend some time alone in nature.

Hippocrates maintained that we are a part of nature and our existence depends on a healthy inter-relationship with our wider planet.

Consequently, well-being and longevity can only be achieved by living by this principle and should be fostered through proper nutrition, rest, sunshine, fasting and the use of herbal treatments. He advocated a daily aromatic bath and massage using essential oils as a form of preventative treatment. Medicine, religion and science at this time were intimately related and humankind was seen holistically: as a physical, mental, emotional and spiritual being. Early naturopaths believed that our body would naturally heal itself given the right conditions. As Hippocrates said: 'Nature is the greatest physician.'

A simple way of feeling a greater sense of contentment and happiness on an individual level is through connecting with the natural world using our five senses. This can be a deeply enriching, healing and transformative experience in itself. Just spending time in nature with a clear and open mind can also help to bring us into the present moment. Paying attention to all the sounds, sights, smells and sensations around us can enable us to let go of distracting thoughts or emotions and become fully immersed in our natural surroundings. Observation of nature enables us to look at the world without any preconceptions. Nature does not judge us or elaborate unnecessarily – it just is – and this experience can be refreshing and healing. Listening to the wind in the trees, seeing the sunrise or gazing into the vastness of a clear blue sky naturally opens our hearts, slows down our breathing and helps us to release any tension we feel in our body or mind.

> *'Live in each season as it passes: breathe the air, drink the drink, taste the fruit, and resign yourself to the influence of the earth.'*
>
> **Henry Thoreau, *Life in the Woods* (1854)**

Spending some periods alone in the wild can also allow us to connect on an essential level with the rhythms of the natural world and our inner self. When we connect with any of the elements using our five senses, we can automatically feel nourished by their inherent vitality and dynamic quality. This is also an effective method for switching our attention away from our constantly churning thoughts to instead focus on everything that we experience via our five senses. Focusing on our sense of hearing is especially effective in this respect since sounds enter into our being in a more profound way than visual stimuli. The idea is here to simply allow all the sounds we hear to be absorbed into us, then gradually to allow all our sense perceptions to enter freely into our being.

I was brought up accustomed to the primeval quality of the Finnish landscape and so it has always provided a place of refuge and nourishment for me. I have also viewed it as my 'spiritual home' because of the raw and elemental quality of the natural environment. The Finnish term *luontosuhde*, which translates as 'nature relationship', is intrinsic to the Finnish people and their culture because of their close relationship with the land – land that is occupied mainly by vast forests and lakes.

> *'In Finland we have this thing where you take a match box and you put some rocks, moss or grass in it, and carry it in your pocket. Whenever you want to feel you are outdoors, you can smell it or feel it and get the sense of nature wherever you are.'*
>
> **Tina Nopanen, 'Women and Nature' by Emma Drady**

Then many years later while living in London, I would frequently visit South Wales to immerse myself in the wilds of nature, and to recharge my batteries. At a certain point, I became aware that as soon as I saw the Brecon Beacons and Black Mountains outlined against the skyline as I approached Powys, I could feel my heart region opening as if I could breathe more fully. Wherever we are, in a city or the countryside, it is valuable to make time to appreciate the aliveness, beauty and interconnectedness with nature, and to perform some form of simple breathing exercise or meditation as part of our everyday routine.

Aromatic Rituals

Botanical aromatics have been used for thousands of years to accompany spiritual rituals, whether this is through prayer, meditation or the act of purifying our outer and inner environment, as in the Native American tradition of the Sweat Lodge. According to this tradition, smudge sticks (*see* Chapter 4) are used to purify people and places where the smoke from the burning herb acts to cleanse the body, an object or a place from any negativity. In the Plains Sweat-Lodge ritual, the floor of the structure is traditionally strewn with white sage leaves for the participants to inhale their fragrance and rub on their bodies during the sweat. In this way, the scent and effect of the herb become intrinsically tied up and associated with the experience of the ritual itself.

Natural aromatics especially have been used in sacred rites since ancient times within different cultures across the world. For example, the aroma of incense subliminally reminds us that we are creating a calm space for meditative practice; applying a favourite perfume, such as rose or jasmine, helps impart a sense of joy and warmth; the smell of a particular flower, such as lavender, may transport us back to a nostalgic memory from our childhood, instantly and unexpectedly.

Throughout our lives, the scents that we encounter also acquire individual emotional meanings and, once these are established, they are inextricably linked to us. This means that whenever we encounter a certain smell, it brings back specific memories and associations. Our other senses can help shape these impressions: an odour can be associated with a particular person, a place, a piece of music, an experience of touch or it can even bring back the memory of a whole scene from our past. When this is a positive experience, then our association with that particular scent can be used to recreate and reinforce our feelings of well-being connected with that mood and moment. This is the power of ritual!

Our sense of smell is processed by the limbic region of our brain, the area that deals specifically with our stored memories and emotions. This is the reason why a certain scent can instantly transport us back to a long-forgotten scene from our childhood and why fragrance is such a powerful 'trigger', instantly connecting us with past experiences associated with a repeated ritual. Juniper, cypress, cedarwood, sage, frankincense, myrrh and sandalwood are but a few of the many natural aromatic herbs, essential oils, woods and gum resins that have been used since antiquity to alter our consciousness, relax our breathing, calm the mind and create a sense of ritual that is conducive to contemplative practice.

All these botanical aromatics can also be employed effectively in a modern-day context, used in oil burners or vaporisers to accompany meditation practice, prayer, purification, yoga or simply a session of relaxation. Bundles of dried rosemary, lavender, sage, juniper and cypress have also been used for thousands of years as natural incense, to perfume and purify the air. Simply dry the herbs, bind them into bundles and throw them onto open fires or barbecues. Other aromatic materials, such as orange peel, pinecones or citrus leaves, enhanced with added essential oils, can be used to perfume the home on festive occasions or cleanse the house as part of spring cleaning. *See* Chapter 4 for instructions on making smudge sticks.

Exploring Our Creativity with Nature

Creativity is an essential part of life. Nature has inspired art from the earliest times: it has been the subject of poems, paintings, stories and songs for as long as civilisation has existed. The earliest known images are buried underground in caves, carved into rocks or transmitted by storytellers and musicians from around the world. Often, these ancient artistic expressions depict animals, plants and all the seasonal changes of life together with our own experience as part of these natural cycles.

To my mind, these primal images are some of the most beautiful artistic human expressions because they are a pure expression of our inherent creativity, stripped of artifice or contrivance. These primitive artworks also express a unique beauty together with a sense of wonder and awe. Here, human being and nature are not separate: they are interdependent and indivisible. The gifts of the earth are all provided by Mother Nature: she is the ultimate creative source for the entire botanical world upon which our existence depends. Nature also provides us with materials by which to create our works of art, such as charcoal, mineral colours, paper, cloth and natural dyes. When we connect with nature in this way and appreciate her riches, we also begin to appreciate her innate intelligence and generosity.

The beauty inherent in nature is an inspiration to pursue our dreams and can be a key to opening the door to our creativity. Not everybody identifies with being an artist, or being a creative person, yet creativity is an inherent part of each of us. Creativity can express itself in all sorts of different ways and is a direct means by which we can discover new aspects of ourselves. It can also enable emotional expression in areas that might otherwise have been suppressed or been sidelined by circumstance. In addition, creative expression strengthens our neural pathways and improves brain function, which is valuable at all stages of our lives. As you read earlier, studies have shown that an intimate observation of nature can improve our overall mental and physical health.

Creating something does not always need to have a purpose, either: it can just be about play

SHOWN TO THE CHILDREN

The Language of Flowers

Bay laurel – success; glory; victory; fame; ambition
Basil – protection; dispels negativity; promotes self-expression
Black pepper – endurance; warmth; tenacity; strength
Cardamom – alertness; aphrodisiac; vitality; 'fire of Venus'
Cedarwood – strength; resourcefulness; steadfastness; fertility; abundance
Chamomile – childhood innocence; simplicity; calm; kindness; gentleness
Coriander – lust; adventure; carefree; immortality
Cypress – mourning; transition; courage; rebirth
Eucalyptus – clearing; purifying; healing
Fennel – cleansing; dispels negativity; longevity; strength; courage
Frankincense – spirituality; meditation; insight; freedom; inspiration
Gardenia – secret love; good luck
Geranium – harmony; balance; gentility; determination
Ginger – warmth; grounding; comforting
Grapefruit – cleansing; refreshing; vitality
Hyssop – cleanliness; sacrifice
Jasmine – sexual passion; creativity; desire; seduction; aphrodisiac; wealth; optimism
Juniper – purification; protection; prayer; youthfulness
Lavender – cleanliness; happiness; devotion; peace; nurturing
Lily (white) – virginity; purity; majesty; beauty; peace
Lime and lemon – vitality; well-being; healing panacea; refreshing
Lotus – enlightenment; wisdom; purity
Marjoram – clarity; 'joy of the mountains'
Melissa/lemon balm – sympathy; calm; 'elixir of life'
Mimosa – chastity; sensitivity
Mint – fresh; invigorating; purpose; sense of direction
Myrtle – love; fidelity; emblem of marriage
Myrrh – healing panacea; preciousness; inspiration
Orange – cheerfulness; happiness; contentment
Orange blossom/neroli – innocence; eternal love; marriage and fruitfulness; serenity; good fortune
Palmarosa – adaptability
Pine – hope; self-worth
Rose (red) – love; desire; passion; compassion; femininity; healing the heart; spiritual attainment, 'queen of flowers'
Rosemary – remembrance; fidelity; vigour; protection
Sage (white) – sacred protection; wisdom; respect
Sandalwood – serenity; majesty; contemplation; masculinity
Thyme – willpower; strength; endurance
Valerian – readiness; relaxation
Vetiver – grounding; stability; 'oil of tranquillity'
Violet – modest; faithfulness; 'I'll always be true'
Yarrow – healing; inspiration
Ylang Ylang – aphrodisiac; euphoria; marriage; never-ending love; 'flower of flowers'

and pleasure. Children create things all the time in their land of make-believe. There is no need to prove anything or even show what we sketch or write in a diary to another person – it can simply be a process of self-discovery and self-revelation. Nature shows us that there is no such thing as perfection or an end product. There are no straight lines or matching colours and no defined way of doing anything. Using nature as our muse, we can allow ourselves to enjoy the freedom of imperfection. This is summed up by the Japanese term *wabi-sabi* – appreciating the beauty in imperfection, individuality and impermanence in nature.

Recording our experiences of the natural world in a notebook as part of an ongoing creative process can be a life-enhancing process. Exploring the symbolism and meaning of any plants or animals we encounter and then researching their meaning in various cultures and spiritual traditions can also be enriching. We often find that we resonate with some cultural traditions more than others, as well their native animals and plants, especially if we have a family connection. Researching our ancestry and finding out what kind of relationship our relatives had to the land can help us to reconnect with an inner meaning within our own life. Learning about the mythologies of our kinsfolk can also provide insights into our deeper self, for example, to understand more fully any associated images or animals that may appear in our dreams. In this way, nature is fundamentally a supportive aid in allowing any hidden, lost or suppressed feelings we might have to emerge and be processed.

Botanical Shrines and Offerings

Nature shrines can be found in diverse cultures all over the world. I remember when I first visited Bali and was fascinated to see simple altars decked with flowers and other beautifully crafted botanical offerings, scattered right across the island. The practice of making natural offerings is a ritual that is intricately woven into the fabric of the Balinese lifestyle. These offerings, known as *bantens*, are seen to express gratitude, seek blessings and maintain harmony between the physical and spiritual realms. It is therefore an inherent part of their culture to make daily gifts to the local deities to ensure the prosperity of the land and people. In Bali, most offerings are meticulously fashioned using natural materials that are an intrinsic part of everyday life in a lush tropical environment. Many shrines are located outdoors in gardens. Exotic leaves, flowers and fruits along with holy water are the key components used for offerings, as specified by Krishna in the Mahabharata. Grasses and leaves are woven together to form mats or baskets to display or contain the offerings.

Within Balinese households, making simple daily offerings at home, which are known as *segehan*, is also a common practice, with the belief that through these tangible acts of devotion, it is possible to establish a connection with the divine. Different types of flowers and specific colours may be chosen based on personal preferences or according to the purpose of the offering. Hindu ceremonies in India, for example, make extensive use of marigold flowers to honour their divinities, since their saffron colour signifies renunciation; they are therefore offered as a symbol of respect, gratitude and surrender.

In many parts of Italy, small shrines can still be seen erected on roadsides beside bridges or dangerous passes to attract the blessing and protection of the Madonna, often alongside floral offerings. Flowers are also a familiar sight at the spot where someone has died, in memory of their passing. Fresh flowers themselves signify the impermanence of life itself since they inevitably fade before too long.

In general, whatever the purpose or context for making an offering, it is having the correct intention of giving unconditionally that is most important. Of course, any botanical materials will naturally decompose after a while, so may be returned to nature without any harm to the local environment. The beauty of living close to nature in this way is that you can be a temporary custodian of these offerings (which can be as simple as a leaf or a flower of a sprig of blossom) for a few days only, as part of their beauty is that they are essentially transient.

Placing natural-found objects in the home is also a meaningful way to connect with the beauty and sacred quality of nature. Smooth stones, skeletal leaves, colourful shells, twisted twigs or attractive seed heads can help to inspire creative expression too. These might simply be for decoration in your home, for example, by placing smooth stones on a mantlepiece or pretty shells into a bowl in the bathroom. I have amassed a collection of white chalk stones from beaches in Kent, which have been carved by the water and tides into amazing sculptural shapes. Natural chalk stones make lovely natural room vaporisers for use with essential oils, as the absorbent nature of the chalk releases the scent gradually as the oils evaporate. These chalk pebbles often also have small holes and indentations in them, which are perfect for inserting a stick of incense, allowing them to be used as a holder on a shrine.

Making a personalised shrine using natural objects can provide a focal point in a room and be a reminder that all life is sacred. It is also possible to make a personalised nature shrine to act as a centrepiece for meditation practice, whether you follow a particular spiritual tradition or not. In this case, it is best to choose a location for your shrine that is peaceful and secluded. To incorporate a natural shrine into your home or to create a nook in the garden for making offerings, using flowers as well as other natural objects, such as crystals or gemstones, is an ancient practice.

The Symbolism of Flowers

Today, it is easy to take for granted the significance of flowers for ceremonial purposes in the West – yet flowers are still the unspoken language we commonly use in our everyday lives to say: 'I love you', 'thank you' 'please forgive me' or 'rest in peace'. The poignant images of thousands and thousands of bunches of flowers laid along the streets of London following the death of Princess Diana is an unforgettable and quite extraordinary event given our largely secularised society. Valentine's Day is another occasion when the language of flowers still speaks loud and clear, as well as at funerals and weddings.

The profound symbolism and inner meaning that certain plants hold in our lives today is also apparent from age-old folk tales that are infused with stories about them. It is interesting to look at the history and ancient lore surrounding botanicals to learn how we can utilise them to create new and healthy everyday rituals.

Apart from our individual associations, our cultural heritage also feeds into these links via our sense of smell in important ways. When I started to look more deeply into the traditional associations and symbolism connected with botanical plants and their fragrances, I was amazed how familiar they seem, often because they are so ingrained within our culture through literature and folklore. A bay tree wreath is associated with victory and bravery, for example, and it is well-known that rosemary is 'for remembrance', to use Shakespeare's phrase. Red roses speak of passion whereas a white lily conveys innocence and purity.

From the Middle Ages onwards, significance was also given to the astrological connection between plants and different planets. In his *Liber de Vita,* Marsilio Ficino (1433–1499) wrote that the sun ruled St John's Wort, rosemary and chamomile; Mercury ruled dill, fennel, honeysuckle and lily-of-the-valley; while Venus ruled mint, thyme and violet. The relationship between herbalism and astrology lasted until the eighteenth century when a more pragmatic, scientific approach became prevalent.

Meanwhile, the 'Doctrine of Signatures' dates back even earlier, originally being developed in the esoteric mystical schools of Alexandria. This connected the shape of a herb with its curative properties and was a doctrine much promoted by Paracelsus in the early sixteenth century. For example, wild pansy with its heart-shaped leaves was said to cure disorders of the heart, whereas plants whose leaves are kidney-shaped were thought to be good for the renal system.

Under the Elizabethans, herbal posies were exchanged between lovers as an object of romance, with different flowers carrying their own secret messages. For example, roses declared love, while lavender meant silence. Marigolds signified happiness and marjoram wished fruitfulness on the recipient. The Victorians formalised the arrangement of the posies known as 'tussie mussies', making the herbs, flowers and leaves more deliberately concentric and symmetrical. As its symbolism and the use of its secret language faded, the posy became simply an offering for special occasions.

To revive the original custom, a fresh posy can still make a unique gift today, and can be offered as a gesture of intimacy, using flowers with a symbolic meaning. Choose each flower according to the message you wish to convey, then tie their stems together with raffia. You can also select dried herbs and flowers by binding the stems together with floristry wire, then push the posy through the centre of a paper doily and secure with a decorative ribbon. For extra fragrance, add a few drops of essential oil into the middle of the posy.

For a guide to the symbolism of some of the most common plants and aromatic oils presented as a compilation taken from folklore and from the herbal tradition, including the 'Doctrine of Signatures' by Paracelsus and the 'Language of Flowers', *see* 'The Language of Flowers' feature earlier in this chapter.

Crafts & Practices

Making a Nature Shrine

Making a simple shrine is a traditional way to introduce natural materials into the home and to pay respect to the sacred qualities inherent in nature. It is also a creative act. A shelf, small table, mantlepiece or a special structure made from clay or stone that can be fixed to a wall all make ideal altars on which to place your chosen objects. To embellish the shrine, collect whatever plants or flowers you are drawn to and, if you wish, add candles, crystals or other natural objects as part of your design.

An altar of this kind can act as a focal point for a regular meditation practice. In many spiritual traditions across the world, it is customary to place a vase of flowers and to light some incense as an offering on the altar. I like to light candles and burn incense, and often offer a sprig of fresh flowers on my personalised shrine in my room every morning, to accompany my meditation session. The use of incense and natural aromatics has also long been associated with the power of ritual.

Ingredients

Pebbles, stones, crystals, flowers, leaves and so on

Equipment

Flat surface to act as an altar, incense, incense holder

Method

1. Decide on a suitable position for your shrine at home. This could be in the bedroom, lounge or on a smooth stone or rock crevice in the garden. Some people have a designated shrine room as a place for contemplation.
2. Set up your shrine as you wish, which can be as simple or as elaborate as you like.
3. If you feel attuned to a particular spiritual tradition, this can be respected by placing items on your shrine that are sacred to that culture. In America for example, eagle feathers are considered sacred by many indigenous people, representing the principles of bravery and spiritual insight. Alternatively, your shrine could reflect a basic affinity with nature itself.
4. A shrine can be used as a focal point for meditation, for example, by focusing your gaze on one specific item, such as a candle; this can act as an 'anchor' to tame the mind.

Naturally Scented Candles

Off-the-shelf scented candles are typically made with synthetic fragrances and paraffin wax, which results in harmful chemicals being released into the home and a potential concern for pets and people with asthma and allergies. A natural candle should typically be more expensive because the price is reflective of the quality of the ingredients inside. Making your own candles using plant-based waxes and natural essential oils is the ideal way to know exactly what is inside your candle and a fun way to experiment with different combinations.

The following recipe makes one candle.

Ingredients

Mixture of soy/jojoba/coconut wax and beeswax flakes or pellets at a 75:25 ratio, 40–50 drops (total) of essential oils of your choice (*see* seasonal suggestions at the end of this recipe)

Equipment

Clean, empty recycled candle holder/glass jar or suitable vessel, saucepan, scales, jug, bain-marie, thermometer, waxed and wired cotton wicks with metal fasteners, two sticks or reeds

Method

1. Mix the soy/jojoba/coconut wax with beeswax pellets or flakes.
2. Pour the mix into the candle vessel until it reaches 2.5cm (1in) from the top, then place into a bain-marie.
3. Turn on the heat and melt the wax mix until

it becomes liquid.

4. Remove from the heat and allow to cool to around 140°C (275°F), checking with a thermometer.
5. Add essential oils one by one, aiming for 40–50 drops in total per candle.
6. Place the metal tab of the wick at the base of the candle vessel and hold the cotton part up while you pour the wax around it to the desired depth.
7. Hold the wick vertically by wedging it between two sticks or reeds until the wax has cooled.
8. Leave the candle to cure for two days, then it can be lit and enjoyed.

Tip: Remember to trim your wick after each use to keep your candle burning efficiently.

Four Seasonal Scents

Trees of the Forest
10 drops of cedarwood atlas
10 drops of cypress
10 drops of juniper needle
10 drops of frankincense
10 drops of elemi

Summer Meadow
20 drops of chamomile
10 drops of hyssop
10 drops of palmarosa
10 drops of geranium

Coastal Breeze
20 drops of lime
20 drops of eucalyptus
10 drops of black pepper

Sleepy Scent
20 drops of lavender
20 drops of bergamot
10 drops of sweet orange

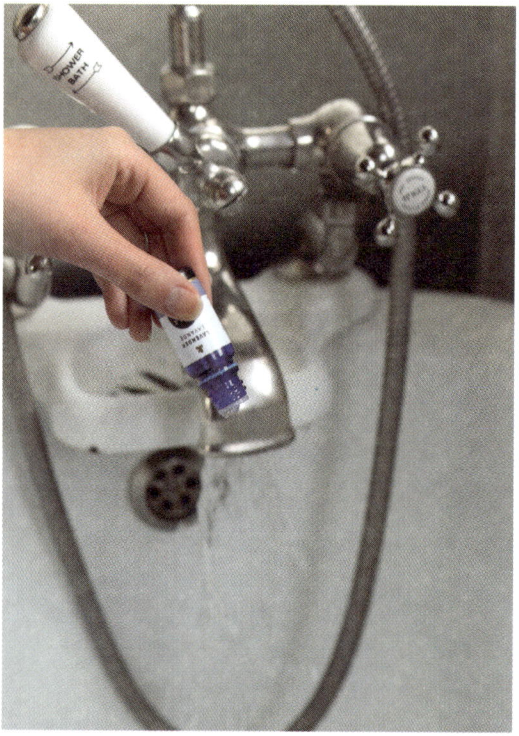
SHOWER
BATH

Ritual Flower Bathing

In spiritual practices all over the world, ritual bathing serves as a form of rebirth, cleansing and healing. Water is used for baptism to cleanse the soul, wash away old habits and change patterns that no longer serve us – ritual bathing traditionally encompasses both a physical and spiritual dimension. Introducing fresh plants into our bathing ritual helps to nourish our mind, body and spirit, and can be practised once a week as a pleasurable means to promote healing, renewal and regeneration. Hippocrates recommended a daily aromatic bath as a preventative treatment for ensuring longevity and this was central to his naturopathic approach to promoting good health. Epsom salts, Dead Sea salts and a little wine vinegar or apple cider vinegar can also be added to the water if you wish.

Adding fresh rose petals to the bath is a classic treat – it is said that Cleopatra would not bathe without hundreds of rose petals floating in the water! However, all kinds of scented fresh flowers or leaves can be gathered from the garden for a ritual bathing experience. Light a candle, relax in the warm water, and treat yourself to some time away from your everyday demands, with a glass of wine on the side. Lemon geranium leaves impart a delicious, sweet and soothing scent to a bath and are a favourite with young children. Other options include fresh lemon balm, jasmine flowers, orange blossom, lavender flowers, rosemary leaves or a combination of your favourite herbs. The warmth of the bath water gently steams the petals and leaves, releasing their fragrances. You can also enhance the scent by adding a few drops (up to ten drops) of the corresponding essential oils to the bath water, such as lavender, rosemary or rose geranium oils.

For a less messy technique (so you don't need to clear up the plant materials afterwards), stuff the plants into a bath bag as described here. Another simple technique is to attach a sprig or bunch of fresh aromatic plants to the shower head or bath taps using a piece of string or ribbon. I like to use a bunch of eucalyptus leaves for their fresh, invigorating fragrance. The hot steam of the shower releases their essential oils, creating a home spa experience.

Ingredients

Fresh plants – flowers or herbs, 10 drops (total) of essential oils of your choice

Equipment

String or ribbon, small square piece of muslin or an empty cloth bag, candle (optional), glass of wine or your favourite beverage (optional)

Method

1. Pick a bundle of aromatic leaves and flowers fresh from the garden.
2. Remove any hard stems and check there are no insects in the material.
3. Make a simple sachet by tying some ribbon or string around a small square piece of muslin cloth. Alternatively, use a ready-made, wide-mesh, drawstring bag approximately 10 × 15cm (4 × 6in) in size, which can be reused easily.
4. Stuff the bag with aromatic leaves and flowers and secure it at the neck.
5. Tie the bath bag under the hot tap (or shower head) while the bath is running.
6. Add up to 10 drops of your chosen essential oil.
7. Soak in the bath and enjoy the aromatic vapours!

Tip: Children especially like concocting their own bath blends and the scent is better than you will find in any commercial or dried preparation.

Keeping a Nature Journal

Keeping a nature journal to document your experiences, thoughts and feelings by sketching or writing about the plants, animals and landscapes you encounter can help to deepen your connection to the environment. We can also discover more about our personal associations with different plants and our surroundings. Artistic expression is a way of making us more observant, aware and still. In addition, it can facilitate a process of inner exploration, as often what emerges can surprise us or reveal unexpected insights. Sometimes it can also be equally rewarding to remain in silence, observing the natural world surroundings without the need for words or explanations.

Equipment

Notebook or sketch pad, pen/charcoal/pencils/crayons, bag for 'found' objects

Practice

1. Find a quiet spot in nature; it could be in a garden, park, beach or forest.
2. Remain still. Quietly observe what you can see, hear and smell.
3. Notice what catches your attention – this may be a tree, a landscape or a single flower, or it might be an idea or feeling that is triggered by your experience.
4. Start to sketch what you can see – patterns, textures, colours and so on – or start to write about your observations as they emerge, or both combined. Don't feel that your sketch or writing needs to match what you see before you or have preconceived ideas about whether your work is good or bad.
5. Make a note of the date and location of your sketch or writing and include any other details you think are relevant.
6. If it is not environmentally damaging, you may want to collect a stone, shell or other item to remind you of your experience once you return home.

Forest Bathing

The Japanese term *shinrin-yoku*, which means 'forest bathing', is the practice of walking slowly through woods and paying attention with all the senses to one's immediate surroundings: the leaves, canopy, sunlight, woodland plants, all the scents and sounds, as well as the creatures who live in the forest. Forest bathing and other types of elemental meditations should be above all relaxing, so it is important to find a natural green space where you feel comfortable. Try visiting several different locations at various times of the day to get an idea of what is on offer locally.

For example, in the UK, the National Trust have specific 'well-being' trails that take in a beautiful landscape or vista, or paths that take a route beside the sea, a lake or a river. Listen to the sounds of all the elements: the rush of a waterfall or the drip-drip of rain falling through leaves; feel the wind on your skin, the soft brushing of grasses against your skin; look into the open sky; watch the light on the smooth surface of a lake. This simple mindfulness practice can also be done in a garden or any space where it is possible to be in contact with all the elements of nature.

Practice

1. Turn off your mobile phone and put aside other distractions so that you can focus all your attention on where you are and what you can see, hear, feel and smell.
2. If you are walking or are in the company of a companion, don't speak for a period of time, which you can agree mutually beforehand.
3. Although it may feel a little contrived at first, the key is to simply slow down. Focus your attention on all of your senses to appreciate everything around you; in this way you can tune into your surroundings more fully and enjoy the strength of each element.
4. Avoid following your thoughts or letting yourself be carried away by trying to name or categorise what you see, hear, feel or smell in this exercise.
5. Enjoy just 'being' with the different qualities of nature and the elements.

Nature-Inspired Breathing Practice

A home sanctuary is a place within which we feel comfortable and relaxed. Even if it is not possible to devote a whole room to creating a calm space for our practice, it is good to find a spot that is quiet and secluded. If we use this place regularly to sit and focus on our breath, then we become more familiarised with the method and routine as part of a daily ritual. This breathing technique helps calm the mind, but it can also help to combat stress, anxiety or panic attacks. It just takes a few minutes and can be done almost anywhere, although you will get the most benefit if you do it regularly as part of your everyday routine.

Practice

1. Find a place to sit where you will not be disturbed and where you can return frequently. This might be a room in your home or a spot in your garden.
2. Switch off your phone and remain still; just become present to where you are.
3. Make yourself as comfortable as you can and loosen any clothes that restrict your breathing.
4. Keep your back straight, whether you are sitting on the floor or on a chair.
5. Bring your attention to your body: feel where it is touching the floor or seat.
6. Gradually start to scan your whole body, relaxing each area one by one: your face, shoulders, chest, legs, arms and feet.
7. Now bring your attention to your breath, and feel the sensation of it entering your nose, mouth and lungs. Breathe gently and regularly, allowing the breath to flow naturally.
8. Start to breathe in through your nose and out through your mouth.
9. Let your breath flow into your lungs and as deep down into your abdomen as is comfortable, without forcing it. It can be

helpful to count steadily from one to five on this inbreath.
10. Then, if you can, hold your breath for five beats.
11. Then breathe out gently from the mouth, counting from one to five again.
12. Remain empty for a couple of seconds after the outbreath, then repeat.
13. Continue for at least five minutes then relax totally.

An Elemental Meditation

Meditation is a practice that has been part of human history for thousands of years, with many different forms of expression. All types of meditation are aimed at bringing the individual back to themselves and back to the present moment. Rather than trying to eliminate all thoughts, the purpose is to recognise when you are lost in your train of thoughts and to gently bring yourself back to the present. Practising meditation outside in a natural environment is a different experience to remaining in an enclosed room. Emerging research suggests that sitting directly on the earth has a grounding effect on our system, soothing the nerves and boosting energy levels. By sitting outdoors in a garden or park, we can simultaneously open ourselves to all the sounds, sights and smells of all of the elements as well as anything that is occurring around us. We might become aware of clouds passing in the sky or become conscious of the birdsong around us. We can then use our senses, for example by listening to the sound of water or wind in the trees, to focus our attention. This is one of the most effective ways of becoming directly integrated with the natural elements around us.

Practice

1. Become aware of your senses and the messages they are receiving.
2. Try to let your train of thoughts drop away as your being becomes integrated into the sounds that you can hear.
3. Start to focus on one of your senses, for example hearing is a particularly useful tool for contemplation.
4. Focusing on one of your senses, such as hearing, can act as an 'anchor' to help quieten your mind. For example, listen to the sound of the waves on the beach, then just remain with that presence and awareness.

Sitting by a waterfall, the sea or a fast-running stream is an effective aid for this type of practice. Alternatively, standing in a shower at home can also allow a taste of this type of experience too.

Chapter 6

Bringing Nature Indoors

'A spring breeze is blowing
I'm bursting with laughter
– wishing for flowers'
Matsuo Basho

The Japanese are renowned for their love of nature. This is epitomised by their annual national festival held simply to view the appearance of the first cherry blossoms in spring. The tradition of *hanami* or 'flower viewing' is the Japanese custom of enjoying the transient beauty of flowers. This is associated with the Zen Buddhist theme of recognising that this life is impermanent and passes swiftly 'like the clouds in autumn' and will soon fade quickly like spring flowers. The annual cherry blossom festival usually lasts for the entire month of April and includes evening events where the trees and their lovely blossom are illuminated. The flowering period usually starts from around the beginning of April and can last into May. Japanese haiku poetry, such as the lines at the start of this chapter by Matsuo Basho, is suffused with references to the natural world, while Japanese Zen gardens and temples show reverence for the inherent serenity that it invokes.

Home Design Elements

The design of traditional Japanese houses shows an appreciation of the natural world. Inner and outer spaces are merged with full-height sliding screens and movable partitions, so each area flows seamlessly into another. Wide sliding doors open onto verandas so the garden beyond can be viewed with ease from the rooms within. Furniture is kept to a minimum and structures are made from carefully chosen materials, such as wood, paper and woven matting, so the immediate surroundings are easy on the eye. A love of natural materials is also exemplified in a traditional Japanese kitchen layout, where bamboo and ceramics along with pot plants transform what is essentially a workshop into a place of refined aesthetic beauty. This ingenious use of space, which often includes additional shelving hung from the ceiling of the kitchen, and integrated wooden poles from which to hang pans, herbs, pot plants and other items, can provide a wealth of design inspiration that integrates natural materials with greenery.

Aesthetic considerations are harmonised with efficiency in Japanese design, where natural materials are not only beautiful but also practical. For example, wood, bamboo and stone often improve with age and develop a unique character, adding individuality and richness to interiors as well as textual sensuality. Furnishings made from organic or raw materials, such as cotton, linen or silk, can also help to bring the natural world into our home. Choosing sustainable and naturally renewable materials, when responsibly sourced,

also has a lower impact on the environment. At the same time, by choosing naturally derived materials, we are reducing the number of synthetic toxins in our homes, thereby creating a healthier space to live in.

Honouring the power and impact of all our senses adds another dimension to our everyday experience. Fresh flowers and scented naturalistic arrangements are plentiful in traditional Japanese homes. Special alcoves are even created within the walls of the main drawing room to house a nature shrine in which to display floral offerings, such as a bud vase with sprig of cherry blossom. This inbuilt reverence for nature and attention to each detail within the home naturally evokes a sense of spaciousness and heightened awareness within the mind as well. Seen in this way, it makes sense that the atmosphere of our home also parallels our inner state.

Taking inspiration from Japanese-style interiors, we can apply similar principles to our own homes by paying attention to detail, embracing simplicity and bringing nature indoors in all sorts of ways. Enjoying a sense of spaciousness and ease is a spiritual as well as a physical sensation. An uncluttered environment makes even a jar of wildflowers placed on the kitchen table a thing of intense beauty. In this way, our home can not only be a source of enjoyment and inner nourishment but also enhance our health in all sorts of ways.

Merging Inner and Outer Spaces

The history of human consciousness can be interpreted through the basic structure of our homes, from the circular shelters of tribal people to the contemporary urban, rectangular buildings of our cities today. A circular type of dwelling mirrors those forms found in nature, being more of an organic structure like a nest, and relates more to our origins, like a replica of our mother's womb. This is the home as a personal sanctuary or refuge in the true sense of the word. The way in which we relate to our interiors also inevitably reflects

Feng Shui Design Principles

Feng shui is an ancient Chinese tradition that has developed the concept of harmonising the relationship between an individual, the home and their immediate environment into a more formalised system. This tradition embodies the Taoist art of living in harmony with the environment, including a reverence for the changing seasons. It is the ancient science of achieving perfect equilibrium with nature; in the East, people have relied on it to build their homes and design their interiors for over 4,000 years. Over time, hundreds of different formulas have developed to solve all kinds of problems relating to the interconnection between ourselves and our surroundings, between the inner and outer spaces of our homes. Using feng shui principles, it is possible to enhance, balance and energise our lives as well as create a beautiful and healthy place in which to live. The home I live in today has been designed and furnished with feng shui principles in mind.

One of the main principles of feng shui is the relationship between the five elements – earth, metal, water, wood and fire – and understanding how they interact with each other and how to harmonise them. In the creative cycle: fire creates earth, earth creates metal, metal creates water, water creates wood and wood creates fire; each element is also associated with a specific colour. However, in the negative cycle: fire melts metal, metal chops wood, wood penetrates earth, earth limits water and water destroys fire. Each element is also related personally to our astrological chart as well as to a compass direction and a specific colour – but colour remedies are only a small part of feng shui design. Decorating a room in a particular colour can instantly change the shape of a room or make it more cosy by introducing a warm tone, such as ochre; however, sometimes it is better to use neutral colours on the walls and instead harmonise a specific space by introducing the element of wood by using plants, for example, or by adding a water feature, lighting candles or incorporating wind chimes, which represent metal.

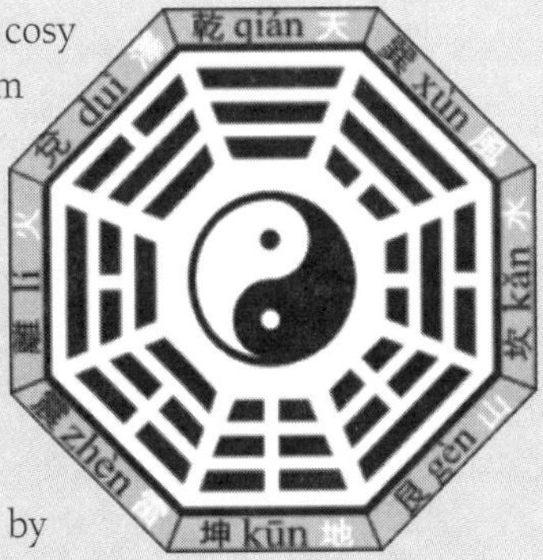

For example, if the bedroom is in the eastern part of your home, which corresponds to the wood element, and has little natural light yet has a beautiful garden outside, it is better to avoid using green on the walls since this might create a rather cold atmosphere in the room. Instead, it is better to draw the eye to the space outside since the wood element is already present in the green of the garden. In this case, one technique might be to use neutral colours on the walls and simply enhance the view of the garden by minimising the use of curtains or blinds, adding some green accents to the furnishings and incorporating some house plants into the room.

According to feng shui principles, all plants can help to enhance our personal energy when introduced into the home. The green colour of their leaves strengthens the activity of the wood element, which brings the energy of growth, freshness and vitality into a space. The energy of the wood element, which is inherent in all plants, can also inspire compassion and kindness, as well as being associated with rejuvenation and renewal.

the quality of our life and our mode of being. William Morris decreed that we should not have anything in our home that we do not consider to be useful or believe to be beautiful. We can go further than this by ensuring that the contents of our home are not only beautiful and practical but are also connected to the natural world.

A wooden veranda or stone terrace is the perfect mediator between inner and outer spaces, bringing nature within arm's reach. This is also the ideal spot to place a table for dining or a casual chair for reading, while still being able to hear the rustle of the wind in the leaves or the scent of jasmine trained against a wall. Open plan design has also become popularised within the last few decades, where the dividing lines between kitchen, lounge, entrance hall and garden have become less static and more flexible. Installing glass sliding doors between the living areas and the garden can further allow a sense of integration with the landscape beyond, thus merging inner and outer seamlessly. The way the inside of our home connects with the outside affects our sense of overall well-being. Bringing nature indoors by introducing design elements that promote contact with the greenery outside is a way of ensuring this connection, alongside welcoming living plants and natural materials into the home.

The Turn End Botanical Gardens at Haddenham in England exemplify the concept of designing the outdoor spaces as a natural extension of the buildings themselves. This garden's interlinked informal spaces and garden rooms with naturalised planting around existing trees, all interwoven with the house, reflect Peter Aldington's hands-on approach as a designer and his deep understanding of materials and plants. Created in conjunction with the house, it is an expression of the architect's belief that architecture and landscape design are an intimate and indivisible whole. The famous Mirror House at Joshua Tree in California, USA, takes this concept to the extreme: it is so-called for its mirror-clad facade, which reflects its desert surroundings so it effectively disappears into the rocky landscape! In this extraordinary design, the mirrored surfaces create the illusion that the home is invisible within the desert itself. However, the Mirror House is far from ecological with its multimillion-dollar price tag. By contrast, the local Pueblo houses of the arid Southwest are made from local stone, plaster and wood, and are organically rounded both inside and out; their traditional adobe-style homes employ earth, water and grass or straw in their construction, often having enclosed courtyards for outdoor living. Likewise, the riad style of traditional buildings in Morocco are constructed around a central courtyard that provides a pleasant outdoor space, often featuring a fountain and an abundance of scented plants, in which to relax or simply view from the windows of the surrounding rooms.

Tucked away in Pittwater, an hour north of Sydney in Australia, is a modern 'forest home' designed for natural living. This miniature low-cost house consists of just two chambers, with living and cooking quarters below and a simple sleeping area above. Outdoor dining takes place on an extended wooden deck protected by a canvas canopy. This innovative naturalistic home constructed by the architect Peter Stutchbury has an elementary steel-frame structure that supports a gently curved roof. Large sliding windows and wooden panels give the interior an unusual lightness and transparency, allowing intimate views into the verdant bush beyond.

In cities, living walls using individual plants placed in specially designed pockets and green rooftops made from low-growing, low-maintenance plants, such as succulents, are now becoming a familiar sight within urban developments, along with rooftop gardens. Habitable tree houses have also become fashionable getaway retreats, where inhabitants can experience living up in the treetops along with the birds! English poet William Wordsworth believed a home for living close to nature should

be: '... a production of nature and rather to be said to have grown than have been created, to have risen, by instinct of their own, out of naked rock'.

Building in harmony with nature is a challenge architects, scientists and interior designers face due to our rapidly warming planet and the high carbon footprint that construction entails. While the industry is shifting towards the use of recyclable and sustainable materials, such as bamboo flooring to reclaimed wood, there is now a demand and a desire to choose materials for the home that are not only durable and aesthetically pleasing but also environmentally responsible. The average homeowner or tenant may not have the means, time or know-how to build an eco-home from scratch, but many of us do want to take the utmost care to ensure that what we use, consume and fill our homes with mutually respects the planet and its creatures as well as our own health and well-being.

Reverence for the Seasons

Since ancient times, the Japanese have divided their year into twenty-four periods, but the natural world comes to life more vividly through their seventy-two micro-seasons. Using poetic references to note the changes occurring in nature, this traditional Japanese calendar marks the passing of the seasons by giving specific names to each miniature section of the year. Originally taken from classical Chinese sources, which are still well known throughout East Asia, the year starts with *Risshun*, 'the beginning of spring', in early February until the end of winter called *Daikan*, or 'greater cold', in January. Each micro-period lasts around four to five days, and in their present form, they offer a poetic journey through the year in which the land awakens and blooms with life before returning to a state of hibernation with the arrival of winter. In April alone, for example, there are seven subdivisions, each referring to occurrences in nature:

- 31 March–4 April: 'distant thunder'
- 5–9 April: 'swallows return'
- 10–14 April: 'wild geese fly north'
- 15–19 April: 'first rainbows appear'
- 20–24 April: 'first reeds sprout'
- 25–29 April: 'last frost, rice seedlings grow'
- 30 April–4 May: 'peonies bloom'.

To relate to the progression of nature throughout the year in this way implies paying close attention to the minute changes happening around us, slowing down and becoming more attentive to the moment. It is possible to apply the same principles to wherever we live and in whatever situation. There are always ways to connect with nature, even in a city, by exploring parks, spending time in a garden or tending window boxes or pots.

At one time, I owned a farmhouse near the Epynt mountains in Wales, with a three-acre garden to tend. The land was totally overgrown and wild when I arrived, so gradually developing the garden was a horticultural adventure. Because of the dramatic seasonal shifts, I also started writing a daily diary recording all the tiny changes that were occurring in the garden. Much like the Japanese seventy-two poetic sketches, I found myself observing the seasons more closely; simply tuning into the details gave me a greater appreciation of all the different moods of the seasons – even the cold, wintry frosts or those days when it never stopped pouring with rain!

In April, for example, the gardens were always full of dark-leaved, violets, creeping purple vinca, and primroses emerging on the grassy banks, while delicate white wood anemones appeared beside the stream in the valley. My mature rosemary bush would also flower in the spring (and again later in the summer so long as it was protected against the southern wall of the farmhouse) and would be covered in beautiful azure-blue flowers in April. Many years later, I still always have a mass of cut flowers, bulbs or pot plants on my kitchen table so I can mark the seasonal changes by witnessing different flowers blooming throughout the year. Potting up spring bulbs, tending house plants or tending window boxes are some of the easiest and most pleasurable ways to bring nature indoors, at any time of the year.

Pots and Container Planting for All Seasons

Displaying house plants in pots and containers full of greenery in or around the home is a traditional method of bringing nature inside. This is also a practical way to enjoy many tender or semi-tender species that can be moved indoors or outside, as the temperature allows. This movable system of gardening greatly extends the flexibility of the growing season for the gardener. For example, containers planted with scented lilies and placed on a terrace can later be plunged into a border to add drama, fragrance and colour wherever gaps appear. Fragrant containers set on a veranda near an open window in summer or on a balcony adjoining a bedroom can permeate a room with their perfume. The additional joy of containers is that they can be removed instantly once the flowering season of the plant is over. With the wide range of aromatic plants available both for the conservatory and for more general container planting, there is the possibility of creating an ever-changing display that can provide interest throughout the year and in all seasons.

Spring

In spring, wild primroses, sweet violets and snowdrops are some of the first flowers to appear in the countryside and the garden, followed by cyclamen, daffodils , grape hyacinths and fragrant narcissi. Together with miniature irises and lily-of-the-valley, these early harbingers of spring make excellent container plants that can be brought indoors to enjoy just as the days start to get warmer. Tulips are not generally scented but there are a few fragrant species worth planting for a spring display. For example, the dwarf tulip *Tulipa humilis* has sweetly scented magenta-pink flowers and is best grown as a pot plant. This is one of my favourite spring flowers and less common than the larger and gaudier tulip varieties.

Hyacinths are some the most exotic of the fragrant bulbs and make a rich statement planted in containers with other bulbs, such as narcissi and daffodils. Some hyacinth bulbs can also be 'forced' for a midwinter display, while many species of narcissi are equally at home in pots or left to naturalise in the wild. It would be difficult to imagine spring without flowering bulbs and tree blossom, and some dwarf fruit trees can also be container grown. Miniature cherries, decorative crab apples and other fruit trees are some of the most beautiful spring-flowering plants to position near the house. For example, the small, pink, double-flowered cherry (*Prunus triloba* 'multiplex') looks lovely underplanted with grape hyacinths or primroses. Alternatively, the downy cherry (*P. tomentosa*) makes a perfect statement specimen planted alone, having beautiful pale-pink flowers and lovely fresh green leaves that eventually turn to a deep maroon.

Summer

The warmth of summer brings with it an abundance of fragrant flowers, including a wide range of old-fashioned, highly perfumed roses – some of the smaller varieties look stunning grown in old terracotta pots. Climbers such jasmine and honeysuckle, together with more humble plants like phlox and wallflowers, burst into flower in early summer, all of which look lovely massed in pots or containers. Popular plantings for summer pots or window boxes include scented geraniums and pinks. Herbs such as chives and mint are also ideal for container planting and often work well planted together in combinations, being especially useful grown on a kitchen windowsill.

Slightly tender species, such as the delicate lavender *Lavandula dentata* or summer savory

and immortelle (*Helichrysum italicum*), can easily be protected from frost when planted in pots too. Sweet-smelling violets such as *Viola cornuta*, which produces masses of flowers over several months, look beautiful trailing from window boxes or hanging baskets. Classical lilies, such as the classic Madonna lily, are perhaps the most imposing and highly scented of all container plants for larger containers, and most flower in the middle of the summer. Sweet peas (*Lathyrus odoratus*) are old favourites too, and look delightful growing up a small, trellised wigwam in a large pot on a terrace or placed in the vegetable garden.

Autumn

Autumn may not have the abundance of full summer, but there are still several aromatic plants that can be enjoyed in the later part of the year that are suitable for pots and containers, including the Elizabethan favourite, sweet woodruff. Many herbs are still flourishing, including purple sage, rosemary and lavender, while culinary herbs such as coriander and parsley will continue on for many months if they are sown in batches throughout the season. The lovely bronze fennel (*Foeniculum vulgare* 'Purpureum') adds height and architectural interest to any container, with its delicately feathered foliage. The sweet bay tree (*Laurus nobilis*), which can be pruned into a number of shapes, including a classic round ball, always looks attractive grown in a decorative pot at the entrance to a doorway and has the advantage of being evergreen.

Winter

In winter, although the choice is more limited, there are still some plants that look lovely during the darkest months of the year that can be planted in containers. The gorgeous spidery flowered witch hazel as well as sweet briar, with its apple-scented leaves, can both be comfortably grown in tubs. Aromatic evergreens, such the low-growing juniper (*Juniperus squamata* 'Blue Carpet') with its aromatic blue foliage and wintergreen (*Gaultheria procumbens*) with its fragrant white flowers, make a welcome sight in the colder months, especially underplanted with flowering bulbs. Early snowdrops push their delicate blooms through in late winter, as does the delicately perfumed miniature iris (*Iris reticulata*) and the grassy-leaved *Iris unguicularis*, with its pretty pale-mauve flowers, which also look stunning grown in shallow pots or under the protection of a wall. Crocuses can also bring a late-winter fragrance to the garden; for example, the cultivar 'E.A. Bowles' is a late-winter- or early-spring-flowering crocus with richly scented yellow flowers.

Fresh Flowers for Arrangements

One of the most enjoyable and simple ways to invite nature indoors is by displaying fresh flowers in your home. Always keep your eye out for vintage glasses, vases and bottles when you are out and about for making unique flower arrangements. Some everyday items, such as glass jars or jugs, are great for repurposing. However, it is important to wash any container in warm water well to remove any debris or soil and to make sure they are scrupulously clean, as cut flowers require crystal-clear water. I like to look for all sorts of containers for arranging flowers in local markets and junk shops, as it is surprising what treasures you can find second-hand. I now have a large collection of different types of containers, including glass vases, ceramic jugs, decorative pottery bowls as well as some large pots for tall arrangements. Large boughs of spring-flowering blossom can look amazing as indoor displays. Avoid using floral foam for arranging flowers as it is non-biodegradable – instead use a flower frog, wire netting or construct a support from hollow stems or woven twigs.

To harvest plants for arrangements, you can either collect them from your garden or buy them individually from a market or a florist. If you gather them from your own garden, this has to be one of the most pleasurable aspects of gardening, in my view. Children also love to pick fresh posies from the garden to place in rooms around the house. You can either pick flowers from amongst those plants already growing in your existing borders or you can design a specific area to use for creating flower arrangements. If you decide to design a specific cutting patch, you will need to work out the size you want to devote to cut flowers and to choose what kind of plants you wish to grow there. Choosing fragrant species always adds another dimension to any garden and to the pleasure of flower arranging.

Ideally for a cutting garden, it is better to pick a prime site in a sunny spot with good soil because much will be demanded of this small area. You will also need a water source nearby, such as an outside tap, a water butt or some form of irrigation system. In this case, straight lines and clean shapes are easier to work with than curved ones as they divide more naturally into smaller sections. Paths should be wide enough to get a wheelbarrow to each area. Plants will grow better and quicker in a sheltered site, but high fences or hedges will also create shade, which will not suit all types of plant.

Once you have made all the structural decisions, you need to decide on the planting design itself. Ask yourself if you want to grow shrubs, perennials or annuals – or a mixture of all three. Most annuals require more work but with minimal capital outlay, and will generally provide flowers only in summer and autumn. It is always possible to extend the picking season by adding spring bulbs. Otherwise, a mix of perennials and shrubs is more suitable in the longer term, as they continue to flower without the need for regular deadheading and require much less maintenance. Of course, growing plants from seed is the most economical way to create a garden if you have the time and inclination to do so.

Directions for cultivating plants from seed and a selection of the best plants to grow for cutting and for use in the stillroom can be found in Part 2 of this book. It is always worth keeping a note of those plants that you particularly like and those plants that like you and grow well in your local soil. If you don't have a separate space to devote to cut flowers, think of integrating them into different parts of your garden, including the vegetable patch. If you have decided to include a full range of colours in your garden, you will need to consider which species look good when they are grown together.

Potager-style gardens, where flowers, herbs and vegetables are grown together to form a community, have become popular in recent years. This is not only a space-saving design option, but also provides an environmentally friendly alternative to using insecticides, by adopting the method of 'companion planting'. Basil, for example, can help protect tomatoes from pests when planted alongside, while chives can help deter aphids from attacking roses.

Crafts & Design

Flower Arranging

When it comes to making flower arrangements, there are no hard and fast rules. There is no need for any elaborate equipment or complicated techniques. All you need is a sense of drama and to follow a few basic principles regarding structure, scale and colour. It is also important to follow the advice for cutting and conditioning plants before placing them in arrangements. Like any art form, it is vital to feel free and be spontaneous when using your chosen materials; arrangements do not need to follow a conventional style. For example, a huge vase of pussy willow or cow parsley is an impressive sight in springtime. I used to pick great swathes of cow parsley in the fields around Stroud when I was living in Gloucestershire to display in massive jugs around the house – and my daughter and granddaughter are now continuing the family tradition.

Equipment

Fresh flowers and greenery, a pinch of sugar or a piece of charcoal, floral scissors or knife, clippers or secateurs, water bucket and gloves if picking flower stems from your garden, suitable vase or container, floral netting (optional, for if you are creating larger arrangements), flower frog (or wiring)

Method

Collect the flowers you wish to use (*see* the tips on colours at the end of this activity). Remember to use sharp scissors when you collect (and condition – *see* step 2) flower stems. Always plunge the stems into water as soon as possible after picking – *see* Chapter 1 for advice on harvesting plants.

1. It is important to first condition each flower stem by freshly cutting them at their base on the diagonal and to remove any leaves below the waterline, as otherwise, the foliage tends to contaminate the water and kill the flowers.
2. Arrange the flower stems in your chosen container. Use appropriate containers or vases to suit different types and sizes or display – floral netting is also useful for larger, more structured arrangements.
3. If, after a few days, any flowers start to die, remove them from your arrangement so they don't cause the other flowers to decay.
4. Change the water every few days and, to keep it fresh, add a tiny pinch of sugar or a piece of charcoal to the water.

Colour Tips

- Greens, blues, whites and yellows make for beautiful and calming combinations when used in arrangements.
- Mixing rich and exotic colours such as oranges, golds, maroons and near-black flowers can be eye-catching and enriching.
- Use contrasts to set off strong colours – for example, the acid-green frothy flowers of lady's mantle can help to counterbalance powerful tones. Lady's mantle is one of my all-time favourite cut flowers as it is also easy to grow and propagate by division, and makes a lovely edging plant spilling over pathways and softening any hard lines.

The Art of Ikebana

The classical Japanese art of *ikebana* – 'arranging flowers' or 'making flowers alive' – is a tradition that dates to the seventh century, when floral offerings were made at altars to honour the Buddha. Later, these exquisite flower arrangements were additionally used to adorn the decorative alcoves of traditional Japanese homes. Being based on Zen principles, this type of flower arranging has a minimalist aesthetic, and choosing each plant piece, including the container, is as essential as the final composition itself. The process is deliberate and reflective (as opposed to a more spontaneous approach), where asymmetry and negative space are just as important as the flowers themselves, as these create a sense of movement and energy. In its most basic form, a triangular shape defines the Japanese style of flower arranging, where three main stems – one long, one medium and one short – are placed to create a dynamic tension within the design.

Ikebana is one of the three classical Japanese arts of refinement, along with incense appreciation and the tea ceremony. This discipline reached its zenith in the sixteenth century under the influence of the Buddhist tea ceremony masters. Acknowledging and appreciating seasonal changes is also fundamental to this form of flower arranging as each piece needs to reflect a specific moment in time, as if it is a portrait paying reverence to a specific season.

Most Japanese flower arrangements include only about five to thirteen items, where crooked stems and uneven shapes can add an extra dynamic. This is part of the Japanese notion of *wabi-sabi*, the Buddhist belief that there's beauty in imperfection. Once you have chosen your pieces – these can be flower stems, blossom branches or foliage – it is time to start putting them together. Remember that Japanese floral arrangements like to emphasise some empty space in the design. Select a suitable container for the size and style of your plants and choose your stems one by one, according to colour, texture and form. If you are gathering them from your own garden, you can select specific flowers as you pick them to suit your chosen design.

Equipment

Fresh flowers, blossom and greenery, a pinch of sugar or a piece of charcoal, a suitable container such as a ceramic pot, decorative jug or glass vase, sharp scissors or knife, flower frog or *kenzan* (for securing stems at the base if required)

Method

1. Choose whatever container you think suits your design – for example, a bud vase, glass jug or ceramic bowl – or whatever you have available.
2. Select one flower stem as the focal point then select others that work well next to it, and that form a relationship. Uneven numbers, such as three, five or seven, are preferred to create a dynamic asymmetrical design, although they still need to complement each other in both colour and form. Refer to step 1 of the previous activity if you are picking the flowers fresh yourself.
3. Condition each flower stem by using sharp scissors or a knife to freshly cut the stems at their base on the diagonal and remove any leaves that will be below the water line.
4. Add the stems to the display one by one, thoughtfully. Take your time, as ikebana is a meditative process – it is all about stillness, simplicity and slowing down.
5. Use a *kenzan* if required – a circular base with upright metal pins to secure stems in place. Alternatively, you could use a flower frog.
6. If, after a few days, any flowers start to die, remove them from your arrangement so they don't cause the other flowers to decay.
7. Change the water every few days and, to keep it fresh, add a tiny pinch of sugar or a piece of charcoal to the water.

Making a Floral Bouquet

A bouquet of fresh flowers makes a beautiful offering for friends or family and provides a traditional gift for all sorts of occasions, such as birthdays, weddings, housewarmings and thank you gifts. It is important when you make any type of bouquet that you prepare the flowers well by placing them in a container of water beforehand to allow them to have a plentiful drink. Select the colours and variety of flowers you wish to use and that are suited to the occasion. Once you have decided on the theme, you can start picking or preparing the arrangement. For example, a Mother's Day bouquet might include scented roses, lavender and lilies for a more traditional floral arrangement. For further inspiration, *see* the 'Language of Flowers' in Chapter 5.

Equipment

Fresh flowers and greenery, scissors, florist wire, decorative ribbon, tissue paper

Method

1. It is important to first condition the flowers by freshly cutting the stems at their base on the diagonal and remove any leaves below the waterline, as otherwise the foliage tends to contaminate the water and kill the flowers.
2. Start to build the bouquet by placing the thickest stems in the middle to create strength and then add a few more sturdy stems.
3. Keep threading the stems in a criss-cross arrangement as this will help the flowers support themselves.
4. Place flowers with slender stems, such as narcissi, towards the centre of the arrangement, threading them through the thicker stems, so they are supported by the rest of the structure.
5. Try to include odd numbers of the same type of flower – for example, three or five of the same species will help to balance one another.
6. Keep reviewing how the flowers look regarding their different heights so the shorter stems are positioned at the front and taller ones are at the back or middle of the posy.
7. To make your arrangement secure, bind the stems together with florist wire and cover this with a decorative ribbon; then carefully wrap the bouquet in tissue paper for full effect.

A Simple Posy

Small, scented posies were once called 'tussie mussies' and were used to combat unpleasant smells at a time when washing was a luxury. Like the pomander, they were used to deter infection as well as for the enjoyment of their fragrance. In medieval times, fragrant herbs were used to prevent the spread of contagious diseases: rue, sage, wormwood, rosemary and lavender in particular were employed in this respect. These herbal posies were frequently hung from the belt as a protection when travelling.

The Victorians formalised the arrangement of these miniature posies, making the herbs, flowers and leaves more deliberately concentric and symmetrical. However, as its symbolism and the use of its secret language faded, the posy became simply an offering for special occasions. This ancient tradition can be reimagined as naturalistic displays of herbs and wildflowers that can be displayed in an unassuming way in a glass, cup or even a jam jar. Children especially enjoy making small posies to place around the home, for example beside beds and in the kitchen. These posies can also be offered as a symbolic gift in the traditional fashion.

Equipment

Flowers, greenery, grasses, seed heads, wildflowers and foraged botanicals, scissors, simple containers (or raffia or ribbon if using as a gift)

Method

1. Gather small, decorative flowers or grasses from the garden or hedgerow, in groups of one, three or five.
2. Take note of their symbolism if you wish to make a traditional statement as a gift.
3. Arrange the flowers in a concentric symmetrical design using greenery at the edges.
4. Arrange the mini floral bouquet in a plain glass jar, simple jug or another suitable container.
5. Alternatively, tie the posy together with raffia or ribbon to offer as a gift.

Creating an Indoor Garden

Indoor plants can immediately lift a space from feeling flat and uninteresting to being alive and vibrant. Many plants also look more attractive when they are massed together, much as they would be in a garden, and often thrive better when they are in the company of others too. There are several reasons why house plants grow better in an indoor garden than in a solitary pot, which include higher humidity levels, protection of the roots from sudden changes in temperature plus a constant water reservoir below. Another obvious advantage of an indoor garden is ease of watering and misting regularly. However, close planting means reduced ventilation, so it is important to look out for signs of over-saturation. A collection of miniature spring bulbs massed in wide bowl then padded out with moss can look stunning as an indoor display, which can later be planted out in the garden. Alternatively, a selection of larger evergreen plants, all with purifying qualities – *see* Chapter 3 – can create a forest of greenery and have a significant impact on the air quality of a room, especially when grouped en masse.

Equipment

Gravel or pebbles, selection of indoor plants of similar size and requirements, potting compost, moss, large watertight container, gardening gloves, watering can, misting spray

Method

1. Select an attractive container that is large enough to hold several indoor plants. There is a limitless range of watertight containers to choose from, including old metal basins, ceramic bowls, ornate *jardinières*, large built-in troughs or wooden handmade boxes lined with a waterproof sealant.
2. Pour a shallow layer of gravel or pebbles into the base of the container for drainage.

3. Choose several plants, for example, air-purifying plants, that require similar conditions for optimum growth. If the plants are all large, then three together will be enough to form an arrangement. If smaller, use five to seven. Make sure the height and shape of the plants are in keeping with the size and shape of the container.
4. Stand the specimen plants onto the layer of gravel or pebbles. Arrange your selection while still in their pots, or plant directly into soil, ensuring larger plants are at the back (or middle) and smaller ones towards the front, so the arrangement looks harmonious.
5. Surround each pot with damp peat, so the top of the pots are no longer visible. Alternatively, the pot plants can simply be massed in a tray or bowl with a pebble or gravel base, then infilled with moss.
6. Finally, water thoroughly to settle all the plants into their new indoor garden.

Planting up a Window Box or Container

Just about everybody has room for a window box or container, which can create a lovely focal point for a room. All kinds of displays are suited to different locations, and using specialised potting compost means you can grow plants that may not suit your garden soil. No matter the size of your space, there is always room for a window box, pot or container. Smaller herbs, such as thyme, dwarf lavender, chives, pinks, parsley and prostrate rosemary make an excellent choice grown in containers for sunny spots, for example, on the kitchen windowsill. The trailing ivy-leaf geranium also looks lovely in hanging baskets or window boxes. Ferns, ivy and some grasses will tolerate shady conditions, such as those on the north side of a house. It is good to select species that have a long season of interest, and if they are flowering perennials, they can later be planted into the garden, as can most spring bulbs. All types will

need watering regularly. For larger container planting ideas, *see* the 'Pots and Container Planting for All Seasons' section earlier in this chapter.

Equipment

Selection of plants that suit your site and combine well, both in texture and colour, potting compost (one that is soil-based will be more free-draining than one that is based on wood pulp or coir), window box or container, some crocks, small trowel, gardening gloves, watering can

Method

1. Identify the conditions in your site, that is, whether it is sunny and dry or shady and damp.
2. Select flowers or herbs that suit your growing conditions. You may wish to stick with a single-colour theme or instead focus on foliage. For example, several different types of miniature grasses or culinary herbs growing together can look striking.
3. Place crocks over the drainage holes to prevent any soil blockages occurring, then use a small trowel to fill the base of your container with compost. Remove the plants from their pots, being careful with their roots.
4. Place the plants into the window box and, when you are happy with the arrangement, begin planting them in; fill in any gaps between the plants with compost, firming it down and making sure the level almost comes up to the top of the container.
5. Once potted up, water your composition thoroughly as this will help settle the compost around the plants.

Tip: Generally, it is good to water plants every three days in summer and feed them with a little liquid fertiliser once a week, or twice during the growing season. Remember that smaller containers tend to dry out quicker than larger ones, especially if they are made of terracotta. And to keep your plants flowering, remember to deadhead and remove any seed heads using secateurs. Herbs such as chives can benefit from being trimmed back several times a year.

Flower Pressing

Picking wildflowers and pressing them in books within sheets of blotting paper is one of my earliest childhood memories. I grew up on the banks of the river Wye in Herefordshire, where wildflowers proliferated. Learning all their names and pressing them into diaries was therefore my earliest hobby. This is one of the most artistic and enduring ways to enjoy and display botanical items around the home – in picture frames, within acrylic sheets (for example those used for displaying photos) or as collages.

Equipment

Selection of colourful fresh flowers and petals that are suitable for drying – *see* Chapter 1. To press fresh materials, individual flowers, petals or leaves, it is important to choose thin, fully opened flowers and avoid thick, succulent material that tends to hold a lot of moisture, heavy books (or flower press), blotting paper, textured paper, picture frame or acrylic sheets

Method

1. Arrange a stack of heavy books – then take some absorbent blotting paper and cut it to a suitable size to fit your stack. Alternatively, you can buy a specially made flower-pressing stack with screws at each corner to keep the flowers in place once you have compressed them.
2. During the early stages of drying, check and change the paper if the moisture from the flowers has made it too damp. This will ensure the petals and leaves are preserved for the best quality possible. Depending on which plant you are pressing, it can take from two days to three weeks for your specimen to dry completely.

3. Once no longer damp and completely dry, store the pressed flowers in an airtight container somewhere dark until ready for use.
4. Take your time to lay out your design on textured paper, which can either be minimalistic, for example by using grasses, or rich and sumptuous, using colourful florals.
5. Display your finished design. One of the nicest ways of arranging pressed flowers is to use a simple wooden or metal picture frame with two pieces of glass, between which the flower design is pressed. Another effective way to display dried pressed flowers is within photo- or poster-size acrylic sheets that slot together.

Making Flower-Petal Paper

This is a really simple process that is lovely to do with children. The resulting paper can look stunning and is ideal for making cards or gift tags. You can also use it as the basis for artworks to hang on the wall of your home, for example using pressed flowers, as described in the previous activity. There are also plenty of other imaginative ways to use fresh flowers creatively, such as hammering fresh flowers onto cotton fabric to create an imprint or pressing their delicate forms into clay to make botanically inspired ceramics.

Equipment

Selection of dried flower petals, ripped-up pieces of paper (experiment with different types), water, blender, large container (needs to be large enough to fit the mesh tray), mesh tray (available at craft supply stores), rolling pin, tea towel

Method

1. Rip your paper into small pieces and saturate them with water.
2. Blend the shredded paper in a blender until it is pulpy.
3. Pour the paper mush into a container that is big enough to fit the mesh tray.
4. Add your flower petals and mix them in with the pulp.
5. Use the mesh tray to scoop up some pulp from the water. Try to make sure the pulp covers the mesh frame evenly.
6. Use a rolling pin to press out the excess water.
7. Let it dry overnight.
8. In one smooth movement, dump the pulp out from the frame onto a tea towel. You now have homemade paper with flower petals embedded.

PART II

A-Z of the Best Botanicals Species to Grow at Home

Directory of Herbs & Flowers

Here is a selection of some of the most useful herbs and flowers that are easy to grow at home, whatever the size of your garden, including some of the best ways to use them.

Floral Craft **Culinary**
Home Care **Herbal Tea**

Angelica (*Angelica archangelica*)

Angelica (*see* left) is one of the most striking, stately plants to grow in the garden. The whole plant is powerfully aromatic: the ferny leaves have a pungent, fresh green scent while the large rhizome or root has a musky-earthy aroma. In early summer, umbels of sweet-scented greenish-white flowers rise from tall branches, which later bear many spicy-scented seed heads. The whole plant can reach a height of about 2.5m (8ft) so it needs to be positioned at the back of a bed. Best planted in dappled shade, it likes a rich soil with plenty of moisture. Although angelica is a hardy biennial (a perennial if it is prevented from flowering), it dies down completely over the winter. It can easily be grown from seed sown in early autumn, although it is also a natural self-seeder and will propagate itself year after year. Plants can also be propagated by root division, which should be carried out at the end of the growing season.

Note: The Deanery of St Paul's was fumigated twice a week with angelica root during the Great Plague of London in 1665.

Home Uses

The flowers make the perfect centrepiece for large naturalistic displays and the dried seed heads look lovely when used in dried arrangements.

The essential oil from the seed has a rich, herbaceous, earthy scent that is fortifying and stimulating when used in room vaporisers. The dried chopped root or root latex also makes an excellent potpourri fixative.

A tea made from the fresh leaves or seeds has soothing, digestive and restorative properties.

Caution: The fresh tea is best avoided during pregnancy and by people with diabetes.

Basil Sweet (*Ocimum basilicum*)

Sweet basil is one of the most valued aromatic herbs with over 160 different varieties found worldwide. Native to India, where it is frequently

Basil Sweet (Ocimum basilicum)

grown outside temples, basil prefers a warm, sheltered side in a well-drained soil and can be frost tender. Sweet basil is generally a tender annual herb with shiny green leaves bearing pinky-white flowers throughout the summer. For a plentiful crop, it is best to sow the seeds thinly in late spring as soon as the soil has warmed up. It makes a good companion plant in the vegetable garden too, especially alongside tomatoes. It is also happy grown in containers and will thrive grown in pots on a sunny windowsill; so long as it is protected from cold, it can be treated as a short-lived perennial. Keep your pot plant moist but not waterlogged and always remember that basil dislikes being transplanted! Ensure you protect your pot basil from scorching sun and pinch out tops to encourage bushy growth. Basil has numerous culinary and therapeutic uses, having a lovely, warm, slightly spicy scent that is uplifting, purifying and reviving.

Note: Basil is considered sacred in many cultures. In India, for example, *tulsi* or 'holy basil' is placed outside the front door as a protection for the home.

Home Uses

A fresh pot of basil growing in your kitchen will help to keep flies away.

An essential oil produced from the leaves is one of the best aromatic nerve tonics for anxiety, depression or insomnia when used in a room vaporiser. *See also* the A–Z of essential oils in Appendix 1.

Fresh or dried basil leaves and flowers are commonly used in culinary dishes, especially Mediterranean dishes. The leaves are best picked fresh and added at the last minute since they can become bitter if cooked for a long time. Leaves should always be picked from the top to prevent the plant flowering and should be torn rather than chopped.

An aromatic tea made from fresh basil leaves aids digestion and helps combat nausea while the herb's scent can help clear the head, relieve intellectual fatigue and give the mind greater clarity.

Caution: The fresh tea is best avoided during pregnancy.

Bay Sweet (*Laurus nobilis*)

Bay is a handsome evergreen shrub with glossy, dark-green aromatic leaves and small black berries. In spring, it bears a profusion of small yellow tufted flowers, smelling sweetly of honey. As a native of the Mediterranean region, the sweet or true bay thrives in well-drained soil in a sunny position, although it will tolerate some shade. A bay tree can be slightly tender and young bushes may be cut to the ground by a hard frost, although they will usually shoot up again. In cold areas, it is therefore best grown in a tub and brought under glass for the winter. However, in a warm site, sheltered from cold winds, a mature shrub can reach more than 6m (20ft) high.

Bay Sweet (Laurus nobilis)

A bay tree is also at home, grown wholly in a warm environment such as a conservatory or greenhouse. New shrubs can be propagated by semi-ripe cuttings in summer or by autumn-sown seeds.

Note: Bay leaves were once used for strewing floors, especially in churches, due to their disinfectant properties. Both the leaves and essential oil repel weevils.

Home Uses

Sprays of fresh bay last well in water (crush the bottom of the stem first) and look good in large, naturalistic arrangements. The leaves retain their shape, colour and scent well upon drying. Harvest them in summer for use in dried arrangements and potpourri recipes. A wreath made of fresh bay leaves hung on the front door at New Year is a traditional symbol of protection and courage.

The essential oil makes an effective room purifier used in room vaporisers. *See also* the A–Z of essential oils in Appendix 1.

Together with parsley and thyme, dried or fresh bay leaves are essential for any bouquet garni.

An infusion of the fresh leaves can be drunk as a tea to stimulate the digestion.

Caution: The fresh tea is best avoided during pregnancy. Use in moderation as narcotic in large doses.

Borage (*Borago officinalis*)

Borage is a hardy annual with a greenish-grey stem and leaves that are covered in a prickly fuzz, which acts as a deterrent for insects. It is easy to grow from seed in spring and will also self-seed freely. The star-

Borage (Borago officinalis)

shaped flowers hanging in downward-facing clusters are a beautiful vibrant blue, and it is these that have given the plant its folk name, 'star flower'. The flowers are brilliant for pollinators. Grown in a potager, it is considered a good companion plant for tomatoes, squash and strawberries. Native to the Mediterranean region, it was a favoured herb of the ancient world with a range of medicinal uses. The seeds are also pressed to make borage seed oil, valuable in skincare and haircare since it contains an exceptionally high content of gamma-linolenic acid (GLA), which helps combat ageing skin and dryness.

Note: Its leaves and lovely blue starry flowers were traditionally steeped in wine to make a tonic and they are still used today to flavour Pimm's No.1.

Home Uses

The flowers can be dried for use in potpourri and dried arrangements.

Both leaves and flowers are edible and have a mild cucumber fragrance and make a pleasant addition to any cool drinks in summer, or frozen onto ice cubes or as a decorative addition to salads. The flowers can also be candied.

The leaves have traditionally been used to make tonic herbal tea.

Chamomile Roman (*Chamaemelum nobile*)

Roman chamomile is a low-growing evergreen perennial with feathery leaves and sweet-scented, daisy-like white flowers. The whole plant has an apple-like scent and is in flower all summer. Chamomile is best planted in the sun and prefers a well-drained soil. It has a beneficial effect on other plants growing nearby and is thus known as the 'physician's plant'. Plants can be propagated easily by seeds planted in spring (both Roman and German species), by cuttings or by division of established plants.

Note: Chamomile is an ancient medicinal plant – it was called Maythen by the Saxons and revered as one of their nine sacred herbs.

Home Uses

Cut flowers last longer if chamomile tea is added to their water while a flower water can be made from fresh chamomile flower heads. Use in soothing bath sachets, either fresh or dry.

Both Roman and German chamomile are used to make essential oils – both with outstanding sedative effects used in room vaporisers. See *also* the A–Z of essential oils in Appendix 1.

Renowned for being a mild herb, it can be used for children's complaints such as insomnia, agitation and so on in the form of a weak tea. Chamomile flowers steeped in boiling water and served with a spoonful of honey make a bedtime nightcap.

Chives (*Allium schoenoprasum*)

Some of the most invaluable plants in the herb or kitchen garden are alliums, which include some decorative varieties. Chives demonstrate many of the same properties as garlic and onions and are mentioned in early Chinese herbals. Chives have a milder flavour and a less intense aroma than either garlic or onions, making them more versatile

Chamomile Roman (Chamaemelum nobile)

Chives (Allium schoenoprasum)

as garden plants. A clump of chives makes a colourful addition to any herb garden or border, with their striking mauve or rose-pink clustered heads. Planted under roses, chives – like garlic – act as an aphid repellent, prevent black spot and can even help intensify the perfume of the roses. Planted next to apple trees, they also help prevent scab. Chives will flourish grown in window boxes or in pots. When planted outdoors, a heavy frost will make them die back in winter, so it is best to bring a pot into the house for a fresh all-year-round supply. They thrive in hot sun and like a rich, moist soil – they also enjoy the addition of left-over coffee grounds to their soil. Easy to grow from seed, chives can also be propagated by bulb division; indeed, it is best to lift established clumps every few years and divide them. Chives can be cut to within 5cm (2in) of the ground up to four times a year for culinary use. This mild but potent herb has been cultivated and used in cooking for thousands of years, dating back to ancient civilisations. It has been employed in China for over 4,000 years for its potential health benefits, including aiding digestion, promoting cardiovascular health and as a good source of vitamins A, C and K.

Note: In Medieval Europe, chives were hung in bunches around gardens and homes to ward off both insects and evil spirits.

Home Uses

The more decorative allium species are valuable for fresh flower arrangements.

A pot of fresh chives makes a useful and decorative windowsill plant, which can also help repel flies and insects from the kitchen. Flower heads can be dried in bunches and used in potpourri.

The beautiful fresh purple flowers can be used as an edible garnish or added to salads. Chives do not dry well but can easily be preserved by freezing for use as a garnish. Like garlic, chives can help to boost energy and aid digestion when added to culinary dishes or flavoured oils or vinegars.

Coriander (*Coriandrum sativum*)

Coriander is a strongly aromatic herb with bright-green leaves and white lace-like flowers followed by a mass of round, green seeds that slowly turn brown as they ripen. It has been cultivated for thousands of years both as a medicinal and culinary herb. Its delicate structure requires a sheltered position and protection from strong winds when grown outdoors, and it prefers full sun and rich, light, well-drained soil. It does not like damp conditions. Plant the seeds in autumn or late spring (or early spring under glass) and water regularly until established. Coriander self-seeds readily, but seedlings do not transplant well, so it is best to sow *in situ* and thin out later. The seeds can be harvested once they turn brown, by shaking them from the flower heads. As an annual, it is easy to grow at home in the garden, balcony or on a windowsill and can also be grown in pots either outside or indoors. Coriander should not

Coriander (Coriandrum sativum)

be planted alongside fennel, as the latter's seed production will suffer. It has a sweet, woody-spicy and pungent flavour, much appreciated in Eastern and Middle Eastern cuisine. The dried seeds were once called 'dizzycorn' because, when freshly crushed, their scent can promote dizziness.

Note: Coriander seeds have been used as medicine and spice and for their aphrodisiac effect since the earliest times. It was among the herbs found in the tomb of Tutankhamun.

Home Uses

Use the fresh or dried seeds in sachets and potpourri.

The seeds are used to produce an essential oil that is valuable in perfume blends in minute amounts.

The leaves are valuable for seasoning and garnishing food, while the seeds can be dried and stored whole for use in flavouring vinegar or oil.

A lovely tea made from fresh leaves can help relieve indigestion and flatulence, and even help prevent infant colic if drunk while breastfeeding.

Note: Use in moderation only – it is a narcotic in large doses.

Dill (*Anethum graveolens*)

Dill is a hardy annual with attractive foliage and flower heads. The flowers have a brilliant acid-green colour that is lovely in naturalistic arrangements. Its feathery leaves are similar to fennel and are delicious added to salads and soups, as well as with fish. It is used a great deal in Scandinavian cuisine, for example in Finnish dishes, especially with salmon – this herb was a staple in my mother's herb garden! Although the leaves are invaluable for cooking, I like to use its flowers too just for decorating salads and as a garnish. Avoid planting dill in very wet soil and water only when needed, for example in extreme times of drought. Plants will self-sow freely and, once established, may eventually require some support.

Dill (Anethum graveolens)

Note: Used as a medicine and a condiment for over 2,000 years, the name dill originates from the Norse word *dilla*, which means 'to soothe'. Dill seeds were once called 'meetinghouse' seeds because they were chewed during long church services. In the Middle Ages, it was believed to protect from witchcraft.

Home Uses

Use the flowers and leaves in naturalistic arrangements.

An essential oil distilled from the seeds of the herb has a light, fresh, spicy scent that is refreshing when used in room diffusers for its purifying effects.

The seeds are aromatic and can be used in wine vinegars or for pickling cucumbers and gherkins, while the leaves can be used as a garnish for salads and fish dishes.

Chew the seeds to freshen the breath and as a pick-me-up. A weak tea made by steeping the seeds in water can soothe stomach upsets, wind or colic.

Elecampane (*Inula helenium*)

This ancient medicinal herb is a tall, bold perennial that grows to about 1.5m (5ft) high, flowering over midsummer. It has oval, velvety green leaves and large yellow daisy-like flowers, similar to a sunflower. It is spectacular planted in a group at the back of a herbaceous border or in a corner of the herb garden, but looks awkward grown as a single specimen. Native to Asia, elecampane is now naturalised across much of Europe and America, having spread through its cultivation as a medicinal herb. In the East particularly it is highly valued as an incense, medicine and as a spice. It prefers a moist soil and sunny position, although it will tolerate most conditions, and may need staking if unprotected from strong winds. Cut the stems down after flowering and remove the leaves in autumn before they start to look ragged – the whole plant dies down completely over winter. Elecampane is best propagated by taking offsets from the large fleshy rhizomes in early autumn.

Note: Known as 'elfwort' or 'elfdock' in the Celtic tradition, it is believed that elves inhabit this plant. Spreading the dried roots around the home was thought to attract good fairies and the roots were hung in children's nurseries as a protection.

Home Uses

The fresh flowers look striking in naturalistic arrangements but the whole plant dries well and the flowers look lovely in dried displays.

Elecampane (Inula helenium)

The roots, which should be lifted in autumn, can be dried and used as incense to encourage intuition.

An essential oil is produced from a closely related species, sweet inula (*I. odora*) is valuable for treating respiratory complaints when used in room diffusers.

The sliced root steeped in boiling water makes a tea beneficial for respiratory complaints, for example, to soothe dry, irritating coughs.

Note: Avoid drinking the tea during pregnancy.

Eucalyptus Blue Gum (*Eucalyptus globulus*)

This beautiful tall evergreen tree can grow up to 90m (300ft) high, having bluish-green oval leaves and yellowish, creamy white flowers. There are over 700 different types of eucalyptus, many of which are grown as ornamentals. Eucalyptus is a great all-rounder in the garden – you can enjoy it as a tree or a shrub, let it grow tall or prune it to fit a container. The most popular UK variety is *Eucalyptus gunnii*, an extremely hardy evergreen. The ideal location for a potted eucalyptus is in a sunny position, positioned where it is easy to water regularly. At least 500 species produce a type of essential oil, which are much used in the production of all types of pharmaceutical and fragrance products, such as soaps, detergents and toiletries. The essential oil from blue gum eucalyptus has a powerful camphoraceous odour with a woody-sweet undertone.

Tip: Eucalyptus essential oil, along with lemon oil, is one of the must-haves for household care and hygiene – *see* 'Bathroom Hygiene – Four Ways with Eucalyptus' in Chapter 3.

Home Uses

The hazy-bluish leaves of several species of eucalyptus are popular as greenery in flower arranging – 'silver dollar' is a wedding favourite, whereas I like the 'willow' eucalyptus with its narrow leaves. The fresh leaves make a lovely naturalistic display and have a beautiful, refreshing aroma. Eucalyptus lasts around three weeks if kept in clean, pure water as a floral arrangement.

Fresh eucalyptus is recommended for keeping your home smelling fresh and hygienic while the essential oil is anti-bactericidal and perfectly employed in all kinds of household cleaning jobs.

Eucalyptus oil is extremely valuable when used in room vaporisers, especially to combat airborne germs. *See also* the A–Z of essential oils in Appendix 1.

Fennel Sweet (*Foeniculum vulgare*)

Sweet fennel is a decorative plant for the back of a border or the herb garden. Its tall growth and bright-green, feathery leaves lend an air of softness to any garden. Reaching up to 2m (6.6ft) high, with umbels of tiny golden-yellow flowers that ripen into aromatic seeds, the whole plant has a sweet, anise-like scent. Native to the Mediterranean region, sweet fennel is naturally a biennial or

Eucalyptus Blue Gum (Eucalyptus globulus)

Fennel Sweet (Foeniculum vulgare)

perennial herb, although it is generally cultivated as an annual. It prefers a well-drained, sunny position but will grow almost anywhere and will seed itself freely. Alternatively, sow the seeds directly in the ground in spring, after all frosts have passed, or earlier under glass. Fennel can also be propagated by root division in autumn. If stems are cut right down in the summer, there will be a second flush of leaves later in the year. There is also a coppery-bronze variety of fennel, *Foeniculum vulgare* 'Purpureum', which is particularly striking. Fennel is one of the oldest medicinal herbs in the world – used as early as 3,000 BCE in Mesopotamia and known as a snake bite remedy in ancient Egypt.

Note: During the Middle Ages, fennel was said to have magical protective powers, so stems of it were hung over doorways to drive away evil spirits. The dried seeds were also placed in keyholes to bar the entrance of ghosts. Fennel is one of the plants in the Anglo-Saxon *Nine Herbs Charm*.

Home Uses

The fresh leaves, especially the bronze variety, look lovely in naturalistic arrangements, while the dried seeds are also a good addition to sachets and aromatic powders. It is best to harvest and dry the whole herb in bunches once the seeds have turned brown – use the dried seeds for potpourri. Fresh fennel when grown in pots indoors helps repel fleas and other insects.

Dried bunches can help to dispel the smell of dampness in a basement area or other areas of the home. An essential oil made from the seed makes a refreshing and purifying room fragrance. *See also* the A–Z of essential oils in Appendix 1.

Both the leaves and seeds have a strong aniseed flavour, much used in culinary recipes worldwide. Bronze fennel gives vinegar a rich claret colour.

Seeds can be chewed to sweeten the breath and as a traditional digestive after eating rich food, or made into a tonic to impart strength. A fresh fennel tea made from the seeds can be used as a nerve tonic.

Caution: Fennel tea should be avoided by people with epilepsy and during pregnancy.

Gardenia (*Gardenia jasminoides*)

A small decorative evergreen bush that is mainly grown for ornamental purposes and bears beautiful fragrant white flowers. Native to the Far East, India and China, the flowers are used to flavour tea, much like jasmine. An aromatic absolute and concrete are produced from the fresh flowers, which have a sweet, rich, jasmine-like scent, mainly employed in high-class perfumery, especially in East Asian fragrances. Gardenia can be grown either as a house plant or planted

Gardenia (Gardenia jasminoides)

outdoors in warmer climates, needing a minimum temperature of 16°C (60°F) and acidic soil. Gardenias are excellent candidates for container culture – although they require a lot of light and moist conditions to thrive. This one is of my favourite fragrant house plants!

Note: The scent of gardenia is said to have natural sedative properties that can help you fall asleep faster. It will also make your entire bedroom smell wonderful!

Home Uses

The freshly cut flowers of gardenia make a perfect posy, with their pretty symmetrical pure-white blooms and attractive, evergreen, dark leaves. It also makes a beautiful house plant with its exquisite and pervasive scent, and relatively easy maintenance requirements. Gardenias also look stunning grown in pots outdoors – for example on a terrace where the scent can be enjoyed. The containers can then be brought indoors during the winter in cold climates.

Gardenia absolute can be employed in making exquisite blends for use in room vaporisers and natural perfumes.

Geranium Rose (*Pelargonium 'Graveolens'*)

Geranium species are some of the most beautiful house plants that are equally happy in a cool conservatory or on a warm windowsill. They do not, however, like hot, moist conditions and beware of overwatering, especially in winter, when the plants should be kept dryish. Generally, it is the leaves that are scented rather than the flowers, as is the case with rose geranium, which has pinkish flowers and soft, serrated leaves that have a sweet, lemony-green, rosy scent. The genus is native to the Mediterranean and the Middle East. They were

Geranium Rose (Pelargonium 'Graveolens')

first grown in Britain by the wealthy in glasshouses and it was only in the nineteenth century that they gained wider popularity. Tender geraniums are best planted in pots in the garden so they can be brought under glass to overwinter. They thrive in containers generally and are ideal to grow in hanging baskets and window boxes, as they like lots of sunshine and a well-drained soil. To propagate, take softwood cuttings from mid-spring right through to late summer. Rose geranium is used for producing an essential oil that has anti-fungal, antiseptic and astringent properties – much used in skincare and for the treatment of stress-related issues and menopausal problems. Pelargonium and geranium species have also been used since antiquity for their medicinal applications, mainly for their styptic, tonic and antiseptic properties.

Note: According to Culpeper, this is one of the plants that symbolises love, and the flowers were traditionally added to herbal love charms, posies and sachets.

Home Uses

The fresh-scented leaves are valuable for making deliciously fragrant bath sachets, and a lovely flower water can be made at home from the fresh-scented leaves for use as a light perfume.

Sprigs of fresh flowers can be used in aromatic posies and the dried leaves impart a long-lasting, sweet, lemony scent to potpourri and other home items.

Lemon-scented geraniums are perhaps some of the most pleasing insect-repellent pot plants to have in the kitchen.

The essential oil from the flowers and leaves has a harmonising, balancing and uplifting effect used in room vaporisers. *See also* the A–Z of essential oils in Appendix 1.

Hops (*Humulus lupulus*)

This perennial hardy climber with deciduous, heart-shaped leaves and aromatic greeny-yellow flowers is grown commercially in vast quantities for beer production. Male and female flowers or cones are produced on separate plants, and it is the female cones or strobiles that are used for brewing. The heady scent of hop flowers on a hot summer's day is unmistakable! It is not a showy garden plant, yet it has many endearing characteristics, not least the fact that it is a quick grower and can cover a trellis or wall in a single season, eventually reaching over 8m (26ft) high. Plants need to be adequately supported and require moist but well-drained soil in sun or partial shade. After harvesting the flowers in autumn, the twining stems should be cut right back to stimulate new growth. The common hop is an important medicinal plant and has a long history of use. It will also thrive as a pot herb and can easily be propagated by taking cuttings of young shoot tips from female plants in early spring. The golden-leaved variety *Humulus lupulus 'Aureus'* is particularly attractive. The flowers are still widely used in herbal medicine for their sedative properties.

Hops (Humulus lupulus)

Note: Hung over beams or arches, hops were once thought to bring good luck to the household. A pillow stuffed with hops was a popular traditional remedy for insomnia across both Asia and Europe.

Home Uses

Simply hung from old beams or hooks, the fresh or dried twining stems make attractive kitchen or household decorations. Fresh sprays may be used in naturalistic arrangements and the cones can also be added to potpourri or used in dried arrangements. The dried flowers or cones are excellent in sleep pillows or soothing bath bags.

Displayed indoors, the flowers help to dispel unpleasant odours such as cigarette smoke or cooking smells.

The hop cones – either fresh or dried – have a profoundly soothing effect, having a rich, warm, spicy-sweet, slightly narcotic aroma.

A herbal tea can be made at home using the fresh flowers – add honey to taste to produce an excellent nightcap.

Caution: Hop tisanes are not recommended for those suffering from clinical depression. It is also a narcotic in large doses – use in moderation.

Hyacinth (*Hyacinthus orientalis*)

Hyacinths originated in the south-east Mediterranean region and are related to the native bluebell of Britain. It is a powerfully perfumed plant, producing spires of fragrant waxy flowers in springtime that last for two to three weeks. The different cultivars range in colour from white, yellow, pink and blue through to violet and purple. Their lovely heady-sweet scent is one of the harbingers of spring for me. Plant the bulbs outdoors in autumn, using new bulbs each year for the most impressive display. They require well-drained soil, like to be planted in a sunny or semi-shaded position, and are generally frost-hardy. Pot-grown plants make a welcome fragrant addition to the Christmas season by forcing them into flower early. For a festive display, in autumn plant three or four specially prepared bulbs in a pot filled with fibre or potting mixture, making sure that the bulbs are almost touching each other and that the tops of the bulbs are just showing. To allow the root system to develop, keep the bulbs cool and damp for some weeks: a garage or shed is ideal for this. Once the first shoots appear and the flower spires are a couple of inches high, they can be brought indoors.

Hyacinth (Hyacinthus orientalis)

Note: In the 'language of flowers', yellow hyacinths are linked to 'jealousy', purple flowers mean 'forgiveness', blue hyacinths mean 'sincere care', pink hyacinths mean 'playful joy' while white flowers represent 'love' or 'prayer'.

Home Uses

The fresh flowers make decorative, sweet-scented posies, traditionally used for their symbolic meaning in the 'language of flowers'.

Dried multi-coloured hyacinth flowers are lovely in potpourri and the fresh flowers can be used to make a home perfume using the enfleurage method.

Note: A decorative way to grow hyacinths indoors is to place a bulb in a vase of rainwater, allowing the hyacinth to root. The base of the bulb should rest just above the water to avoid rotting. Keep the vase in a dark cupboard until the first small green flower shoots have formed, then bring it into the light. Beware when handling hyacinths as the bulbs are toxic.

Hyssop (*Hyssopus officinalis*)

Hyssop is an attractive, highly scented evergreen herb with a slightly camphoraceous, spicy-herby aroma, and comes originally from the Mediterranean and Asia. With its decorative vivid blue flowers and small lance-shaped leaves, hyssop forms a neat compact bush that is equally at home in a herb garden, border or pot. Since in its natural habitat it is found on dry, rocky hillsides or on old walls, it will thrive in containers placed on a sheltered patio or on a sunny windowsill – in fact, it needs hot sunshine to really flourish. Reaching a maximum of 1m (3ft) high, it flowers continuously throughout the summer and early autumn, especially if it is dead-headed. To maintain a compact shape, trim plants back after flowering or in spring if grown in cold areas. Hyssop is grown easily from seed sown under cover in spring or later directly into the soil, once it is warm. Alternatively, it can be propagated by softwood cuttings in early summer. The whole plant is much beloved of butterflies and bees for its strong, aromatic fragrance.

Note: Hyssop has been revered as a sacred plant of purification since ancient times: Dioscorides called it a 'holy herb' as it was used in cleansing ceremonies in the form of an incense. During the fifteenth century, it was employed as a strewing herb due to its disinfectant properties and it was used in the consecration of Westminster Abbey.

Hyssop (Hyssopus officinalis)

Home Uses

Hyssop makes a lovely pot plant for a sunny kitchen windowsill, with vivid blue flowers and a long flowering season. Use bundles of the dried twigs as a purifying, space-clearing incense. It is best to harvest the flowers when in bud, so they can be used in decorative arrangements and potpourri.

The fresh leaves and flowers made into bath bags are good as a pick-me-up for nervous exhaustion. The essential oil from the leaves and flowering tops of the blue hyssop has a purifying, restorative, refreshing quality when used in room vaporisers and is especially beneficial for clearing respiratory infections.

The pretty blue flowers can be used sparingly in salads.

A tea made from the leaves and flowers of hyssop is one of the best remedies for nasal congestion and other respiratory complaints, as it is an excellent antiviral agent. A tisane can also help those suffering from nervous debility and during convalescence.

Caution: Best avoided in pregnancy and by people with epilepsy and those with high blood pressure.

Immortelle (*Helichrysum Italicum*)

Closely related to the sunflower, this Mediterranean plant has yellow ball-like flowers that give off a strong curry-like scent. It is one of the best plants for drying, hence its common name 'everlasting'. The flowers retain their bright-yellow colour long after drying and for this reason it is frequently used in dried flower arrangements. Plant the seeds indoors in early spring or directly into the ground after all frost has passed. This herbaceous perennial will grow as tall as 0.6m (2ft) high to 1m (3ft) wide and needs to be cut back after flowering to stop it from becoming leggy. Immortelle thrives in full sun and prefers a well-drained soil. It does not put up with waterlogged conditions, so it flourishes in gravel and rock gardens, as well as in containers so long as the soil contains plenty of grit. It has long been considered a valuable medicinal plant since earlier times for its healing and restorative skincare properties.

Note: The name *Helichrysum* is derived from the Greek words *helios*, meaning 'sun', and *chrysos*, meaning 'gold', referring to its clusters of small bright-yellow flowers. According to myth, the flowers were offered to the sun god Apollo in ancient Greece, who wore them as a crown to symbolise his immortality.

Home Uses

Use as a decorative plant for containers or pots, blooming throughout the summer. Display the dried bright-yellow flowers in aromatic posies and potpourri. Collect and dry the flowering stems just as they are coming into bloom for use in dried flower arrangements.

Used in vaporisers, the essential oil has a warming and opening effect, which supports deep abdominal breathing, together with an elevating effect on the mind. The oil is also said to stimulate the intuitive side of the brain, thus its use in meditation, yoga and creative rituals.

Iris Florentine (*Iris Florentina*)

This much-loved flower is one of the oldest cultivated plants – it is depicted on Egyptian temple walls dating from 1,500 BCE. This genus can be subdivided into those species that have a

Immortelle (Helichrysum Italicum)

Iris Florentine (Iris Florentina)

rhizome and those that grow from a bulb. The Florentine iris is a beardless iris that has dark-green sword-shaped leaves, a creeping fleshy rootstock and grows to about 1m (3ft) high. It has delicate, highly scented white flowers tinged with blue and a yellow fall, which are borne in summer. This species is also known as orris because its large rhizomes are used for making orris powder, a valuable fixative and perfumery material with a distinctive violet-like scent. Like most iris species, the Florentine iris is a native of southern Europe and prefers to grow in a rich but well-drained, sunny position and benefits from having some lime in the soil. It should not be planted too deeply, for it likes the surface of its rhizomes to bake in the sun. It is best propagated by removing offsets in late summer or by seed sown in autumn. The roots should be lifted in early autumn if they are to be used for drying. An absolute is produced from the dried rhizomes of Iris Florentina, having a sweet, honey-floral aroma. However, it is extremely expensive and often adulterated.

Note: The name iris derives from the Greek word meaning 'rainbow' and refers to the multicoloured nature of the flowers. In Greek mythology, Iris was the name of the goddess who was said to deliver messages to the gods across a rainbow bridge. Today there are numerous cultivars available flowering throughout the year

Home Uses

The beautiful fresh iris flowers are a mainstay of flower arranging with a mass of colours to choose from – it is one of my favourite flowers to include in bouquets! The rhizomes can be dried and then ground to make orris powder, although the roots only develop their violet-like aroma once they have been dried for three years.

Powdered orris has traditionally been used to scent sachets, linen, clothes and so on, and as a fixative for potpourri.

Caution: The fresh leaves and roots of all irises are harmful if eaten.

Jasmine (*Jasminum officinale*)

Jasmine is undoubtedly one of the most sweetly intoxicating perfumed plants, with a wide range of species, some tender and others hardy. The common jasmine is native to the Himalayas and has an intensely sweet, honey-floral scent. It is a deciduous or semi-evergreen vine with delicate bright-green leaves, bearing hundreds of tiny star-shaped, fragrant white flowers from summer through to autumn. The scent of the flowers increases at dusk – in India, jasmine is known as 'queen of the night' and it is often planted in courtyards, on verandas or beneath windows where it can be enjoyed in the evening. Despite its fragile appearance, a jasmine vine can climb to more than 10m (32ft) high, and care must be taken if it is grown against a house as it may lift the roof tiles. It looks lovely when allowed to scramble over a porch or pergola or arch. Outdoor varieties like full sun and a fertile, well-drained soil, while

Jasmine (Jasminum officinale)

tender species require a minimum temperature of 10°C (50°F). Most species need to be pruned back vigorously after flowering. Propagate plants taking semi-ripe cuttings in late spring or by seeds sown in early spring.

Note: In Indian mythology, Kama, the God of love, tipped his arrows with jasmine blossoms to pierce the heart. The perfumed oil is renowned as an aphrodisiac.

Home Uses

Jasmine makes a lovely addition to fresh naturalistic flower arrangements. In the East, especially in India, fresh flowers are worn in the hair, and made into wreaths and posies at religious festivals.

Grow this exquisite climber by doorways and around windows so its scent can be enjoyed in the evening.

An exotic flower perfume can be made at home using the enfleurage method which has a warm, uplifting, aphrodisiac, almost narcotic quality.

Jasmine absolute used in room vaporisers or worn as a perfume helps promote feelings of optimism and well-being. *See also* the A–Z of essential oils in Appendix 1.

Flowers from *J. sambac*, the tender Arabian jasmine, can be used to flavour tea.

Juniper (*Juniperus communis*)

The common juniper is a small evergreen tree that can be found growing wild from the Mediterranean to as far north as the Arctic Circle. It is a tenacious plant that can thrive on bare rocky mountain slopes, moorland and in cold conditions where few other shrubs survive. It has small flowers and little round berries, which are green in the first year and turn blue-black in the second and third. Only the female tree bears berries. The flowers of the female tree are green and the male, yellow: both male and female plants are necessary for berries to be produced. Juniper prefers to grow in an exposed, sunny site, but it will tolerate stony, dry or shady conditions in both acid and alkaline soils. It is also hardy and can survive strong winds, ice and snow, so it is an extremely useful garden shrub for awkward places where little else will grow. Growing up to 6m (20ft) high, with bluish-green, narrow, stiff needles, the whole plant exudes a lovely, fresh, resinous aroma. Although it is possible to propagate a juniper tree from seed, it may take two to three years to germinate. Since they are such slow growers, it is more practical to take semi-hardwood cuttings in late summer or to buy a small plant at the garden centre. There are now a great many cultivars of *Juniperus communis* available to suit every garden. Juniper has a long history of herbal use, notably as a purification incense.

Juniper (Juniperus communis)

Note: Both the Tibetan people and Indigenous Americans burn sprigs of dried juniper in ritual cleansing ceremonies, while in Europe the burnt twigs were used to combat infectious epidemics and to keep evil spirits at bay.

Home Uses

The dried berries can be added to potpourri and the dried needles are excellent for burning as a purifying incense, as they have a wonderful scent.

An essential oil can also be produced from the needles of the common juniper, although the most highly prized oil is from the berries, which is purifying, stimulating and restorative when used as a room freshener or vaporiser. *See also* the A–Z of essential oils in Appendix 1.

Harvest the berries when they turn blue and store in airtight jars for use in all sorts of stillroom preparations. The berries are traditionally used sparingly in pickles and when cooking game or poultry – and famously for flavouring gin. It is also easy to make a juniper-flavoured vinegar or oil using the berries.

Caution: Avoid using juniper during pregnancy and if there is kidney weakness.

Lavender (*Lavandula officinalis*)

Lavender is a classical and vital ingredient of a herb garden for all aromatic enthusiasts. Its hazy blue flowers and silver foliage together with its soft, floral scent seem to capture the scent of summer. It is one of the few herbs that has never gone out of fashion, having a multitude of uses. The whole plant is highly aromatic with a sweet, floral-herby, balsamic-green, slightly camphoraceous scent that is soothing and relaxing. All lavender species – and there are many cultivars of lavender – like full sun and well-drained soil but will tolerate partial shade. The more compact species make good hedging plants for the front of a border or for lining a path. In colder climates, tender species are best grown in terracotta pots that can be moved to the shelter of a greenhouse or conservatory for the winter months. It is important to cut bushes back after flowering to maintain their shape and prevent them from getting woody (but avoid cutting into the old wood); then trim them again in the spring. Seed can be sown in the spring, but this method does not tend to result in plants that are true to species. Instead, take softwood cuttings in spring or semi-ripe cuttings later in summer or early autumn, and keep the young plants protected over winter before planting out the following year. Lavender will also thrive in pots grown on a sunny windowsill or in a window box. The flowering tops are used to produce an essential oil that is the most popular oil used in aromatherapy today, being extremely versatile for a range of conditions, especially skincare. Harvest the flowers just as they open then dry them either by hanging the flowering tops in bundles upside down in a well-ventilated area or by laying them out on trays in a dark place.

Lavender (Lavandula officinalis)

Note: The origin of the name lavender comes from the Latin *lavare*, meaning 'to wash'. Sheets are still traditionally hung out to dry over lavender bushes in the Mediterranean.

Home Uses

Fresh lavender flowers can be put directly into bath sachets under a warm running tap for a deliciously soothing bath. A favourite with children!

The dried flowers make lovely sleep pillows and wardrobe sachets. The dried twigs make a good burning incense and bundles of the dried herb can be used to scent household drawers and cupboards to keep moths away. Lavender water can also be used for scenting linen and as eau de toilette.

Traditionally, lavender flower water has been used in the production of eau de cologne, which can be made at home from the fresh flowers.

The most popular application of all types of lavender oil when vaporised is for use in stress-related disorders such as insomnia, migraines and headaches. *See also* the A–Z of essential oils in Appendix 1.

Small amounts of the flowers can be added to vinegars or oils.

Lavender tea is drunk in France for its tonic effect and its antidepressant, antispasmodic, nervine and sedative properties.

Lemon (*Citrus Limonum*)

Lemons are one of the most important fruit crops grown internationally. The origins of the lemon can be traced to South-East Asia but the wild citron or cedrat is said to be the original citrus

Lemon (Citrus Limonum)

species. Lemon trees are widely cultivated in the Mediterranean and other warm regions as they are not frost tolerant and will only thrive at temperatures above 7°C (45°F). The 'Meyer' lemon is easier to grow than other types and can also survive modest freezes. Lemon trees require a sheltered spot in full sun with moist soil containing plenty of enriched organic matter, and good drainage is essential. Dwarf lemons are happy grown in containers in colder climates when the plants should be moved into a greenhouse or sunroom over winter. Lemons, like other citrus species, are heavy feeders that are best fed with a high-nitrogen organic fertiliser to avoid any yellowing of the leaves. Prune plants in spring or early summer as it is good to keep them compact so it is easy to bring plants indoors for the winter. The individual fruits are ready to pick when fully ripe with a bright-yellow colour. If possible, it is best to place pot plants outside during the summer months to expose them to heat and pollinators. Soft soap sprays can help protect against scale insects and mealybugs. Like with other citrus, it is possible to grow lemon trees from seed, although this requires a lot of patience (I know this from experience), as it takes ten to fifteen years to be mature enough to produce fruit. Lemons have a multitude of medicinal, household and culinary uses.

Note: According to Greek mythology, putting some dried lemon leaves in your pillow encourages sweet dreams. In Hindu culture, it is traditional to offer the host a lemon before entering someone's house as a symbol of good luck and prosperity. The lemon is also believed to ward off evil spirits and bring positivity to the home.

Home Uses

Lemon is a beautiful plant to keep on the terrace in the summer so long as you have a warm place to overwinter it – the blossom has a lovely floral scent. Both leaves and the fruit can easily be dried for use in potpourri and other decorative creations, such as a lemon pomander – a lemon stuck with cloves.

The leaves can be used fresh and tied in a bundle under a hot tap for an uplifting, refreshing bath.

Traditionally, the dried peel is also used to perfume clothes and repel moths and other insects. Fresh lemons are also a fantastic, fresh, cheap and green way to keep your home clean – a section is dedicated to their many applications in Chapter 3.

The essential oil is a powerful antiseptic with purifying qualities when used in room vaporisers to kill airborne germs. *See also* the A–Z of essential oils in Appendix 1.

Lemons have numerous culinary uses – especially as a garnish for fish dishes. Fresh or dried lemon peel can be used to flavour oil or vinegar.

Combine fresh lemon juice with ginger and a teaspoon of honey to make a tea that is good for warding off colds, sore throats or chills combined.

Caution: The essential oil is phototoxic, that is, it should not be applied to areas of skin exposed to direct sunlight.

Lemon Verbena (*Aloysia citrodora*)

Lemon verbena is one of the most beautiful semi-hardy deciduous shrubs for a sheltered spot in the garden, with a gorgeous lemony, fruity-floral, sweet scent. It has slender green aromatic leaves and small white flowers – but is tender so needs protection from cold winds over winter and from frost. It has similar medicinal properties to lemon balm, being good for conditions such as depression or anxiety and uplifting in its effect overall. It is one of my favourite herbs, as apart from its beautiful, sweet, lemony-floral scent, it has a profoundly soothing effect on the whole nervous system. A native of South America, in tropical conditions, it

Lemon Verbena (Aloysia citrodora)

will reach a height of 5m (16½ft) or more but in cooler climates it will not usually grow higher than 2m (7ft). It will not tolerate temperatures below –10°C (14°F). In Britain, it is best to grow lemon verbena as a container plant, so it can simply be moved under glass at the end of the summer. It thrives in a rich but free-draining soil, in a sunny position and likes to be kept moist during the growing season. Trim the branches to about half their length in autumn to encourage bushy growth the following season. Plants are best propagated by softwood cuttings taken in late spring or by semi-hardwood cuttings taken in late summer, as the seeds do not set well in cool climates.

Note: This citrus-scented plant was traditionally used in magic rituals as a protection and in love spells. It was said that having a sachet under your pillow would also ensure a good night's sleep.

Home Uses

This is a lovely plant to keep as a pot plant in the kitchen or on a windowsill, because of its delightful scent. It is also the perfect plant to position near an entrance or by a seat in the garden, where its fragrance can be appreciated.

The leaves can be used fresh tied in a bundle under a hot tap for a soothing bath. One of my favourites!

The dried leaves retain their fragrance for many years and so are ideal for use in for all kinds of scented sachets around the home.

The fresh leaves can be used to flavour oil or vinegar.

A refreshing and soothing tea can be made from the leaves – either fresh or dried. Sharing similar medicinal properties to lemon balm, the tea is also good for digestive upsets and stress-related conditions of nervous origin.

Lily Madonna (*Lilium candidum*)

The Madonna lily is one of the earliest exotic garden plants brought to Britain by the Romans. It has a honey-like, rich, exotic, floral scent that is intoxicating and euphoric. The oldest of the cultivated lilies, it originally came from Ancient Egypt and Greece and is now an endangered species in the wild. The bulb produces a rosette of dark-green base leaves in autumn, then in spring a flowering stem shoots up to 1.5m (5ft) high with as many as twenty trumpet-shaped flowers that bloom around midsummer. Despite its stately appearance, it is relatively easy to grow, although it can be temperamental, and prefers to have some shade at its base. It will naturalise in a semi-shaded position and is equally at home in a border or herb garden, infusing the surrounding air with a heavy honeyed fragrance akin to honeysuckle. Plant the bulbs in early autumn with no more than 5cm (2in) of light alkaline soil covering them.

Lily Madonna (Lilium candidum)

Plants can be propagated by seed sown in spring or autumn, or by division of mature bulbs, using the offsets or outer scales, in late summer. The Madonna lily resents disturbance once it has become established. It has an ancient history of medicinal usage in both the East and West. The fresh flowers of *Lilium candidum* are used to produce a costly absolute used in exclusive perfumery work.

Note: As its name suggests, the flower is startlingly white with golden stamens, and is symbolically associated with the Virgin Mary and with the qualities of purity and innocence.

Home Uses

Lilies make ideal container specimens for a patio or conservatory – the pots can then be moved around so their scent can be enjoyed to the maximum, especially after dark. They are one of the most long-lasting and attractive flowers for indoor arrangements, with a pervasive perfume; the scent of some species can be overpowering.

Fresh lily flowers can be used to make an exotic home perfume using the enfleurage method.

Caution: Beware of the pollen, which can stain surfaces or clothes.

Marigold (*Calendula officinalis*)

Marigold is a familiar herb of ancient medical repute, now often cultivated as a decorative plant, having a green-herby, sharp, pungent scent. The whole plant is strongly aromatic, especially the leaves, while its bright golden-orange, daisy-like flowers are in bloom almost continually and will bring a splash of colour to a herb garden or border whatever the time of the year. In fact, the marigold is named *calendula* from the Latin calendae, the first day of the month, since it is said that the plants can be found in flower at the beginning of every month. The common marigold is a hardy annual, growing up to 2ft high with soft bright-green leaves and a mass of flowers. Found growing wild right across the Mediterranean region, it will tolerate most situations, but prefers a well-drained, loamy soil and a sunny position. A single plant will flower over a long period if it is dead-headed regularly but will eventually die down in winter. Marigolds self-seed readily but can easily be propagated if required by seed sown in autumn for early spring flowers or in spring for a later show. It makes an excellent companion plant, as it helps to keep away insect pests, especially whitefly, from surrounding flowers, herbs and vegetables. Marigold has been used traditionally for its potent skincare properties in medical herbalism. Calendula was used extensively during the First World War to treat wounds and to prevent sepsis, where the flowers were made into a poultice. In aromatherapy, the infused oil or cream is more commonly used for the treatment of a wide range of skin complaints.

Marigold (Calendula officinalis)

Note: In the East, marigolds are used to decorate altars and the surroundings of temples on sacred sites. The vibrant colours of marigolds represent the brightness of life, good fortune, wisdom and the path to enlightenment.

Home Uses

Marigold flowers make a colourful addition to fresh posies and arrangements and are the perfect addition to floral garlands for their bright, decorative effect.

With their exotic colouring, the dried flower heads make a lovely addition to potpourri.

Use the fresh flowers in bath bags as a natural skin healer.

The dried or fresh flowers can be used to make an infused oil as a stillroom healing agent.

Add fresh petals to fish dishes and salads; the flowers can also be cooked with rice to add a golden colour – they are often used as a saffron substitute.

A tea made from the flowers stimulates the lymphatic system and helps cleanse the body of impurities, and can help heal mouth ulcers.

Caution: Avoid the tea during pregnancy.

Marjoram Sweet (*Origanum marjorana*)

Marjoram is a plant with numerous species and can cause much confusion for the gardener in identifying the different sub-species. Sweet marjoram is a bushy herb with soft fresh green

Marjoram Sweet (Origanum marjorana)

leaves and the whole plant is highly aromatic. This low-growing plant, which is native to the Mediterranean, makes a good groundcover or edging plant. In early summer, small knot-like flowers appear along the stem, ranging in colour from lilac to white. It grows well in containers too and is one of the best culinary window box herbs along with parsley, basil and chives. Since sweet marjoram is slow growing, it is better to start with young plants instead of seed. Plant out in spring after the last frost in a sunny spot with fertile, well-drained soil. Check soil moisture every few days and water when the top of the soil becomes too dry. Since sweet marjoram is tender, it is best propagated by softwood cuttings annually. With a warm, sweet-spicy flavour, both marjoram and oregano species are used extensively in Mediterranean cooking. It can be harvested on an ongoing basis about four weeks after planting.

Note: The botanical name derives from the Greek, meaning 'joy of the mountain'. In Greek myth, it was associated with Aphrodite as a symbol of love and honour, so it was customary to crown young married couples with the herb. In England, it was used as a strewing herb right up to the end of the seventeenth century. It was one of Elizabeth I's favourite scents and used in all kinds of sweet bags and herbal waters. Bunches of the herb were also hung up in the dairy to keep milk fresh, especially during warm weather!

Home Uses

It is ideal grown in containers or pots near to the kitchen or in window boxes. Use the fresh flowers in herbal posies.

Add the fresh leaves and flowers to bath bags to reduce fatigue.

The leaves and flowers of sweet marjoram dry well and can be used in dried arrangements, household sachets and potpourri. The oil has a soothing effect as a room fragrance. *See also* the A-Z of essential oils in Appendix 1.

Use the fresh herb or make a sweetly flavoured vinegar or oil.

A tea made from the leaves of sweet marjoram helps to combat colds and respiratory infections.

Melissa/Lemon Balm (*Melissa officinalis*)

Melissa/Lemon Balm (Melissa officinalis)

Melissa or lemon balm is a delightful, citrus-scented herb with soft, bushy, bright-green serrated leaves and tiny white flowers, native to the Mediterranean region. This perennial plant will thrive in virtually any soil or situation and will happily grow in pots where it forms a compact shape if it is trimmed regularly. Not only does it seed itself readily, it can also spread rapidly by root runners to form new clumps, so can be invasive if it is not kept in check. Unlike mint, however, it is easy to pull up and control, so it is not necessary to keep it confined. Despite its rampant nature, lemon balm remains a first choice for the herb garden as it is both decorative and useful. Growing up to 1m (3ft) high, the bright foliage of lemon balm looks best when planted next to herbs of a contrasting colour and texture, such as purple sage. Lemon balm is easy to propagate by root division or by cuttings taken from mature shoots. Cut to ground level after flowering and a new crop of leaves will be produced before the whole plant finally dies back in winter. The sweetly scented flowers are attractive to bees, which explains one of its folk names – 'bee balm'. In aromatherapy, the oil is used mainly for stress-related conditions, including insomnia, migraines and shock. Lemon balm has a long history of medicinal use, most famously as a cure for melancholy and to promote longevity. It has been called the 'elixir of life' and several people who have lived to more than 100 years old swear their good health is due to drinking lemon balm tea daily. Melissa is also one of the main ingredients of traditional eau de colognes, including Carmelite water.

Note: The name derives from the Greek nymph Melissa, protectress of the bees, as they find the scent of the tiny white flowers irresistible! Rubbing the fresh leaves on wasp stings is said to bring pain relief.

Home Uses

The leaves should always be harvested just before flowering, then they can used for drying to make potpourri and so on. The fresh leaves stuffed in muslin bags release a sweet and refreshing citrus aroma, especially when used in the bath. A light eau de toilette or perfume can be made at home by infusing the fresh leaves.

The dried leaves retain their scent for a long time and can be used to deter moths from clothes when used in sachets. The scented juice from the stems when rubbed on oak furniture will give it shine.

An essential oil is made from the leaves and flowering tops in minute quantities, having an intense, fresh, lemony scent with an uplifting, refreshing and restorative effect when used in blends in vaporisers.

Add the fresh leaves to summery drinks for a fresh lemony flavour.

The fresh leaves make an excellent soothing herbal tea – good for headaches, insomnia and easing cramps caused by indigestion or period pains.

Mimosa (*Acacia dealbata*)

This attractive, small tree, growing up to 12m (39ft) high, has a greyish-brown bark and masses of clusters of delicate ball-shaped bright-yellow fragrant flowers in early summer. Native to Australia, it was brought to Europe as an ornamental plant in the early nineteenth century but now it grows wild in warm regions. It is slightly frost tender so needs a sheltered site to thrive. An aromatic concrete and absolute are extracted from the blossom, mainly for use in high-class perfumery – principally produced in southern France. This natural fragrance material has a slightly green, sweet-floral scent and exhibits good fixative properties. This is one of my daughter's favourite garden plants. It also makes a beautiful and popular house plant due to its relatively easy maintenance, just requiring full sun and moist soil.

Mimosa (Acacia dealbata)

Note: *Mimosa pudica*, more commonly known as the 'sensitive' or 'touch-me-not' plant, makes a fascinating house plant, as it closes its leaves instantly when touched.

Home Uses

The freshly cut flowers of mimosa (*dealbata*) make a perfect naturalistic display, since the leaves are also attractive. The yellow blossom is also attractive in mixed flower arrangements.

Mimosa absolute can be employed in making exquisite blends for use in room vaporisers and natural perfumes.

Myrtle (*Myrtus communis*)

The common myrtle is a beautiful shrub or small tree up to 3m (10ft) tall, with many tough but slender branches, a brownish-red bark and small evergreen, pointed leaves. It has simple five-petalled ivory flowers with dense golden stamens, followed by small blue-black berries; both leaves and flowers are fragrant. Myrtle is a Mediterranean plant and is almost frost hardy: it can survive outdoors in a warm, sheltered position but prefers a minimum average temperature of not less than 5°C (40°F). In colder climates, it is best grown as a conservatory plant or brought under glass for the winter, where it makes a lovely specimen shrub, especially as a topiary plant. Trimming back growth in late spring will maintain a pleasing shape. Myrtle is easily propagated by softwood cuttings in spring or hardwood cuttings in mid- or late summer, set in free-draining compost. The essential oil is valued primarily as an antiseptic and skincare agent – myrtle leaf oil is mainly used in skincare and for respiratory conditions.

Note: According to myth, the goddess Aphrodite hid her nakedness behind a sweet myrtle bush and the plant has always been associated with the qualities of beauty, innocence and love. Its name is derived from the Greek *myrtos*, the 'herb of love'.

Myrtle (Myrtus communis)

Home Uses

Use the sprays of the fresh white blooms in naturalistic flower arrangements. The fresh flowers are popular in bridal bouquets, as a symbol of love and chastity. Dried leaves and flowers can be included in sleep pillows and potpourri.

The fresh leaves hung up in bunches act as an insect repellent. Use the essential oil in room vaporisers for its fresh, green-floral, slightly camphoraceous scent, which has an uplifting and reviving effect. *See also* the A–Z of essential oils in Appendix 1.

The fresh leaves and flowers can be used to make a refreshing facial tonic – it is an ingredient in the classical 'Angel Flower Water.'

The berries can be dried and used as a spice, much like juniper. Preserve the fresh leaves in oil or vinegar for cooking.

A tea made from the leaves is said to preserve youthfulness, which is the reason why some French women still drink myrtle tea!

Orange Tree (*Citrus aurantium*)

The bitter orange tree or Seville orange is one of the most versatile aromatic species. Eventually it can grow into a handsome evergreen tree up to 10m (33ft) high, with dark-green, glossy, oval leaves and long but not sharp spines. It has a smooth greyish trunk and branches, and fragrant large white flowers. The bitter fruits have an aromatic rind which is smaller and darker than the sweet orange. Native to China and north-east India, the Seville orange is now cultivated all over the world, especially in the Mediterranean. In colder northern European climes, most citrus species, including the Seville orange, need protection against frost and must be overwintered under glass. They require a minimum temperature of 7°C (45°F), plus a rich but well-drained soil, plenty of sun and they like to be well watered during the growing season (but sparingly in winter). Plants can be propagated by seed – although cultivars do not come true from seed – or by semi-ripe cuttings taken in summer. The bitter orange tree produces three different types of essential oil, each with a distinct perfume from various parts of the plant: orange oil from the fruit, neroli oil from the flowers and petitgrain oil from the leaves. In aromatherapy, the most valuable oil is from the flowers, as it has a profoundly soothing effect on the entire nervous system and is used to treat anxiety, depression, nervous tension and other emotional problems, plus it has a wide range of skincare benefits. Petitgrain also has excellent skincare qualities as it tones the complexion and is also a classic ingredient of eau de cologne.

Orange Tree (Citrus aurantium)

Note: Neroli oil is named after the princess of Nerola in Italy, who loved to wear it as a perfume, while the distilled water, known as orange-flower water, has long been a popular cosmetic and household article.

Home Uses

The fresh flowers are traditionally used in bridal bouquets and wreaths and are good for small posies and arrangements. Dried oranges, either sliced or whole, have many decorative uses, especially on festive occasions. Dried peel from all citrus species, including oranges, can be used in potpourri. Orange-flower water can be made at home from the flowers.

Place an orange tree where the lovely orange blossom scent can be enjoyed.

Make a natural neroli perfume from the fresh flower petals using the enfleurage method.

Orange essential oil, neroli and petitgrain can all be used in room vaporisers for their individual properties and fragrances: the scent of the fruit is fresh, warm and comforting; the flowers have a lovely floral, honey-like fragrance that is soothing yet uplifting; the leaves, by contrast, have a fresh green citrus slightly herby aroma that is stimulating and reviving. *See also* the A–Z of essential oils in Appendix 1.

A tea made from an infusion of dried citrus flowers can be used as a mild tonic for the nervous system.

Oregano (*Origanum vulgare*)

Oregano or wild marjoram is a bushy perennial herb that grows to around 45cm (18in) high, with upright purplish stems and oval leaves that are sometimes flushed with red and dark purple-pink flowers. The whole plant is highly aromatic, with a warm, woody, spicy camphoraceous, herby scent that is stimulating and refreshing. This common herb can be found growing wild from Europe right across to central Asia, and thrives in the warm Mediterranean region. Most oregano species are hardy and will tolerate a range of situations, so long as the soil is not waterlogged. Softwood cuttings taken in spring are the best way to propagate plants or by root division after the plant has flowered. Trim the plants back after flowering to maintain their shape. There are numerous cultivars of *Origanum vulgar,* including the lovely golden-leaved marjoram *Origanum vulgar* 'Aurum', which adds lustre to any herb garden with its bright, fresh foliage. It forms a compact low-growing mound and has a mass of mauve flowers. Spanish oregano (*Thymus capitates*) is a perennial creeping herb with a woody stem, small dark-green leaves and pink or white flowers borne in clusters. Although this herb is strictly thyme, it serves as the source for most so-called 'oregano' essential oil production. Oregano has powerful antiseptic properties and was much favoured by early herbalists such as Culpeper and Turner due to its powerful antiviral and tonic properties.

Oregano (Origanum vulgare)

Note: Oregano was used in spells to bring happiness, protection, joy and to deepen love – it was also used in marriage wreaths to bless the couple with happiness. Sleeping with oregano under the pillow was said to bring psychic dreams. It was also placed on graves for the deceased to find happiness in the next life.

Home Uses

Use the fresh flowers in small posies. The leaves and flowers also dry well so the more decorative species are lovely used in dried flower arrangements and in wreaths, potpourri and so on.

Added to bath sachets, the fresh flowering tips are reviving and uplifting. The essential oil produced from the herb helps combat respiratory infections when used in room vaporisers.

Infused in vinegar, oregano was once used as a substitute for smelling salts.

The fresh leaves, when chewed, can relieve toothache.

Both marjoram and oregano are used extensively in Mediterranean cooking – either fresh or dried; they are one of the main ingredients of bouquet garni.

Oregano tea supports digestion and the immune system.

Caution: Not to be used during pregnancy.

Parsley (*Petroselinum crispum*)

Parsley is one of the most widely used of all culinary herbs, especially as a garnish. A biennial or short-lived perennial herb, with crinkly, bright-green foliage and small greenish-yellow flowers producing small brown seeds. Usually grown as an annual, as its bright-green leaves are tougher in the second year. Its seeds need moisture and warmth to germinate and the plant likes fertile soil, preferably in full sun or dappled shade. A tip to help encourage the seeds to germinate is to pour a kettle full of boiling water into the earth before planting. I have found this really helps germination – I have also found that it does not like being transplanted. There are different varieties: some are flat leaved and some curly. Parsley seeds are used to make an essential oil that has a detoxifying effect on the whole body.

Note: The ancient Romans placed fresh parsley on their plate to protect food from contamination or poison – a sprig was also tucked inside their togas to protect against inebriation! The scent of parsley counters the smell of garlic. Parsley does not like to be transplanted and it was considered bad luck to uproot it.

Home Uses

Dry the herb in bunches before flowers for the leaves or leave to set if you wish to collect the seeds.

The essential oil from the seed has a warm, woody-spicy scent that is purifying and cleansing when used in room vaporisers.

In the kitchen, the fresh or dried herb is versatile for flavouring all types of savoury dishes. Use as a fresh garnish for most dishes. An infused culinary oil or vinegar can be made from the seeds.

Weak parsley tea is diuretic and a good detox aid.

Peony (*Paeonia officinalis*)

The common peony is a perennial plant growing up to 70cm (28in) tall, bearing beautiful bowl-shaped deep-pink or deep-red flowers in late spring. In the East, it is revered, much like the rose in the West, as it symbolises beauty, love, honour and prosperity. Historically, peonies were

Parsley (Petroselinum crispum)

Peony (Paeonia officinalis)

planted and enjoyed by Chinese emperors and later were also grown as a popular medicinal herb in Europe until the sixteenth century. Today, peonies are mainly grown as garden and cut flowers and there are many different cultivars available, either having single or multi-petalled blooms. The common peony prefers a rich, well-drained soil in partial shade. It can be propagated by seed sown in autumn, by division in autumn or by root cuttings in winter – although the seeds may take three years to germinate. It is said that peonies don't like to be transplanted, but I have never had an issue with this so long as there is a large enough root ball. Some species are fragrant, such as the lovely single pale-yellow peony 'starlight', while the superb 'Molly the Witch' variety, together with the stately tree peonies, are among my all-time favourite garden plants.

Note: In Western folklore, peony root was believed to ward off evil spirits and protect against misfortune, so it was often grown in gardens as protectors against the unseen.

Home Uses

Peonies are extremely popular as cut flowers and considered to bring good luck and represent love at first sight as well as the sanctity of marriage, so are often used in bridal bouquets and wedding decorations. The petals of the darker-flowered varieties dry well and can be used in potpourris and other floral crafts, such as paper making.

Peonies also look stunning grown in pots outdoors. It is best to place the containers in a sheltered spot in a semi-shaded position.

Peppermint (*Mentha × piperita*)

Mint has been cultivated since early times and is still one of the most popular aromatic herbs today, with both culinary and medicinal uses. There are many types of mint but peppermint is the most commonly used for its refreshing, invigorating effects. Peppermint is a perennial plant up to 1m (3ft) high, with dark-green leaves and purple-tinted stems, which dies down over the winter period. Most mints will quickly take over an area of the garden via their spreading underground runners if they are not confined. If you plant it in the garden, it is therefore best to sink a container into the soil. With a fresh, green and slightly camphoraceous scent, peppermint will thrive in a pot on the terrace or in a window box. It is easy to propagate and grow from root cuttings and prefers a moist soil in sun or partial shade. It is best to harvest the whole plant just as it begins to flower. In aromatherapy, peppermint oil is produced from the leaves and used for its cooling and stimulating effects as an inhalation for colds, bronchitis and asthma. In perfumery, it is employed and principally in colognes and toiletries. Middle Eastern dishes use a lot of fresh mint – drinking fresh mint tea is also popular.

Note: Peppermint was cultivated by the ancient Egyptians and remains of it have

Peppermint (Mentha × piperita)

been found in the tombs dating to 300 BCE. It is also an ingredient in their famous perfume Kyphi. The Greeks and Romans used it for making garlands and it was also worn by brides. Mint was traditionally used like smelling salts for its fresh, stimulating effect.

Home Uses

Use fresh sprigs in tiny bouquets. The leaves retain their colour and scent well when they are dried so can be used for making herbal sachets.

A bunch of the fresh leaves can also be hung directly beneath the hot tap of a bath for a reviving tonic effect

A fresh pot plant of peppermint in the kitchen is good as an insect repellent. Peppermint oil makes an excellent refreshing room fragrance. *See also* the A-Z of Essential Oils in Appendix 1.

Leaves may be added to flavour vinegar and oils.

Use to make a herbal tea to promote digestion as well as ease nausea, nervous fatigue, colds and flu, or just for a pleasing, uplifting drink.

Roses *(Rosa centifolia* and *Rosa damascena)*

The rose is renowned as the 'queen of flowers' and has been prized by all cultures alike for thousands of years. It is associated with beauty and love, due to its perfect form and alluring scent. Roses are some of the earliest cultivated plants although it is difficult to locate the exact origin of the first wild rose species. There are now numerous cultivars of the rose with different characteristics, some dwarf species and some climbers. In terms

Roses (*Rosa centifolia and Rosa damascena)*

of cultivation, however, nearly all roses prefer an open, sunny position with shelter from strong winds and a loamy, rich soil. Most roses can be propagated by hardwood cuttings taken in autumn. They also need to be pruned in spring and deadheaded regularly to encourage a long flowering period. The fragrant hybrid roses developed by David Austin are recommended for their superb scent and long flowering period. Several highly scented species of rose are used to produce essential oils and absolutes, as well as the classical rosewater, mainly the *Rosa centifolia* and *Rosa damascena* species. Rose has always been a mainstay of perfumery work – there is an old saying, 'no perfume without rose', and it is highly prized in aromatherapy too. The *centifolia* rose, with its numerous tightly packed petals – thus the name 'cabbage rose' – has a rich, sweet-floral and slightly spicy fragrance that is uplifting and heart-warming. It is renowned as an aphrodisiac and more generally employed for stress-related complaints as it has a pronounced euphoric and soothing effect on the heart, making it good for grief and depression. The essential oil, known as rose otto, has a slightly sweeter and lighter fragrance while the absolute produced from *Rosa damascena* has a deeper, more sophisticated scent and is considered superior for perfumery work. Rosewater has been employed for thousands of years used extensively in skincare. The leaves, but especially the hips, of the common dog rose (*Rosa canina*) are a common European folk remedy.

Note: To mystics, the rose was a symbol of divine love. The Romans scattered masses of rose petals during their banquets, weddings and funerals and wore garlands of them at feasts – they even put rose petals in their baths and in their wine. The petals were also used for strewing floors in Elizabethan times in Britain.

Home Uses

All types of roses are indispensable for fresh flower arrangements and posies. Most roses dry well, and rosebuds and dried petals are one of the main ingredients of potpourri. Make your own rose oil from fresh petals using the enfleurage method, an exquisite perfume that has a heart-warming effect.

It is easy to make your own rosewater at home by floating the scented petals in water and leaving them for a few days. A quicker method for making your own rosewater is also shown in Chapter 2.

Rose petals can be ground into a fragrant powder for scenting the home or used in the bath. Rosewater has traditionally been used to perfume a range of household items, such as linen, paper and cloth, since early times.

The absolute of rose maroc (*Rosa centifolia*) from Morocco is the most popular aromatherapy rose product and adds warmth to virtually any perfumery blend (*see also* the A–Z of essential oils in Appendix 1)

Petals of the apothecary's rose (*Rosa gallica* var. *officinalis*) can be added to salads or used in jam-making. The hips can be made into a syrup at home that is rich in vitamin C or used to make rosehip-seed-infused oil..

Rosemary (*Rosmarinus officinalis*)

Rosemary has been called the 'prince' of aromatic herbs and it is one of the most beautiful fragrant plants for the kitchen and garden – it is one of my favourite herbs. Rosemary has been much loved by gardeners throughout the ages. Historically, its pungent scent has been associated with the qualities of faithfulness and fidelity; as Shakespeare noted: 'There's rosemary, that's for remembrance'. It has also been used traditionally as an aid to memory or mental alertness. Rosemary also has an ancient history of medicinal usage. It was burnt in early religious ceremonies to purify the air and its powerful anti-infectious qualities were employed during the plagues of Europe to ward off illness. Of all the different rosemary varieties available,

Rosemary (Rosmarinus officinalis)

Rosmarinus officinalis is still considered to be the most valuable species, medicinally and for culinary use. The spires of its dark-green needle-like leaves have a pungent, fresh, pine-like and slightly camphoraceous scent that is stimulating, restorative and purifying. The evergreen leaves are complemented by pale-blue to dark-blue flowers; the whole plant is strongly aromatic, with a scent like a warm, resinous incense. Since rosemary is evergreen, it can be used throughout the year and has a multitude of uses. There are many cultivars available to the gardener today, such as Tuscan Blue or Severn Seas (which has brilliant bright-blue flowers), and most species like to be protected from the frost and chilling winds. The native habitat of wild rosemary is Asia Minor and southern Europe and, like lavender, it thrives in the Mediterranean region. Given the right warmth and protection, it can grow up to 1.8m (6ft) high, but in more northerly climes it rarely grows taller than 1.2m (4ft). Since rosemary can be slightly frost tender, it is best grown in a sunny position, beneath the shelter of a wall if possible, in well-drained soil. In a protected situation it can be grown as a hedge or topiary specimen but needs to be trimmed regularly to promote bushy growth and to retain its shape. In fact, all rosemary plants benefit from being clipped back, but avoid doing this in autumn or they may be killed by frost. Growing rosemary from seed takes some skill: it is much easier and more reliable to propagate from either softwood cuttings taken in spring, or semi-hardwood cuttings in summer. Rosemary is also happy grown in pots or tubs, although it will not tolerate waterlogged conditions, so it is vital to ensure good drainage. An essential is produced by steam distillation from the flowering tops, invaluable in aromatherapy for a wide range of conditions. Rosemary is famous as the main ingredient in the traditional 'Hungary Water', or 'Spirits of Rosemary', one of the first alcohol-based European perfumes renowned as a youth-promoting elixir.

Note: Rosemary was traditionally burnt as a fumigant in hospitals and during epidemics to disinfect the air. A sprig of rosemary was often carried to ward off evil spirits and in Elizabethan times it was also used in place of smelling salts. According to folklore, if a rosemary bush thrives outside the door of the home, it means the woman 'wears the trousers'.

Home Uses

As rosemary is an evergreen, it can be harvested throughout the year for decorative use in bouquets or fresh flower arrangements. It is an indispensable ingredient of potpourri, retaining its scent and colour well on drying.

The dried twigs can be burnt on barbecues or open fires for a lovely incense-like aroma and a bunch of the fresh needles in a bath sachet gives a wonderful uplifting scent.

Use the essential oil as a room purifier and air freshener as, being bactericidal and antiviral, it is highly efficient at combatting colds, bronchitis, flu and other infections. The vaporised oil is also invaluable in its capacity to raise the spirits and to combat listlessness, mental fatigue and nervous exhaustion. *See also* the A–Z of essential oils in Appendix 1.

Rosemary is used a great deal in Mediterranean dishes and is also excellent for flavouring oils and vinegars.

The tonic qualities of a tea made from the fresh flowering tips may be used as a pick-me-up, especially good for hangovers, and as a general tonic, especially for the nerves and circulation. Use the tisane as a gargle for mouth and throat infections.

Caution: Avoid using the tea during pregnancy and it should not be used by people with epilepsy.

Sage Common (*Salvia officinalis* and *Salvia sclarea*)

Sage is a valuable herb to grow at home as it is one of the most ancient medicinal plants – the name *salvia* derives from the Latin meaning 'to save', indicating its well-established reputation as a healing herb. The common sage has soft evergreen leaves and light-bluish flowers, with a fresh, reviving, warm and purifying scent. There are over 750 species of sage, but many are purely ornamental, and most require full sun to thrive. Native to the Mediterranean region, sage has soft silvery oval-shaped leaves and a mass of deep-blue or pinky-violet flowers in late summer. It has a woody base and evergreen leaves and reaches a height of about 60cm (24in), lending structure to the kitchen or herb garden when other plants die down in winter. Sage is also a decorative shrub for the herbaceous border, especially since there are numerous species to choose from. Most sages require full sun and a well-drained soil to really flourish, although they are not fussy plants and will grow virtually anywhere. Clipping plants back hard every spring (after all danger of frost has passed), as well as later in the summer, helps to keep them compact and stop them becoming leggy. It is best to replace plants every four years or so or when the stem becomes too woody. Sage is a fast grower and is easy to propagate from seed sown outdoors in spring or from softwood cuttings in late spring. Essential oils are produced from the flowering tops of several species of sage, including *Salvia officinalis* and clary sage (*S. sclarea*), each having slightly different characteristics and properties. Clary sage oil has a sweet, nutty-herbaceous scent and is used more frequently in aromatherapy than common sage oil, which is altogether harsher. Clary sage is also a lovely plant to grow at home as a pot plant and there are also a wide range of tender or semi-tender varieties of sage with an array of intriguing scents; for example, *Salvia elegans* is a subtropical species with a pineapple scent and bright scarlet flowers.

Sage Common (Salvia officinalis and Salvia sclarea)

Note: The generic name *'salvia'* is derived from the Latin meaning 'to save' due to its ancient cure-all reputation. It was a sacred herb of the Romans and Greeks while the Chinese believed it conveyed longevity. In traditional Celtic lore, sage is a symbol of wisdom and immortality and it was believed that it could provide spiritual protection.

Home Uses

Clary sage is striking as a cut flower in fresh arrangements and the dried flowers and leaves (of all varieties) are perfect for potpourri and herbal sachets. The leaves of clary sage make an excellent flower water for use in eau de cologne, light perfumes or eau de toilette.

A sprig of common sage leaves kept in the wardrobe will help repel moths. Use bundles of dried sage for space clearing or thrown on the fire purify the air in a room. The vaporised essential oil of common sage for purifying the air in the home, especially after sickness, for its camphoraceous, spicy-herby, fresh aroma, which is reviving and stimulating. (*See also* the A–Z of essential oils in Appendix 1.)

In the kitchen, common sage is best known as a stuffing for savoury dishes.

Fresh sage leaves, boiled in water and drunk with honey and lemon juice, are excellent for relieving a sore throat and colds. A tonic tea made from the leaves is good for indigestion, cramps and nervous exhaustion.

Caution: Avoid using sage during pregnancy. Do not use clary sage oil if you have been drinking alcohol or plan to do so, since it can induce a narcotic effect.

Savory *(Satureja hortensis* and *Satureja montana)*

Summer savory (*Satureja hortensis*) is a popular annual culinary herb with slender green leaves and small pale lilac flowers. Although it is more delicate than winter savory (*Satureja montana*) and needs to be replanted each year, summer savory is preferred for culinary purposes, since it has a more refined flavour – it is also favoured for medicinal purposes. Winter savory is the perennial version with white flowers and smaller dark-green leaves. It forms a neater, more compact plant, making it a good edging plant in the herb garden or border, especially as it is semi-evergreen. Natives to southern Europe and North Africa, both winter and summer savory will tolerate most conditions (except extreme cold and wet), but prefer a light, well-drained soil in a sunny position. Both herbs will grow to a height of about 30cm (12in), although summer savory needs to be picked or trimmed regularly to prevent it from getting leggy. Both types can easily be grown from seed sown under glass in early spring, then planted outdoors once any danger of frost is past. Winter savory is the best choice for container planting as it is an altogether tougher plant, requires less water and will thrive even in poor soil – although it is best given some protection over winter. It can also be propagated by softwood cuttings taken in spring. The essential oil has a fresh, green-peppery scent but is not employed in aromatherapy because it can cause skin irritation.

Savory (Satureja hortensis and Satureja montana)

Note: Savory is known as the 'herb of love' – the Romans believed it was a natural aphrodisiac and used it to make love potions. In folklore, it was gathered on Midsummer's Eve as a form of divination where leaves placed together foretold affection.

Home Uses

The flowers of both summer and winter savory are lovely in posies and potpourri.

A tea made from the fresh leaves of summer savory is good for digestive complaints, and a tisane made from the fresh or dried leaves can be used as a gargle for sore throats.

Tip: Applied externally, the fresh leaves help bring relief from bee or wasp stings.
Caution: Avoid use during pregnancy.

Sweet Cicely (*Myrrhis odorata*)

This is a delicate perennial herbaceous herb that was one of the plants used in the stillroom for household purposes, traditionally used extensively for polishing furniture. Its name means literally 'fragrant perfume' and the plant is still used to make an essential oil used in high-class perfumery work. Sweet cicely has light-green, soft, feathery leaves and umbels of white flowers, followed by distinctive long seed pods. It prefers moderately fertile, moist but well-drained soil and thrives in dappled shade. The plant eventually reaches a height of about 1m (3ft) tall – a great ground cover plant – but dies down completely over winter. It is easy to propagate from seed in the spring or by division.

Note: Sweet Cicely is associated with midsummer festivals when its leaves were added to drinks to aid digestion. During the Great Plague the plant was used with angelica (*Angelica archangelica*) to prevent the spread of infection.

Home Uses

The leaves dry well when hung in loose bunches for stillroom preparations and the fresh flowers look stunning in naturalistic arrangements.

Sweet Cicely (Myrrhis odorata)

The crushed unripe green seeds have traditionally been used for polishing and scenting furniture as they have a fine, nutty, anise-like aroma.

It is an attractive and useful addition to the kitchen garden: the seeds taste like a sweet liquorice and the sweet leaves can help to counteract acidity in fruits such as gooseberries or blackcurrants.

Tarragon French (*Artemisia dracunculus*)

Artemisia is a large genus that contains some of the bitterest aromatic herbs known, including tarragon, wormwood (*Artemisia absinthium*), southernwood (*Artemisia abrotanum*) and sagebrush (*Artemisia californica*). Many have pronounced medicinal properties, possessing powerful antiseptic and anti-infectious properties, and were previously used to combat epidemics such as the plague. French tarragon (*Artemisia dracunculus*) is a half-hardy perennial herb, with narrow green aromatic leaves, small yellowish flowers and a unique bitter-sweet, peppery, warm-herby, slightly anise-like aroma. It is the unique scent and sharp herby-

Tarragon French (Artemisia dracunculus)

green flavour of French tarragon that makes it indispensable for the fragrant herb garden. In warm climates, it will grow all year round, but in colder regions, it will die back after the first frosts. As a native of southern Europe, French tarragon is slightly tender and in cold areas it is a good idea to cover the roots with a mulch before winter sets in. Alternatively, it is happy to be grown outside in big pots over summer and then moved to the protection of a cold frame or greenhouse in autumn. It likes plenty of warmth and free-draining soil, so plants grown in pots need plenty of crocks for drainage. French tarragon grows to about 1m (3ft) tall in a single season and although it does not have the most decorative of flowers, its fine dark-green leaves and bushy shape contrast well with the foliage of other kitchen herbs, such as sage or chives. For culinary use, the flowers should be pinched out to encourage leafy growth. It is best to propagate French tarragon from cuttings or by root division, since it does not seed itself readily, and plants should be replaced every three or four years as the flavour gradually deteriorates. It is good to be aware that most of the commercial seed sold as French is the Russian species (*Artemisia dracunculus dracunculoides*). The latter is, however, a completely hardy plant and will survive even the coldest of winters.

Note: The name *Artemisia dracunculus* means dragon, from the Latin 'dracoin', referring to its coiled roots. Mugwort (*Artemisia vulgaris*) is a renowned 'magical' herb – it was once common to hang a sprig of mugwort over the doorway or to burn it as an incense to protect against illness and evil spirits.

Home Uses

Apart from French Tarragon, most of the Artemisia species dry well for use in decorative arrangements. White mugwort (*Artemisia lactitlora*) is especially valuable for dried flower arrangements.

Most *Artemisia* species have moth, flea and insect-repellent properties, making them ideal for linen sachets.

French tarragon can be used fresh all year round for culinary use (if protected from frost) and is excellent infused in oil or vinegar.

A mild tea made from the leaves of French tarragon can be safely used in moderation to boost the whole system and stimulate the appetite.

Note: Avoid using all *Artemisia* species during pregnancy.

Thyme *(Thymus vulgaris)*

In the scented garden, thymes are essential for both their hardiness and their pungent, fresh, aromatic scent. A whole area of the garden can even be devoted to a specific thyme bed or a thyme lawn, for there are many species and varieties, mostly edible and nearly all with valuable medicinal properties. They are obligingly

Thyme (Thymus vulgaris)

evergreen perennial subshrubs that thrive in dry, sunny areas, in borders or amongst paving and on the edges of paths, where they release their strong fragrance when crushed. Most thyme species are native to the Mediterranean region and require little to thrive except good drainage and sun, with minimal nourishment. The common thyme is a bushy evergreen herb up to 30cm (1ft) high with a woody root and stem, small grey-green, oval aromatic leaves and pale-purple or white flowers. It will spread quickly to form a thick mass, especially if it is trimmed lightly after flowering – this will also prevent it from becoming woody. Common thyme makes an excellent ground cover plant and is ideal for rockeries and all types of container planting. It is also popular with bees and makes a good companion for cabbages, as it helps keep away insect pests. Most thymes are easily propagated by softwood cuttings in summer or by division in autumn. There are many different varieties, all with individual therapeutic properties, although most thyme species are low growing and evergreen. The wild creeping thyme (*Thymus serpyllum*), with its lilac-pink flowers, is perfect for making a scented lawn or grown between paving stones. All thyme species will thrive in containers in any sunny dry, position, for example on a terrace or in a window box along with other herbs. Essential oils are produced from various species of thyme due to its powerful antiviral, antiseptic and purifying properties.

Note: The ancient Greeks burnt thyme in front of temples, in public squares and at the gates of wealthy houses as a protection against misfortune. The Egyptians used it as a purifying incense and believed it made the souls of their dead eternal.

Home Uses

Common thyme makes a lovely pot plant and when kept in the kitchen, it also keeps insects away. Lemon-scented thyme (*Thymus × citriodorus*) is frequently used in potpourri for its fresh, uplifting scent.

The fresh herb is refreshing used in bath bags for its tonic, refreshing and cleansing effect on the skin.

Dried sprigs can be laid in linen closets, in which it acts as a repellent to moths and flies. The essential oil of common thyme has a warm, spicy-herby, woody-green scent that is refreshing, stimulating and purifying used in room vaporisers. *See also* the A-Z of Essential Oils in Appendix 1.

Thyme is one of the mainstay herbs of Mediterranean cuisine, being an essential ingredient in bouquet garni – it is also excellent added to mulled red wine. The fresh herb can also be added to oils and vinegars to flavour them, imparting a delicious, aromatic scent.

A herbal tea can be made from the fresh leaves and is good for headaches. Add a little honey and the tea is also good for sore throats, chesty coughs and colds – it is also supposed to be useful in cases of drunkenness.

Caution: Avoid the fresh tea during pregnancy.

Valerian *(Valeriana officinalis)*

Common valerian, also known as garden heliotrope, is a stately perennial herb up to 1.6m (6ft) high with a hollow stem, deeply dissected dark leaves and dense clusters of small pink or white flowers. It has short thick greyish roots, largely showing above ground, which have a strong aroma. The scent of the roots, especially when dried, attracts cats who find their pungent, musky smell quite irresistible. They will also roll in the leaves, flattening the plant if given the chance. It prefers a moist, loamy soil and some sun but will also tolerate a shady position. As an ornamental plant, *Valeriana officinalis* forms an attractive backdrop to a floral border or the herb garden, sending up tall elegant flowering shoots in midsummer that have a honey-sweet scent, attracting butterflies and bees with its long blooming period. It is generally beneficial to the garden as it attracts earthworms. By nature, it is also suited to woodland sites or naturalistic plantings, for it likes to be cool around its roots and prefers to grow near water. In aromatherapy, the oil is used in moderation, mainly in blends, for nervous conditions including insomnia, nervous indigestion, migraines, stress and nervous tension. It has a pronounced painkilling and tranquillising effect on the entire nervous system and is mildly narcotic, so it must be used with caution. Common valerian (*Valeriana officinalis*) should not be confused with red valerian (*Centranthus ruber*), a plant that seeds itself freely on sunny banks and walls.

Valerian (Valeriana officinalis)

Note: As its Latin name *Valeriana* suggests, this plant was thought to promote valour or strength in the face of distressing times. During the First World War it was given to soldiers to help treat shell shock and to civilians to help relieve stress. In Norse mythology, valerian was used as an ingredient in the love potion brewed by the goddess Freya to make her suitors fall in love with her.

Home Uses

For drying, lift the rhizomes in the plant's second year after the leaves have died off, then clean, slice and dry them, discarding all pale, fibrous roots for use in stillroom recipes.

An infusion of the rhizome of *Valeriana officinalis* added to the bath is good for unwinding. Alternatively, add the powdered roots to a bath bag or to sleep bags to aid relaxation and sleep.

The essential oil from the rhizome has a pungent, warm-woody, musky scent that is profoundly relaxing and can be included in blends for room vaporisation to induce a soothing effect.

To make a sedative tea, crush one teaspoon of the fresh or dried root then allow to steep for five to ten minutes, preferably covered.

Caution: Do not use valerian for more than two weeks at a time or in conjunction with sedatives or sleeping pills. Valerian is also contraindicated for those with liver problems.

Violet Sweet (*Viola odorata*)

The sweet violet is one of the most beautiful early spring flowers. *Viola odorata* is native to Britain and is fragrant and easy to grow, making it an intrinsic part of any naturalistic garden. The sweet violet is a small hardy perennial plant with dark-green, heart-shaped leaves, fragrant violet-blue flowers and an oblique rhizome root. Though barely 8cm (3in) high, it spreads rapidly by sending out root runners, eventually forming a sweetly scented green carpet. Violets thrive best in a fairly rich, moist soil, in semi-shade and do not like heat. They are easy to propagate, either by seed sown in the autumn under glass then planting out in spring, by dividing established clumps after flowering or by taking root cuttings in late spring. Violets also display the additional blessing of self-seeding abundantly. Sweet violets often flower twice, in spring and again in autumn and sometimes through a mild winter. Cultivars of *Viola odorata* come in a variety of colours, from white to pink and purple. Parma violets make good container plants for scenting a room or conservatory, but the double varieties are not fully hardy and are easily spoiled in wet weather, so need to be protected under glass. An aromatic absolute is made from both the fresh leaves and the flowers: both are valuable perfumery ingredients. The roots and leaves are also used in herbal medicine.

Violet Sweet (Viola odorata)

Note: Sacred to Aphrodite and Venus, the delicate violet remains an enduring symbol of love – Empress Josephine had her wedding dress embroidered with violets for her marriage to Napoleon.

Home Uses

A posy of fresh violets is one of the traditional tokens of love. A scented water made from the fresh flowers using the effleurage method can be made at home as a light perfume.

The scent of the fresh flowers is said to 'comfort and strengthen the heart' – good for nervous exhaustion, headaches and stress-related complaints.

The dried flowers and leaves can be used in potpourri, especially combined with violet-scented orris root.

The fresh flowers can be added to salads or crystallised violets can be used to decorate cakes or puddings.

Woodruff Sweet (Galium odoratum)

Woodruff Sweet (*Galium odoratum*)

A delightful plant for the kitchen garden, sweet woodruff is one of the few herbs that prefers shade. It is a low-growing perennial with small white flowers and can easily be grown from seed. It can also be found growing wild in woodlands throughout the UK. Although it is not a culinary herb, it has many household uses: it was once much employed as a 'strewing' herb in Elizabethan times to scent and disinfect rooms or remove musty smells. Its aroma of new-mown hay comes from its high coumarin content, which is most pronounced when the plant is dried, and which intensifies the longer it is kept.

Note: In the Middle Ages, dried sweet woodruff was stuffed into mattresses and pillows, used to refresh clothing and employed in potpourris, sachets and wreaths. Known as 'our Lady's lace' or 'our Lady's bedstraw', sweet woodruff was commonly strewn in churches and was believed to have lined Christ's manger, imbuing it with a sacred aura and association with the Virgin Mary.

Home Uses

Hang the fresh leaves and flowers from the ceiling to perfume and cool the air.

The dried herb can be made into pouches and placed amongst bed linen to impart a fresh and clean scent. The dried herb is also excellent added to potpourri for its distinctive aroma and useful for removing musty or damp smells. It also has moth-deterrent and insect-repellent properties so it is effective in sachets in the wardrobe.

Yarrow (*Achillea millefolium*)

Yarrow is an unassuming perennial herb, with a straight stem up to 1m (3ft) high and finely dissected greyish-silver leaves, giving it a lacy appearance. It bears numerous pinky-white dense flower heads from summer into autumn. Common throughout Europe, Asia and North America, where it can be found growing wild on wastelands, yarrow is an easy plant to grow and will survive even the most inhospitable conditions, such as dry, salty or windswept situations – though it does not like heavy soils. It is a prolific grower and spreads rapidly via its creeping rootstock. However, although it is invasive, it is not hard to control by digging up established clumps each spring and dividing or discarding surplus growth. Yarrow thrives in a sunny position where the warmth of the sun draws out the plant's aroma: both the flowers and the leaves are richly pungent with a fresh, green, sweet, herb-like, slightly camphoraceous scent that is restorative, revitalising and tonic. *Achillea filipendulina* makes a lovely, tall plant for the back of the border with stiff, erect stems and yellow flowers; *Achillea grandifolia* is the giant of the yarrows and makes a dramatic statement.

Note: Yarrow is one of the oldest known medicinal plants, named after the heroic warrior Achilles due to its outstanding healing qualities – the leaves can be made into a poultice. Its dried straight stems are used to make the divination sticks for the Chinese 'I Ching' oracle and, in the West too, it has also traditionally been associated with divination and magic.

Home Uses

The many cultivars of yarrow are perfect for fresh floral arrangements, with a wide range of colours to choose from. Yarrow dries well and the cut stems are also ideal for dried flower arrangements. The flowers of all forms retain their colour well on drying and can be used in potpourri, posies, sleep bags and so on.

A flower water with a toning effect can be made at home.

The essential oil used in room vaporisers can help ease stress-related conditions and promotes relaxation.

Yarrow makes an uplifting tonic tea from the fresh flowers – infuse well and add honey to taste.

Caution: Avoid drinking yarrow tea during pregnancy.

Yarrow (Achillea millefolium)

Appendix 1

A–Z of Essential Oils

Essential oils are highly aromatic, volatile plant oils that are used in the practice of aromatherapy. These oils tend to evaporate easily at room temperature, and it is this volatile character that allows their aroma to be perceived as fragrant. All essential oils, such as basil, rosemary and sage, have a unique phytochemical composition that is responsible for the highly distinctive aroma of the plant. Many essential oils can effectively be used in room vaporisers and diffusers to scent and purify the air in the home or workplace, and are valuable additions to household cleaning products and modern stillroom recipes.

Basil Sweet *(Ocimum basilicum)*: This oil has a sweet-herbaceous scent. It has a refreshing, clearing, purifying and stimulating effect on the mind when used in room vaporisers. It blends well with bergamot, clary sage, lime, marjoram, lavender and geranium.

Bay *(Pimenta racemosa)*: This oil has a fresh spicy top note and sweet balsamic undertone – extensively used in fragrances, especially for men. A valuable culinary oil with many stillroom uses. It blends well with lavender, geranium, ylang yang and spice oils.

Benzoin *(Styrax benzoin)*: A resinous, rich essential oil with a sweet vanilla-like aroma. It has a comforting and soothing effect on the heart and an energising effect on the systems of the body. It blends well with rose, sandalwood, frankincense, jasmine, myrrh, cypress, juniper and spice oils.

Bergamot *(Citrus bergamia)*: A penetrating, sweet, citrus-scented oil that has a soothing effect on the nervous system, although it is reviving and uplifting to the spirits. It blends well with other citrus oils, also geranium, clary sage and chamomile.

Cedarwood Atlas *(Cedrus atlantica)*: A woody-balsamic oil having a sedative effect on the nerves, traditionally burnt as an incense and used to repel insects and moths. It blends well with cypress, jasmine, juniper, clary sage, vetivert, rosemary and ylang ylang.

Chamomile German *(Matricaria recutica)*/ Chamomile Roman *(Chamaemelum nobile)*: These oils have a rich apple-green scent where both types of chamomiles share similar properties. They are both excellent sedative oils, which aid relaxation. They blend well with lavender, bergamot, clary sage, jasmine, neroli, rose and geranium.

Citronella *(Cymbopogon nardus)*: A powerful, fresh, lemony-scented oil. It has a stimulating effect on the nervous system and is traditionally used to repel mosquitoes. It blends well with geranium, pine, cypress and other citrus oils.

Clove *(Syzygium aromaticum)*: The oil has a warm, strong, spicy smell that is stimulating to the mind, helping lift depression. It masks unpleasant odours and repels insects. The oil is useful to add a warm spicy, element to blends added in small amounts.

Cypress ***(Cupressus sempervirens):*** A sweet, smoky-balsamic fragrance with a soothing effect on the nervous system, traditionally used as an incense. It blends well with cedarwood, pine, lavender, juniper, orange, marjoram and sandalwood.

Eucalyptus ***(Eucalyptus globulus):*** A clear, camphoraceous oil with a strong, penetrating, stimulating odour, well known for its decongestant properties and as a powerful anti-infectious oil used in room fragrances. It is an important essential oil for household hygiene and blends well with rosemary, lavender, clary sage, marjoram and herbal oils.

Fennel Sweet ***(Foeniculum vulgare):*** A sweet, anise-like scented oil: it has a cleansing effect on the systems of the body and is a valuable stillroom ingredient. It blends well with geranium, lavender, rose, chamomile and sandalwood.

Fragonia ***(Agonis fragrans):*** A pale oil with a slightly citrus, fresh, clean scent. It displays most of the medicinal characteristics of 'tea tree', being an excellent anti-infectious, bactericidal and fungicidal oil, yet has a pleasing fragrance. I highly recommend it for household hygiene uses – it blends well with citrus oils.

Frankincense ***(Boswellia carteri):*** A warm, rich, sweet balsamic oil with a sedating effect on the nervous system. It helps to calm the mind and is well known as an ingredient of incense in the East and West. It has a healing, rejuvenating effect on the skin. In blending, it makes a useful base note, especially in combination with other resins such as elemi or myrrh.

Geranium ***(Pelargonium graveolens):*** A sweet, rosy-green scented oil that has a balancing and harmonising effect used in room vaporisers. It is valuable in blending work as it combines well with most oils.

Ginger ***(Zingiber officinale):*** The oil has a warm, spicy-woody aroma with a strong, stimulating and warming effect on the entire system when used in vaporisers. It is valuable used in small amounts in perfumery formulations to add a hint of warmth and body to a blend.

Grapefruit ***(Citrus paradisi):*** A fresh, sweet citrus aromatic oil, characteristic of the fruit. It has a purifying effect and is a useful perfumery ingredient in fresh, uplifting blends, especially in combination with lemon, palmarosa, bergamot, cypress, lime and mandarin.

Jasmine ***(Jasminum orficinale):*** An exquisite perfume oil, with an intense floral fragrance. It has an uplifting, soothing quality yet has a stimulating effect on the nervous system – reputed as an aphrodisiac. It blends well with other florals such as neroli and rose and also has the quality of 'rounding off' just about any blend.

Juniper ***(Juniperus communis):*** A fresh, woody-balsamic oil that has a purifying effect when used in vaporisers. It was traditionally used as an incense and for space clearing. It blends well with vetiver, sandalwood, cedarwood, clary sage, geranium, benzoin and citrus oils.

Lavender ***(Lavendula angustifolia)***: A familiar oil with a sweet, floral fragrance and a multitude of uses. It has a marked sedating effect on the nervous system and is a multipurpose household hygiene agent. It blends well with most oils so is therefore perhaps the most useful oil to keep in your home essential oil kit.

Lemon ***(Citrus limon):*** A fresh, clean-scented citrus oil that is refreshing and purifying when used in room vaporisers. An essential item for your botanical home cleaning kit. It blends well with lavender, neroli, ylang ylang, rose, chamomile, juniper and other citrus oils.

Lemongrass *(Cymbopogon citratus):* A fresh grassy-lemony scented oil that has a soothing effect on the nervous system. It blends well with other citrus oils but can be quite overpowering in blends if not used in moderation.

Lime *(Citrus aurantifolia):* A fresh, sweet, fruity citrus scent that has an uplifting effect on the mind and a cleansing effect on the systems of the body. It is employed in blends in stillroom recipes to add a pleasingly sweet top note as it combines well with most other oils.

Mandarin *(Citrus reticulata):* An intensely sweet citrus fragrance, characteristic of the fruit. This oil is especially recommended for children and during pregnancy due to its low toxicity levels, and can be used in baths or room vaporisers. In blends it adds warmth, combining especially well with neroli and spice oils.

Marjoram Sweet *(Origanum majorana)*: A warm, nutty aroma that has a soothing effect when used in room vaporisers. A valuable stillroom oil, it blends well with lavender, rosemary, bergamot, chamomile, cedarwood and cypress.

Myrrh *(Commiphora myrrha):* A rich, warming oil with a spicy balsamic aroma that has been used for over 3,000 years. A traditional incense material, it blends well with frankincense, benzoin, sandalwood, cypress, juniper, patchouli, lavender and spice oils.

Myrtle *(Myrtus communis):* This fresh-smelling essential oil makes an effective air freshener used in a room vaporiser, plus it helps clear congestion resulting from airborne germs. It blends well with lavender, rosemary, clary sage, bay, lime clove and other spice oils.

Neroli *(Citrus aurantium var. amara):* An intensely rich, floral perfume, reputed to have aphrodisiac properties. It is uplifting to the mind and spirit but is soothing to the nervous system when used in room vaporisers. A useful stillroom ingredient that blends well with benzoin, jasmine, myrrh, lavender, rose and all citrus oils.

Orange Sweet *(Citrus sinesis):* A sweet, familiar citrus-scented oil that has a soothing effect used as a room fragrance. Adds warmth to any blends and combines well with lavender, clary sage, neroli, myrrh, frankincense and other citrus oils.

Palmarosa *(Cymbopogon martinii):* A light green oil with a sweet, floral, rosy-green scent – valuable in the stillroom. A useful oil for blending as it 'rounds off' other scents and combines especially well with citrus oils.

Patchouli *(Pogostemon patchouli):* This rich, musky, earthy oil has strong associations with the East, where it is used to scent cloth. It soothes the mind, supports the nervous system and is a potent aphrodisiac. It may be used as a perfume on its own or combined with other exotic oils.

Pepper Black *(Piper nigrum):* One of the most ancient spices, which has been in use for over 4,000 years. The pungent light amber essential oil has a warming and stimulating effect used in room vaporisers and blends well with most oils used in small amounts.

Peppermint *(Mentha piperita):* This penetrating, minty oil is cooling and refreshing – it clears the head and revives the spirit. An essential stillroom oil for the home, it blends well with rosemary and other refreshing herbal oils.

Petitgrain ***(Citrus aurantium var. amara):*** A fresh, floral, citrus scent – somewhat similar to neroli. A classic ingredient of eau de cologne, it gives a unique twist to an otherwise flat composition, having a unique quality as a top note in blends.

Pine ***(Pinus sylvestris):*** This fresh, balsamic scented oil is a good antiseptic, with a stimulating and refreshing effect – effective used in household cleaning recipes. It blends well with other woody and spicy oils.

Ravensara ***(Ravensara aromatica):*** This oil has a fresh, slightly lemony, slightly camphoraceous scent with powerful antiviral, anti-fungal and bactericidal properties. Valuable for combatting airborne infections used in room vaporisers. It blends well with rosemary, eucalyptus, tea tree, fragonia, bay and spice oils.

Rosemary ***(Rosmarinus officinalis):*** A penetrating oil with a warm herbal fragrance and strong, stimulating, fortifying properties. In blends, it is one of the most useful medicinally active essential oils and combines well with most other herbal oils such as clary sage, marjoram and lavender.

Rose Maroc ***(Rosa centifolia):*** This beautiful, warm-rosy, rich floral scent has long been associated with love. It warms the heart and soothes the nerves. There is a saying – 'no perfume without rose' – as it blends well with virtually everything!

Sage Clary ***(Salvia sclarea):*** A pleasing, sweet, nutty-herbaceous scent. It is especially good for stress and anxiety states, in comparison to Spanish Sage, which is more stimulating. It blends well with juniper, lavender, geranium, sandalwood, cedarwood, frankincense, bergamot and other herbal oils.

Sandalwood ***(Santalum album):*** This incense, cosmetic and perfume material has enjoyed over 4,000 years of uninterrupted use. The oil has a deep, soft, woody-balsamic scent that is soothing and long-lasting. A well-known aphrodisiac, it combines well with rose, lavender, black pepper, bergamot, patchouli, myrrh and jasmine.

Tea Tree ***(Melaleuca alternifolia):*** A useful household oil with a fresh, camphoraceous, powerful odour. It supports the immune system and is active against bacteria, fungi and viruses. It blends well with other medicinal or herbal oils, such as rosemary, peppermint and ravensara.

Thyme White ***(Thymus vulgaris):*** There are numerous varieties of thyme, but of these the 'white' thyme oil is recommended for home use. It has a herby, fresh, green scent used in vaporisers and is a valuable stillroom oil. It blends well with other herbaceous oils, including rosemary, lavender, marjoram and clary sage.

Vetiver ***(Vetiveria zizanoides):*** A soothing and relaxing oil with a soft, earthy undertone and a sweet, woody top note, known in the East as 'the oil of tranquillity'. It blends well with patchouli, rose, sandalwood, lavender, ylang ylang and clary sage.

Ylang Ylang ***(Cananga odorata var. genuina):*** An exquisite perfume oil, with a deep, soft, floral-balsamic fragrance. It has a marked sedating effect on the nerves but is reviving to the spirit – a traditional aphrodisiac. This oil is a well-balanced perfume in its own right but can also be used to add an exotic, rich and sensual element to blends.

Appendix 2

Measurements and Conversions

Essential Oil Measurements

Using drops of essential oils as measurements, there are approximately 20 drops in 1ml of essential oil.

Ounces/millilitres		Drops
⅛oz (3.75ml)	=	75 drops
¼oz (7.5ml)	=	150 drops
½oz (15ml)	=	300 drops
1oz (30ml)	=	600 drops

Conversion Tables

When it comes to using measurements, there is a difference between countries, for example, the British tablespoon is about 17.7ml while the US tablespoon is about 14.2ml. In Britain, it is also common to use fluid ounces or millilitres for liquids in recipes, but in the US the term 'cup' is commonly used both for liquid and dry ingredients, where criteria for measurements can vary slightly – *see* below.

UK/US Conversions

1ml (UK)	=	0.035fl oz
1fl oz (UK)	=	28.4ml
1fl oz (US)	=	29.6ml
1 cup (US)	=	250ml

Quick US to Metric Conversions

Liquids

1 tsp	=	4.929ml
1 tbsp	=	14.787ml
1fl oz	=	29.57353ml
1 cup	=	236.59ml
1 cup	=	0.2366 litres

Liquid measurements (approximate)

1 tsp		⅓ tbsp	5ml
1 tbsp	½fl oz	3 tsp	15ml, 15 cc
2 tbsp	1fl oz	⅛ cup, 6 tsp	30ml, 30 cc
¼ cup	2fl oz	4 tbsp	59ml
⅓ cup	2 ⅔fl oz	5 tbsp + 1 tsp	79ml
½ cup	4fl oz	8 tbsp	118ml
⅔ cup	5 ⅓fl oz	10 tbsp + 2 tsp	158ml
¾ cup	6fl oz	12 tbsp	177ml
⅞ cup	7fl oz	14 tbsp	207ml
1 cup	8fl oz/½ pint	16 tbsp	237ml
2 cups	16fl oz/1 pint	32 tbsp	473ml
4 cups	32fl oz	1 quart	946ml
1 pint	16fl oz/1 pint	32 tbsp	473ml
2 pints	32fl oz	1 quart	946ml (0.946 litres)
8 pints	1 gallon/128fl oz		3785ml (3.78 litres)
4 quarts	1 gallon/128fl oz		3785ml (3.78 litres)
1 litre	1.057 quarts		1,000ml

Dry weights

1oz	=	28.35g
1oz	=	453.59g
1oz	=	0.454kg
1g	=	0.035274oz
1g	=	0.0022046lb
1kg	=	35.274oz
1kg	=	2.2046lb

Dry weight measurements (approximate)

1oz		30g
2oz		55g
3oz		85g
4oz	¼ lb	125g
8oz	½ lb	240g
12oz	¾ lb	375g
16oz	1lb	454g
32oz	2lb	907g
1kg	2.2lb/35.2oz	1,000g

Dry measure equivalents

3 tsp	1 tbsp	½oz	14.3g
2 tbsp	⅛ cup	1oz	28.3g
4 tbsp	¼ cup	2oz	56.7g
5 ⅓ tbsp	⅓ cup	2.6oz	75.6g
8 tbsp	½ cup	4oz	113.4g
12 tbsp	¾ cup	6oz	0.375lb
32 tbsp	2 cups	16oz	1lb

Volumes for US Standards to Metric

Volume: Liquids

US standard (cups and quarts)	US standard (ounces)	Metric (millilitres and litres)
2 tbsp	1fl oz	30ml
¼ cup	2fl oz	60ml
½ cup	4fl oz	125ml
1 cup	8fl oz	250ml
1½ cups	12fl oz	375ml
2 cups or 1 pint	16fl oz	500ml
4 cups or 1 quart	32fl oz	1,000ml or 1 litre
1 gallon	128fl oz	4 litres

Volume: Dry

US standard	Metric
⅛ tsp	0.5ml
¼ tsp	1ml
½ tsp	2ml
¾ tsp	4ml
1 tsp	5ml
1 tbsp	15ml
¼ cup	59ml
⅓ cup	79ml
½ cup	118ml

US standard	Metric
⅔ cup	158ml
¾ cup	177ml
1 cup	225ml
2 cups or 1 pint	450ml
3 cups	675ml
4 cups or 1 quart	1 litre
½ gallon	2 litres
1 gallon	4 litres

The author running an aromatic botanical workshop at 'Botany', London.

Supplies and Resources

Aqua Oleum/Julia Lawless: Aromatherapy Supplies

Aqua Oleum Ltd was founded by biochemist Kerttu Ajanko (Julia's mother) and is today owned by Julia Lawless and her daughter Natasha. As such, it is a company with a heritage spanning over three generations, based on expert family knowledge of essential oils. Today Aqua Oleum supplies a range of over 200 premium-quality pure and organic essential oils, plus a wide range of top-quality vegetable oils, salts and other botanical materials. Julia is directly responsible for selecting and checking the quality of all the oils that are sold; she is also in charge of the formulation of all products. For over 50 years, Aqua Oleum has built its reputation based on outstanding product expertise and high ethical standards, together with a real commitment to providing premium-quality oils at a fair price.

Aqua Oleum, Unit 9, Griffin Mill Industrial Estate, London Road, Thrupp, Stroud, Gloucestershire GL5 2AZ, UK

Website: aqua-oleum.co.uk Tel: 01453 885 908

General enquiries: info@aqua-oleum.co.uk

20A Botanical Workshops

Hands-on workshops in aromatherapy blending and making botanically based recipes. Founded by Abi Titterington-Lough with expertise in beauty and skincare, 20A strives to educate and inspire individuals through the medium of aromatherapy, to foster a sense of curiosity and creativity, and to show people how pleasurable it can be to integrate ingredients from Mother Nature into everyday life, and all the benefits it can bring to the skin, body, mind and soul. Through interactive workshops, whether in person or online, 20A aims to engage our senses and dive into the alchemy of scent and the world of natural botanicals.

Website: 20a.co

General enquires: abi@20a.co

Jekka's Herb Farm

Suppliers of herbs, seeds and ongoing education advice on using and growing a wide range of herbs. Founded by Jekka McVicar, Jekka's Herb Farm in Somerset has been described as 'a living book of herbs' and offers a variety of educational and inspiring aromatic experiences for the amateur, enthusiast and professional. Open days, workshops and talks at Jekka's provide a way to learn about growing sustainable culinary and medicinal herbs, as well as how to use them.

Jekka's Herb Farm, Rose Cottage, Shellards Lane, Alveston, Bristol BS35 3SY, UK

Website: jekkas.com

Tel: 01454 418 878

General enquiries: sales@jekkas.com

Kindred House: Creative Workshops & Events

A creative location house and retreat space founded by Natasha Lawless, hosting events, workshops, exhibitions and artist residencies throughout the year. The schedule of creative retreat weekends plays a key role in the spirit of Kindred House, by crafting an environment that actively inspires and encourages creativity and learning, as well as connection to oneself by working with the hands. Inspired by the seasons, the sea and the coastline on which it sits, all of the rooms are uniquely furnished and there is an emphasis on the use of natural materials throughout, encouraging an atmosphere of rest and calm. The house is also available for private rentals and location hire.

Website: kindred-house.com

General enquiries: info@kindred-house.com

Further Reading
– Books by Julia Lawless

Several of the books listed here have been published in various editions and translated into a variety of different languages. Signed copies of many of Julia's books can be bought from the Aqua Oleum website. Most of her books are available from good bookstores while some are also available as e-books, including her all-time best-selling aromatherapy classic: *The Encyclopaedia of Essential Oils.*

Lawless, J., and Allan, J., *Aloe Vera: Natural Wonder Cure* (Thorsons, 2000).

Lawless, J., *Aromatherapy and the Mind: The Psychological & Emotional Effects of Essential Oils* (Thorsons, 1995).

Lawless, J., *The Aromatherapy Garden & The Fragrant Garden: Growing and Using Scented Plants* (Kyle Cathie).

Lawless, J., *The Blending Notebook: An Introduction to the Art of Formulating your own Aromatic Creations* available from Aqua Oleum, 2017).

Lawless, J., *The Complete Aromatherapy & Essential Oils Sourcebook: A Practical Approach to the Use of Essential Oils & Aromatherapy for Health, Beauty and Well-Being* (Harper Collins, 2016).

Lawless, J., *The Complete Essential Oil Sourcebook* (Harper Collins, 2016).

Lawless, J., *The Complete Illustrated Guide to Aromatherapy: A Practical Approach to the Use of Essential Oils for Health & Well-Being* (Thorsons, 1998).

Lawless, J., *The Encyclopaedia of Essential Oils: A Complete Guide to the Use of Aromatics in Aromatherapy, Herbalism, Health & Well Being* (Harper Collins, first published 1992; new revised & extended edition published 2014).

Lawless, J., *The Essential Aromatherapy Garden* (Thorsons, 2019).

Lawless, J., *Essential Oils: An Illustrated Guide* (Element Books).

Lawless, J., *Heaven Scent:* (Thorsons).

Lawless, J., *Home Aromatherapy: A Step-by-Step Guide to Using Essential Oils at Home* (Kyle Cathie, 1995).

Lawless, J., *The Illustrated Encyclopedia of Essential Oils* (Element Books, 1995).

Lawless, J., *Lavender Oil* (Thorsons, 2001).

Lawless, J., *Mud, Salt + Medicine: Essential Oil Blends & Recipes for Natural Healing* (Oh Life!, 2023).

Lawless, J., *Rosemary Oil* (Thorsons, 2014).

Lawless, J., *Rose Oil* (Thorsons, 2014).

Lawless, J., *Tea Tree Oil* (Thorsons, 2001).

Acknowledgements

Many people have helped contribute to the process of creating this beautiful book. Firstly,. I would like to acknowledge my Finnish grandmother 'Mama' whose knowledge of herbs and native plants home was extensive. She passed on her botanical wisdom to my mother Kerttu, a research biochemist who specialised in the study of essential oils long before their use became fashionable. It was her hand-on approach to aromatics plants that in turn encouraged me to train in herbal medicine and aromatherapy in my early twenties. Having spent much of my childhood summers in the wilds of Finland and grown up on the banks of the river Wye on the border of Wales, I've always considered the natural world as my refuge.

As an artist and designer, my daughter Tasha's work is also primarily inspired by nature and her love of the outdoors. I'd like to thank her for taking many of the stunning photographs in this book and for collating all the images found within it. It is her design skills combined with my botanical background that have combined to produce The Botanical Home. Many thanks are also due to my granddaughter Anouk whose stunning photographs feature in the foraging section, and to Aloha for her beautiful images, courtesy of Bloom. In addition, I would like to thank my friend Abi, whose help especially in the home hygiene chapter, has helped bring this project to fruition.

Finally, it has been a pleasure to work with everyone at Crowood in the editing and production of this book.

Picture Credits

Aloha Bonser-Shaw for Bloom magazine: 44;45;49;71. Natasha Lawless: 25; 55/top left; 61;63/top left & bottom right; 68/bottom; 82; 97/top left; 101/right; 109/top; 113/bottom; 130; 135; 186;188. Anouk Lawless-Monnot: 16; 21. Shutterstock: Sophie CY 32; Chatham172 39/top; Wirestock Creators 47; Girts Ragelis 64; Olga Gudumac 74; JohnatAPW 138; Teresa Kasprzycka 139; Tamu1500 140; JirikV 144; Smirnova Elizaveta 145; Peter Turner Photography 146/right; Photostock_88 147; RukiMedia 148; Sashartua 151; Konstantinos Livadas 153; Kateryniuk 154; Wasilisa 157; Kylbabka 159; Nahhana 160; Simona Pavan 163; Mira Kos 165; Adriana Iacob 167; Sergey V Kalyakin 168; Manfred Ruckszio 173; Tobias Arhelger 174; Joanna Tkaczuk 176; Fotomarekka 178. Unsplash: Truog Dieu 4; Marisa Harris 8/9; Priscilla du Preez 10; Annie Spratt 13, Christine 14; Anouk Lawless-Monnot 16; Getty Images 19; Annie Spratt 19/bottom; Aaron Cook 22 /top; Pascale Amez 22/bottom; Yukon Haughton 23; Charlie Harutaka 24; Yellow-Cactus 26/left; Kura Tregenza 26/right; Edward Howell 28; Anshu a Loki 30/top; Anne Nygard 30/bottom; Getty Images 31; Annie Spratt 35/top left; Ehud Neuhaud 35/top right; Michaela Murphy 35/bottom left; Clem Onojeghuo 35/bottom right; Jan Antonin Kolar 36; Gaelle Marcel 37; Michal Balog 39/bottom; Odiseo Castrejon 41/left; Luisa Brimble 41/right; Rohtopia-com 42; Annie Spratt 43; Monika Grabkowska 50; Polina Kuzovkowa 52; Svitlana Lglgec 55/top right; Josh Massey 55/bottom left; Raoul Croes 55/bottom right; Mesut Cicen 56; Keytion 57; Getty Images 59; Hyeongju Seo 63/top right; Monika Grabkowska 63/bottom left; Marina Raspopova 65/left; Julia Berezina 65/right; Karolina Grabowska 66; Blake Cheek 67; Polina Kuzovkova 68/top; Karolina Grabowska 72; Milada Vigerova 76; Anup Ghag 77/top; Volant 77/bottom; Giulia Bertelli 79/top left; Joanna Kosinska 79/top right; Nordwood Themes 79/bottom left; Mustafa Akin 79/bottom right; Conscious Design 84; Daiga Ellaby 85; Yeshen Venema (Aqua Oleum) 86; Spenser Sembrat 87/top; Alex Simpson 87/bottom; Mary Skrynnikova 89; Ray Albrow 90; Kayla Maurais 93; Maxime Amoudruz 97/top right; Ashley Batz 97/bottom left; Alberto Cattani 97/bottom right; Jake Johnson 98/top; Bastien Herve 98/bottom; Chris Ensey 101/left; Annie Spratt 102; Polina Kuzovkova 104/top; Sarah 104/bottom; Annie Spratt 107; No Revisions 109/bottom; Carolyn Carter 110/top left; Florencia Potter 110/top right; Ivana Cajina 110/bottom left; Elly Johnson 110/bottom right; Karolina Grabowska 113/top; Ricorado Resende 114; Milan Popovic 115; Olivie Strauss 116; Winged Jedi 118/top; Nakaharu Line 118/bottom; Gabriella Maurer 121/top left; Kevin Charit 121/top right; Spenser Sembrat 121/bottom left; Smrithi Rao 121/bottom right; Ryan Ancill 123/top; Anna Jakutajc Wojtalik 123/bottom; Khanh Do 124/left; sj Objio laCoxr 124/right; Patrick Langwallner 126; Annie Spratt 127; Oriento 129; Rashid 133/left; Cassidy Phillips 133/right; Anna Jakutajc Wojtalik 136 &137; Julietta Watson 141; Yoksel Zok 142/left; Meg Macdonald 142/right; Chandan Chaurasia 143; David Clode 146/left; Bohdan Stocek 149; Sheelah Brennan 150; Melissa Brown 152/left; Juliet Sarmiento 152/right; Ira Ostafiichuk 155; Yuliya Matuzava 156; Sharon-co-images 158; Phillip Larking 161; Nina Luong 162; Gabriel Bodhi 164; Marina Yalanska 166/left; Annie Spratt 166/left; Olya Mn 169; Phillip Larking 171; Alejandro Pinero Amerio 172; Anja Junghans 175; Gerg Eiermann 177; Olli Kilpi 179; Natalie Behn 180; Maja Petric 185/right; Calum Lewis 185/ left; Masha S.186; Valeria Bold 190.

First published in 2025 by Robert Hale, an imprint of
The Crowood Press Ltd
Ramsbury, Marlborough
Wiltshire SN8 2HR

enquiries@crowood.com
www.crowood.com

British Library Cataloguing-in-Publication Data
A catalogue record for this book is available from the British Library.

For product safety-related questions, contact productsafety@crowood.com.

ISBN 978 0 7198 3169 0

Cover design by Sergey Tsvetkov
Front cover image: Shutterstock
Photographs by Natasha Lawless

Disclaimer
This book is not intended as a substitute for the medical advice of physicians. The reader should consult a physician in matters relating to their health, particularly with respect to any symptoms that may require diagnosis or medical attention.

Designed and typeset by Catherine Murray
Printed and bound in India by Parksons Graphics